Kiowa Humanity and the Invasion of the State

Jacki Thompson Rand

Kiowa Humanity and the Invasion of the State

UNIVERSITY OF NEBRASKA PRESS · LINCOLN & LONDON

Chapter 4 previously appeared in a different form as "Primary Sources: Indian Goods and the History of American Colonialism and the Nineteenth-Century Reservation," in *Clearing a Path: Theorizing American Indian Studies*, ed. Nancy Shoemaker (New York: Routledge, 2002).

Chapter 5 previously appeared in a different form as "The Subtle Art of Resistance: Encounter and Accommodation in the Art of Fort Marion," with Edwin L. Wade, in *Plains Indian Drawings, 1865–1938, Pages from a Visual History*, ed. Catherine Berlo (New York: Harry N. Abrams, 1996).

Library of Congress Cataloging-in-Publication Data
Rand, Jacki Thompson.
Kiowa humanity and the invasion of the state /
Jacki Thompson Rand.
p. cm.
Includes bibliographical references and index.
ISBN-13: 978-0-8032-3966-1 (cloth: alk. paper)
ISBN-10: 0-8032-3966-1 (cloth: alk. paper)
1. Kiowa philosophy. 2. Kiowa Indians—History.
3. Kiowa Indians—Government relations.
4. United States—Social policy. 5. United States—Race relations. 6. United States—Politics and government. I. Title.
E99.K5R36 2008
323.1197073—dc22
2007033431

Set in Quadraat.

Contents

Illustrations

Acknowledgments

Having completed the manuscript, I can look back and see the debt I have racked up over the years. This debt, unlike the national debt, second mortgages, and credit card debt, is the good kind, a consequence of better angels who have laughed with me in fabulous times and held me up when I was unable to do so alone. I extend my gratitude to numerous fellow travelers, many of whom fall into multiple categories—loyal friend, colleague, relative, intellectual and professional mentor, archivist, librarian, and Kiowa. Thus, the necessary sorting that follows disguises these overlapping rich relationships.

If I approach these acknowledgments as a journey, I would plot the way with the people who have appeared at just the right time. All things begin in Oklahoma. Thank you to my beloved women, Martha Skeeters, Kelly Lankford, Melissa Stockdale, Linda Reese, and Leanne Howe; to Aunt Rosalie Imotichey, Uncle Tony Byars, Aunt Christine Keel, all the cousins, Buster and Jerri Jefferson, and Charles Rand. Thank you to Robert Nye for his unwavering support and intellectual generosity when it was most needed. Thank you to Vanessa Paukeigope Jennings, the late Jacob Ahtone, the late Alice Littleman, Gus Palmer Jr., the late Parker MacKenzie, and Richard Aitson for taking the time to talk with me about beadwork, Kiowa language, and Kiowa history.

My stay at the University of Iowa has produced an equally stellar list of companions on the journey. Beginning with the Department of History, warm appreciation for the friendships of Lisa Heineman, Johanna Schoen, Shel Stromquist, Colin Gordon, Susan Lawrence, Mark Peterson, Leslie Schwalm, Rosemary Moore, and Henry Horwitz; thank you to the remaining members of a department filled with accomplished, productive, generous, and kind colleagues whose intellectual generosity has enriched my life. Others at the University of Iowa round out my community. Thank you Helena Dettmer, Jean Aikin, Patricia Goodwin, and Mary Strottman.

Thank you Susan Hauer and our community of fellow travelers, Elizabeth Clark, David Kearns, Ann Stromquist, Mary Neppl, Lori Muntz, Debra Johnson, Oliviah Walker, Quanah Walker, Sarah Walker, their generous relatives at Tama, Nicole Leitz, Sydney Switzer, Christine Nobiss, and Angie Erdrich for your friendships.

My acknowledgments include a list of scholars with intellectual heft and infinite humanity whom every person should be so lucky to call friends, mentors, and colleagues. Thank you Jean M. O'Brien, Frederick Hoxie, Patricia Albers, Laura Rigal, Rudi-Colloredo Mansfeld, Laura Graham, Susan Sleeper-Smith, Andrea Smith, Audra Simpson, Lisa Hall, J. Kehaulani Kauanui, Brenda Farnell, Marsha Weissiger, and Ray Fogelson.

Where would I be without all the patient and smart librarians and archivists? Thank you, Debra Baroff, Museum of the Great Plains, Lawton, Oklahoma; Bill Weir, Oklahoma State Historical Society; John Lovett, Western History Collections, University of Oklahoma; the staffs of Hampton University Archives, Southwestern Area Regional Archives, Smithsonian Anthropology Archives, Smithsonian Archives; Newberry Library; Herman Viola; Bob Kvasnicka, National Archives, Washington DC; Charles Rand, National Cowboy and Western Heritage Museum. Thank you to the University of Iowa College of Liberal Arts and Sciences for research support.

Thank you to the University of Nebraska Press, especially Elisabeth Chretien and Ann Baker.

This project and I have benefited from the conscientious and cheerful contributions of Anita Gaul and Catherine Denial. Anita Gaul took over where I left off on the federal appropriations research. I am forever indebted to Anita for her sustained and substantive contributions.

Professor Ken Cmiel of the History Department assigned himself the job of being my friend and mentor when I arrived at Iowa. I greatly admired his approach to academia. Tales of even the worst antics of academics and administrators, foolish and malevolent alike, prompted Ken's mile-wide smile, outstretched arms, and a cheerful, "I know!" Beneath Ken's comical response beat a warrior's heart. That I am still upright and moving forward is a testament to his infinite empathy. Like many, literally throughout the world, I mourn Ken's passing on February 4, 2006. I cherish the memory of his unexpected appearance at my office door and our last conversation the day before he took ill. I hope he knows that, thanks to him among others, but him especially, I made it over the finish line in one piece, with him, his constant companion and wife Ann, and his rock-steady children in my thoughts.

Thank you to my mother, Lorene Jefferson Byars Thompson, and brothers, J. D. Graciano and Kenneth Thompson, for their pride in my work, and to my father, Jack Thompson, who told me I would go to college.

Anyone who knows me will attest that Thomas Rand and Amelia Rand are the brightest stars in my universe. We share a profound love for our Oklahoma-born companion, Buster, a beautiful black sanctuary dog with a self-acquired regal bearing. His death one week after Ken Cmiel's memorial service ended an eleven-year-old journey, but he will forever be a part of us. I've worked on this project through well over half of the children's lives. My completion of the manuscript coincides with Amelia's departure for college; Thomas has been out in the world for a year. Mama, thanks you for your trust, goodness, faith, encouragement, all-around swell companionship, and for growing me up while keeping me current in all things cool. May we never forget where we came from. As for where we're going and what we're doing, let's remember our shared appreciation for Mos Def's "Fear Not of Man," and seek the clear idea.

I optimistically dedicate this book to ya'll.

Kiowa Humanity and the Invasion of the State

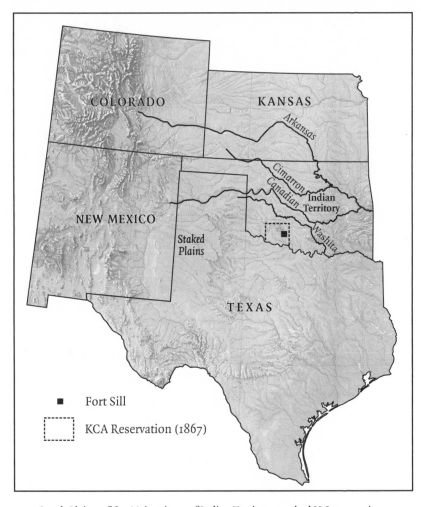

South Plains, 1867. Major rivers of Indian Territory marked U.S. expansion
and Kiowa land cessions stipulated in treaties with the United States. Prior
to land cessions, the Kiowas' land base included contiguous portions of
the five illustrated states and territories.

Chapter 1. **The American Problem**

While working on this project I read Primo Levi's *Survival in Auschwitz*.[1] Levi was an Italian Jew caught in the Nazi net near the end of World War II. He spent ten months at Auschwitz, surviving to see the allied forces liberate the death camp and later writing a stunningly detailed account of life within its walls. Auschwitz was a place of unimaginable horrors, but even there, prisoners developed social organization, an economy, habit, and practice, crafting a version of day-to-day life. The prisoners' daily routines, carried out against a backdrop of genocide, required them to experience simultaneously death and creation, exploitation and human connections, self-interestedness and shared values. Levi's attention to the painful details of the Jews' practices and routines within Auschwitz illustrates the significance of small measures. The practices of Levi and his fellow prisoners constituted a means of self-preservation. Separated from Levi and others' experiences, we possess the luxury of using small measures as a lens into the lives they constructed, preserving their humanity under a regime that saw them as inhuman.

Consider Levi's description of the strategic nighttime rituals of men who shared the tight physical spaces of the prison dormitories. Nights in Auschwitz were dominated by dreams that released desolating grief, interrupted every few hours by the need to relieve oneself of the watery soup served from the camp's kitchens. The nightly procession to the common bucket became a performance of "obscene torment and indelible shame." The bucket bound the men in their mutual misery, but also called for calculation and foresight cultivated by experience.

Each man wanted to avoid carrying an overflowing bucket to the latrine for emptying since the waste of many men inevitably would slop onto one's feet and legs. Given that men slept two to a narrow mattress, their feet at opposite ends, each became invested in teaching the rules for elimination to his bunkmate. Misery, calculation, and social relationships of unknowable duration between men threatened with the possibility of death at a moment's notice converged into a gray space of victimization, agency, choices, and unequal power.

I visited the still new Holocaust Museum soon after finishing Levi's book and rushed to the research center to find what I could about the author. I received a slim file, which opened to an account of his death some five years before. I naively had assumed that a person who could write *Survival in Auschwitz* was impervious to the kind of torment that leads to suicide. Scholars and admirers were left to ponder the reasons for his death without benefit of explanations from Levi himself, without certainty that his death was self-inflicted. The stories he left behind ask us to reflect on irreconcilable experiences: destruction and creativity, dehumanization and dignity, peace of mind in the midst of constant calculation. The probability that Levi killed himself also reminds us that the mark of victimization can never be totally erased.

Levi's account of the death camp led me to look at the American Indian reservation with fresh eyes. Levi, though much closer to his material than I am to the Kiowas' experience, set me on a search for the commonplace in uncommon circumstances where uncertainty, deprivation, and unknowable outcomes dominated life. *Survival in Auschwitz* challenges limited and limiting frames of victimization, agency, and resistance, each on its own an inadequate model for examining matters of genocide and self-preservation. Levi's account of creative human energy transformed into self-replication infused with social values inspired my search for the Kiowas' humanity as they faced a genocidal invasion by the state.

In 1856 the Indian agent for tribes south of the Arkansas River confronted Dohausen, one of the most respected Kiowa leaders of the nineteenth century. The agent threatened to withhold goods from the Kiowas if raids against American settlers continued. Dohausen rebuked the agent for threats he saw as indicative of the Americans' impetuosity[2]:

> The white chief is a fool; he is a coward; his heart is small—not larger than a pebble stone; his men are not strong—too few to contend against my warriors; they are women. There are three chiefs—the white chief, the Spanish chief; and myself. The Spanish and myself are men; we do bad towards each other sometimes stealing horses and taking scalps, but we do not get mad and act the fool. The white chief is a child, and like a child gets mad quick. When my young men, to keep their women and children from starving take from the white man passing through our country, killing and driving away our buffalo, a cup of sugar or coffee, the "white chief" is angry and threatens to send the soldiers. I have looked for them a long time, but they have not come.

Dohausen did not fear violence from the Americans. The Kiowas were strong and respected; the Americans were all talk. But the man with decades of experience began to see the emerging shape of a threat he could not yet name.

The subtext of Dohausen's statement contained his assessment of an unfolding conflict between oppositional systems. Traditional southern Plains diplomacy, politics, and economy centered on a principle of exchange. The law of revenge and specific types and levels of violence—taking horses, captives, and scalps—resolved conflict. The Americans' smallness of heart, material stinginess, and disregard of reciprocity, seen by the Kiowas in the act of refusing the Indians a cup of sugar, were characteristics that the leader observed with concern. The Americans were different from the peoples of the southern Plains. They did not know how to get along, deal with hard feelings, gain respect from others. The Americans reacted to conflict with revenge.

The Plains tribes had already begun feeling the consequences of crude American intrusions. Twenty years of open warfare between the

Sioux and the United States Army had begun in 1854 when an army officer overreacted to the killing of an immigrant's cow. Lt. John Grattan and his men subsequently traveled to the perpetrator's village and opened fire.[3] Grattan and his troops died in the firefight. The U.S. Army retaliated, setting the stage for decades of conflict on the Plains.

Dohausen read the Americans' unpredictable behavior, like the retaliatory attack on an entire village, as the product of emotional immaturity. They did not behave like serious leaders who thought out human costs and consequences before acting. Tribal leaders could not trust the Americans' pronouncements about their intentions or the promises they made. Americans were impetuous, dismissing the give and take of relations on the Plains and the weight of words in this exchange-ordered environment. The Americans' rigidity and sense of entitlement to Native lands, as Indians experienced it in American policies and practices, conflicted with the Kiowas' history of political autonomy and patterns of exchange with others, patterns that sustained the region's economy and external relations. Dohausen could not have known that what fed the Americans' hubris, seen by him as a sign of immaturity, was an American manipulation of the doctrine of discovery first articulated in the famed Cherokee cases that resulted in the removal of southeastern Indians to Indian Territory.[4]

American expansion and hegemonic goals were the root causes of the collision between Americans, Kiowas, and other Plains tribes throughout the remainder of the nineteenth century and into the twentieth. American colonialism was at odds with the ideological foundations of the United States as a nation of law. Treaties signed between Indian tribes and the federal government shrouded American colonialism, especially land transfers, in a veil of legitimacy. The language of cultural conflict established a hierarchy in which Indians held the subaltern position. Tribalism sat at the center of the Americans' critique of Native societies. Native people, from an American capitalist perspective, were communal and nonproductive and organized into tribes lacking self-governance, social organization, systems of law, and economies. The American rejection of tribalism was similar to medieval papal legal discourse of just war against non-normative infidels.[5]

Maureen Konkle argues that "Indian difference" barred them from the path of "endless trajectory toward great perfection" open to Europeans. Europeans and Americans assigned Indians to a "hypothetical trajectory . . . toward the only perfection they can achieve, which is to recognize the superiority of European society and accede to its authority." Americans adopted this teleological logic. Since Indians could not be civilized (not that the Americans had actually expected they could), the most advantageous strategy was, according to President George Washington's secretary of war, Henry Knox, to attach "them to the interest of the United States."[6] Treaties, gift exchanges, and selfless missionaries were strategies to effect the transfer of American ideas of property and Christianity.

Throughout the nineteenth century, American faith in progress justified state-sponsored actions aimed at reducing Indian territories, restricting Indians to reservations, and asserting control over non-consenting Native peoples. The language of Manifest Destiny and Americans' moral responsibility to civilize Indians justified invasion, occupation, and land taking. Too much land, Americans argued, allowed Indians to persist in unproductive tribal practices and obstruct the Americans' introduction of civilizing pursuits. Throughout the nineteenth century, lands passed rapidly out of Indian possession, but the attack on tribalism continued. American public policies crafted in the last quarter of the nineteenth and early twentieth centuries supported eradication of persistent internal tribal autonomy. In a parallel, but not entirely disconnected sphere, anthropologists worked to salvage what they could of Native language, material culture, and Native culture as practice before its presumed vanishing.

For many historians, the term *colonialism* has generally been applied to specific modern historical periods: the American colonies' revolution against British rule; late-nineteenth-century U.S. imperialism in the Philippines; and European colonial rule in faraway Africa and south Asia. U.S. historians have described the establishment of the United States as a history of exploration, discovery, and frontier settlement, omitting colonialism and genocide as agents of nation building. Despite the literature's move toward diverse reassessments of a predominantly homogeneous white male history, the language of Western civilization conquering indigenous wilderness persists.

Native peoples played the part of "the Indian problem," which was synonymous with the plaguing question of how to civilize them, but in reality translated into how to take their lands. The Americans had two choices: war, which the United States could not afford, or the acquisition of lands with promises of peace, protection of Indians against white intruders, and government annuities and commodities. Late-nineteenth-century lawmakers and bureaucrats carried out their attack on Indians with a discourse of tribalism. The term itself connoted for Americans the Indians' rejection of all values associated with capitalism and Christianity: competition, acquisitiveness, recognition of God, and individualism. But, for Indian people, tribalism expressed their social values and humanity.

We do not yet have a very clear picture of how internal colonialism actually worked at the level of personal interactions between Indians and U.S. colonizers. Since the early 1990s, a group of scholars in American Indian studies has had limited success including the United States' colonial relations with American Indian tribes within the theoretical areas that had historically only recognized exported U.S. economic and political colonialism. This early group has largely failed to push beyond generalized transhistorical statements to methodologically instructive scholarly studies of Native North America's experiences with colonialism in its many historically specified locations. Meanwhile, a growing body of literature shows that Native and non-Native scholars are tackling problems of source availability, methodology, and interpretation in their examinations of historically specified studies. Jean Kehoe O'Brien's work on Natick, Claudio Saunt's work on the Muscogee Creek, and Frederick Hoxie's work on the Crow tribe are examples of the recent scholarship that is delving into the complications of colonial relations and breaking out of paradigms framed in binary explanations.[7] Jeffrey Ostler's recent book *The Plains Sioux and U.S. Colonialism from Lewis and Clark to Wounded Knee* uses theory to show that the history of Native America and the United States is rooted in colonialism. The Kiowa experience in the late nineteenth century offers another opportunity to explore how colonialism works, beginning from the premise that the Kiowas, like other tribes, are a sovereign people who were forced to confront an invasion by the colonial state.

Pierre Bourdieu's concepts of habitus and symbolic capital, Nicholas Thomas's framework for colonial societies, and Arjun Appadurai's articulations on exchange and value have also contributed to the shape of this study. Appadurai demonstrated the social significance of things and the ways they circulate, an area of inquiry I have extended to things associated with previously invisible historical actors—Kiowa women and young men. Thomas guided this study away from the progressive academic trends of victimization, resistance, and agency in American Indian history to another vocabulary that simultaneously recognizes and reckons with both the destructive aspects of colonialism and the creative or productive results of indigenous engagements with a colonial project. This creative focus does not overlook resistance and agency, but emphasizes a more holistic picture that includes the unexpected, life-sustaining outcomes of everyday life routines—Bourdieu's habitus—that absorb colonial assaults and carry colonized peoples into the future.[8]

Colonialism is a process both destructive and productive. Indigenous economies are destroyed and new indigenous economic patterns arise. Indigenous institutions that protect and perpetuate community identity are undermined, and other forms of identity expression and validation emerge. Social and political persistence coexist with overt and sometimes violent acts of indigenous resistance. In these ways, the colonized affect the trajectory of genocidal colonial projects insofar as daily life strategies meet changing conditions and preserve collective identity. Thus, indigenous agency is expressed in the give-and-take of struggle. By widening the historian's lens, we enable a larger picture of colonialism to emerge with its multitudinous forms and their connections, its discursive and political operations, and its varied intensities of prejudice and paternalism. The project becomes more than a limited and limiting study in domination. Rather, to return to Thomas's idea, colonialism is the context in which both the colonized and the victimized do the work of creating a new set of conditions in which they both exist, albeit in unequal relations, heavily weighted to the Americans' advantage.

I have approached the question of how nineteenth-century U.S. internal colonialism worked on two levels, the national and the local, and in three sectors: in terms of the state, the commercial sector, and the emerging field of anthropology. Rather than approaching the subject as a chronological narrative, I study three separate but related situations that occur roughly between 1867 and 1910. They tell a common story of late-nineteenth-and early-twentieth-century colonialism, of mutually reinforcing work at the national and local levels, and of local, historically invisible actors. I have produced these interrelated histories by focusing on things associated with the lives of these subjects, traditional documentary sources, anthropological studies, and institutional histories. First, however, the book begins with a chapter on how the Kiowas imagined and practiced their lives before the invasion of the state, followed by a chapter on the values of the state that destroyed the Kiowas' economy and drastically limited their opportunities through the reservation system. The next three chapters, which constitute the heart of the book, focus on Kiowa women and young men.

Kiowa women and young men are not prominent in the documentary record, but the roles they played in the realm of everyday life through the reservation and postreservation periods illustrate the importance of life-sustaining habits of mind and practice and self-imagining under a colonial regime. Young Kiowa men, especially prior to 1874, were repeatedly accused of perpetrating depredations, an undefined category that captured all Indian acts of resistance. Except for the occasional headman's son, their names are unavailable, and specific acts are not linked to specific individuals in documentary sources. As the predominant labor force for raiding, revenge, and hunting parties, young men were associated particularly with horses and mules, which had long been important trade items. The circulation of horses, mules, and other items followed a new trajectory after many Kiowas settled within the reservation boundaries. Young men were carrying out work they had always done, but by the 1860s the United States had criminalized their work and acts of resistance as depredations and the men as outlaws. Following their surrender to Fort Sill in 1874 as prisoners of war and their later incarceration in Florida, young men left a material trail (described in chapter 5) in the form of drawings that have preserved a source of insight into their ideas. Simultaneously, the 1876 Philadelphia Centennial Exhibition exhibited the complex interrelations and colonial collaborations between private, academic, and state sectors. Seemingly separate sectors forged collaborative relationships that mutually reinforced the colonial work of the state.

Kiowa women also felt the impact of American Indian colonialism. Federal Indian policies of the last quarter of the nineteenth century attacked Native culture, tribal law, gendered work roles, and the environment in which Indians lived. The net effect of federal Indian policy and the civilization program was the extension of a Western patriarchal system over Native communities. Kiowa women's work was greatly changed, but not entirely destroyed. After the late 1870s, they no longer had access to valuable buffalo hides. Women did continue to bead for their families while diverting a portion of their labor to the external tourist trade, which was facilitated by licensed Indian traders. In chapter 6, traders' ledgers, diaries, and correspondence shed light on the contribution Kiowa women continued to make to their households and to the preservation of Kiowa material culture traditions.

By 1900, academics, politicians, and government officials had formed a chorus pronouncing with regret and satisfaction, prematurely, the death of Native America. The dramatic decline of Native populations since first contact to some 250,000 gave reason for their predictions. However, in 2006, Kiowas and other recognized and unrecognized tribes continue to exist within the boundaries of the United States, over two million at the last census. Indian people survived the genocide, but were erased from United States history as a national narrative. In the late twentieth century the American public and U.S. political and educational institutions were better prepared for a museum singularly devoted to the Holocaust, carried out by another regime in another time and place, than for its own history of colonialism and genocide. At the time of this writing, the Smithsonian Institution's National Museum of the American Indian, sitting in the shadow of the nation's capital, avoids controversy and confrontation with the United States through exhibits on culture and art while ignoring the colonialism that brought Native people to the brink of extinction. Such projects reinforce the colonizers' sanitization and erasure.

Because the non-Native American public knows very little about Native American history and modern Indian people, they now speculate on a different kind of extinction: authentic, traditional Native culture. One only has to have a conversation or two about casinos and pow-wows to get the drift of this discourse. With that, non-Natives imagine a backward minority population as a sorry legacy of once great Indian nations. The corrupt lobbyist Jack Abramoff, whose clients included such Indian tribes as the economically successful Mississippi band of Choctaws, characterized his tribal contacts as troglodytes in his communications with accomplices.[9] Even if non-Indians can only embrace the memory of Native America in a former time and imagine the continuation of only inauthentic Native Americans, perhaps that still represents progress if measured against the nearly successful genocide of the nineteenth century. At the same time, the continued erasure of Indians in historical scholarship, in the realm of public history abetted by an American-centric popular culture, and in a misleading black-and-white racial paradigm frames a bittersweet legacy.

Chapter 2. **The Kiowa Scheme of Life**

Before their lives were irreversibly disrupted and transformed by the invasion of the United States and its forces, the Kiowa people enjoyed considerable freedom of movement, an independent means for provisioning themselves, and the sovereign right to advance their own interests and choices. Notwithstanding a long history of international trade, first with the Spanish, then Mexicans, and much later Americans, they had retained a large measure of economic independence and political autonomy. And even as they forged a position for themselves in the rapidly expanding mercantile markets of the nineteenth-century southern Plains, the Kiowas continued to engage life inside and outside their own communities according to their own values and habits of mind.

The Kiowa believed themselves to be defined by principles that maintained stability in internal relations, ensured the tribe's security in the material and spiritual realms, respected the individual's dignity, focused their ambition on respect and honor, and distinguished them collectively as Kiowas. The ways in which Kiowa people imagined and lived their lives when they met the American invasion of their territory informed their responses to later assaults on their autonomy. Understanding some of the terms on which they did this is critical to the discussions that follow in later chapters.

By the 1850s the Kiowas inhabited a large territory west of the ninety-eighth parallel, covering much of southeastern Colorado and northeastern New Mexico as well as southern Kansas, western Indian Territory, and northwestern Texas. Once thought of as an inhospitable subregion

of the "Great American Desert" marked by flat, dry, and windy conditions, the southern Plains has emerged from the pages of scholars and
travel writers as a complex and diverse environment. Far from a barren
flat land, the southern Plains varies in elevation and contains microenvironments associated with rivers and streams. Flora and fauna species
adapted to the various conditions of the southern Plains demonstrate
that it is an environment capable of supporting diverse human communities, who, like the Kiowas, successfully exploited its resources
and left their own imprint on the land through their practices.[1]

According to their oral traditions, Kiowa were recent transplants to
the southern Plains, arriving around 1790. Their earliest known history
placed them at three forks of the Missouri River in western Montana.[2]
Following a quarrel between two rival leaders, one band broke off, and
migrated to the country of the Crow tribe with whom they established
an alliance. European Americans reported encountering the Kiowas
(Manrhout) in the northern Plains at the middle of the eighteenth century. Others identified the Manrhout (Kiowas) in 1681 as horse-trading
people who visited New Mexico.[3] From there, they moved to the Black
Hills, where they remained until 1760. From the northern edge of the
Black Hills, they moved to the South Fork of the Cheyenne River. The
Kiowas then traveled to the Platte River country where they remained
until 1790. Eventually, they crossed the Republican and Smoky Hill
Rivers until they reached the Arkansas and finally established themselves on the headwaters of the Cimarron River.[4]

Rufus B. Sage, a deacon's son born in Cromwell, Connecticut, set
out from Ohio in 1841 for what would become a three-year exploration of the central Rocky Mountains. His written account provides a
description of the Kiowa territory on the Cimarron River:

> The Cimarone raises in the range of table lands thirty-five or forty
> miles east-southeast of Taos, and, after following a serpentine
> course for nearly six hundred miles, empties into the Arkansas
> some distance above Fort Gibson. As it emerges from the moun-
> tains, (where it is a stream of considerable depth and a rapid cur-
> rent, confined to a narrow space between high clayey banks, with
> a bed of rock and pebbles,) it expands to a great width, and, in a

short distance, its waters become brackish and unfit for use, till
they finally disappear among the quicksands, and leave a dreary
waste of worse than emptiness, to mark the course of the tran-
sient volumes produced by the melting snows of spring and the
annual rains of autumn.

During its course through the Great American Desert, not a
tree or shrub graces its banks. Its mountain valley, however, is
ornamented with numerous and beautiful groves of cottonwood,
that present among their underbrush a profuse abundance of
plum, cherry, gooseberry, and current bushes, with grape vines;
while the adjoining hills afford oak, pine, pinion, and cedar.[5]

Sage's description captured the complexity of the Kiowas' surrounds
and simultaneously explained their ability to subsist in the southern
Plains—a puzzlement to Americans like Lt. James William Abert. In
1845 Abert led an army reconnaissance that started at Bent's Fort. His
explorations of the Arkansas River, Canadian River, and headwaters of
the North Fork of the Red River took him to the Grand Canyon, eastern New Mexico, the Texas panhandle, and Oklahoma. Abert's assessment of the southern Plains led him to write: "From the idea impressed
by the barrenness of the country, it appeared incredible that so many
Indians could obtain their subsistence from it."[6]

The Kiowas' southward migrations were a result of a combination of
forces.[7] Conflict with the Lakota had developed as they pushed into the
Black Hills and crowded out the Kiowas. The Kiowas were also seeking
better pasturage for their expanding horse herds and trade opportunities with European Americans who had established a presence on the
upper reaches of the Platte and Arkansas Rivers.

The Kiowas had moved into a seemingly difficult environment with
little protection from sun and southwesterly winds, little water, and
little to eat other than game. But Sage's account shows that the southern Plains environment was complex rather than simply barren. River
valleys and creek bottoms broke up dry open lands blown by hot winds.
River microenvironments gave shade and protection, game, water for
humans and animals, and botanical sources for food, medicines, and
manufactures. In 1844, Sage found prairie potatoes, a hairy herba-

ceous plant the size of "our common potato . . . . [that] is dry and sweet tasted [when cooked]," near the Council Grove stream, a tributary of the Osage River, along the Santa Fe Road.[8]

Lieutenant Abert also found a "profusion" of resources in the Kiowa territory located in the contiguous corners of New Mexico, Colorado, Oklahoma, and Texas.[9] He found trees, including cottonwood (excellent tipi pole material), oak and black walnut, and numerous fruits such as plum, cherry, current, grape, persimmon, hackberry, and prickly pear associated with the country's multiple rivers and streams. Abert noted evidence of abundant game and Indian camps in the vicinity of water. Richard Dodge's journals of his travels through the Kiowa country contained details about the numerous grasses that the southern Plains offered. Blue grama and buffalo grass, short grasses of the western Plains grasses, were extremely nutritious sources, "and a favorite with graminivorous animals at all times and seasons."[10] He added admiringly, "It makes up in thickness, what it lacks in length, and horses and cattle not only eat it greedily, but fill themselves much quicker than would seem possible."[11]

A literature devoted to the grasses of the prairies and Plains typically organizes the environment into three zones. The zones that constitute the prairie grasslands reflect adaptations to aridity: the tall grass region east of a mixed-grass prairie running from Saskatchewan to Texas, and the short grass region that borders the Rockies. The edges between zones shift according to drought cycles. The tall grasses farthest east include big bluestem and needle grass, which can grow as high as seven feet in the eastern prairies.[12] Blue grama and buffalo grasses have shorter blades than the big bluestem and needle grass. Their narrow, two-to-three-inch leaves are crowded together at the base of the stems, and grow in small irregular clusters. The unimpressive appearance of blue grama and buffalo grasses belie their highly nutritious, fat-producing properties and hardiness, which assure buffalo year-round grazing.[13] The dominant species of the mixed-grass Plains are little bluestem and needle-and-thread, which grow to heights of one to two feet. In wet years little bluestem and needle-and-thread dominate the mixed-grass Plains; blue grama and buffalo grass dominate the middle region in drought years. Short grasses of the farthest, and driest, west zone have dense root structures close to the surface, which enable them to take advantage of sudden, intense rainstorms, common to the arid southern Plains south of the Arkansas River. The smaller leaf surface minimizes evaporation and allows the plant to devote most of its carbon to the fibrous root system. Severe drought kills such grasses as the buffalo and blue grama in the far western region of the Plains. The various adaptations of the grasses to drought and mixed conditions allowed the region to support large buffalo herds, antelopes, and deer as well as small game.[14]

Following the establishment of their bands on the southern Plains, the Kiowas were able to exploit the grasses' longer growing season, making the region much more ideal for grazing horses than the northern Plains. Their adaptations to conditions are evident in their social organization, subsistence patterns, and divisions of labor, which exhibit traits of opportunism and flexibility well suited to the extremes and variability of the environments they relied upon.

As the Kiowa traveled over wide stretches of territory from one season to the next to hunt, harvest, herd, and trade the resources they depended on, they divided much of their work along gender and age lines. Kiowa labor patterns were marked by interdependence and complementarity across generation and sex. Men and women, the young and old, typically performed different tasks, but the products of these efforts were put to the use and benefit of all. Ethnographic descriptions and historic accounts of Kiowa labor practices reveal that men were the ones who hunted the large game animals, but the capturing of small game was work to which both sexes contributed. Men were the primary caretakers of the horse herds, although women were involved in this work as herders. Women carried out most of the plant harvesting and processing, however, even though men participated in this type of activity when it contributed to their own hunting and herding labors. Women owned and managed their camps.[15]

The buffalo was a critical resource until approximately 1878.[16] The importance of the buffalo to the Kiowas' subsistence is evident in the tribe's social organization and annual movements within the southern Plains environment. Kiowa social organization and seasonal rhythms paralleled that of the bison herds.[17] In late summer, the buffalo formed expansive herds that blanketed large areas of the Plains. In their rutting season, males engaged in ritual combat and mated with the cows. Throughout the summer and rutting season, while the spring calves, now two to four months, grew amid the protection of the herd, the adults became fat and vigorous. They shed their old winter coats for dark-gray and black short-hair coats. At the same time the Kiowa ceremonial bands coalesced for the Sun Dance; afterward, the Kiowa fragmented into *topadoga* (kinship groups) that followed the mating herds until they dispersed for winter. With the coming of winter, nuclear and extended family groups separated from the bands to hunt the scattered herds as they broke up into small male and female groups. Early spring brought on the calving season, and after several months, the herds would again aggregate for the rut, beginning another annual cycle.[18]

Along with the locations of bison, the pasturing places for horses played a critical role in determining the movements of Kiowa bands.[19] Kiowas likely obtained horses from the Crow people after they came down from the Black Hills east of the Crow. In 1682 LaSalle observed plentiful horse herds belonging to the Gattacka (Kiowa Apaches) and Manrhoat (Kiowa).[20] Wissler believed Kiowas might have had horses as early as 1600 based on LaSalle.[21] The Kiowa had mounted warriors by the mid-eighteenth century.[22] Throughout the eighteenth century, Kiowas accumulated horses in such numbers that others observed herds large enough to enable Kiowas to trade them to other tribes such as the Arikara and Mandan for European goods.[23] By the turn of the century Kiowas had migrated into the mountains on the head of the Platte and Arkansas Rivers. After 1800, evidence of large Kiowa horse herds is indisputable. Zebulon Pike reported "immense herds of horses," and in 1831 Jacob Fowler reported that Kiowas had been in possession of large herds ten years earlier.[24] The 1840 peace the Kiowas entered into with the Cheyenne involved a significant giveaway of horses. Cheyenne men, women, and leaders received numerous horses, including 250 from Sa Tank' alone.[25]

Having acquired horses, the Kiowas built a huge economy with
horse herds numbering in the tens of thousands, which they traded
to whites, Indians, and Mexicans. Kiowa dependence on pastoralism
shaped their movements seasonally. They considered locations and
seasons for trading until at least the 1830s when Kiowas began meeting other tribes at large trade fairs. Even after trade fairs ceased to exist, Kiowas traveled to predetermined areas to trade horses to Indians
and to white traders. The persistence of the Kiowas' historical trade
with Mexicans and comancheros sustained an important market for
horses and buffalo hides and sources of goods. Puebloan Indians provided the Kiowas with *biscocho*, a well-liked bread.[26] Kiowas exchanged
goods with white traders. Sometimes they traded on credit against
future horse and mule acquisitions and buffalo hides.

Tribes developed extended relations with individual traders whom
they came to regard as trustworthy. Hatcher, a trader who worked
for the Bent brothers, enjoyed friendly relations with the Kiowas.[27]
Traders contributed an array of materials to the circulation of goods in
the Kiowa economy: a steady supply of beads, awls, blankets, vermil-
ion, and comestibles. Traders encouraged the procurement of horses
and mules from Texas and the production of processed buffalo hides.
Following later treaties and the buffalo extermination, traders became
dependent on payments from Indian annuities. Agents customarily
paid traders who had Indian accounts before spending funds on the
Indians themselves.

Within this environment, the Kiowas relied on a diverse range of
faunal and floral resources for use and exchange. Kiowa women's procurement of plants that were ripening, most productive, and potent
was another important consideration in charting band movements.
Just as there was a seasonal rhythm to buffalo hunting, so there was
a similar tempo to plant collection. For food Kiowa women harvested,
processed, and preserved countless plants, fungi, lichens, and moss,
including numerous roots, tubers, fruits, berries, herbs, plant leaves,
seeds, and nuts. In mid-to-late spring, sumac, wild onion, and prairie potato roots were at their prime.[28] Indian cucumber, a prairie-
growing vine with rough green fruit that looks like a gherkin, comes

in May.[29] Indian sweet potatoes, which also grow on a vine and have narrow, oblong fruit that is sweet, are also available in May.[30] Blazing star is also procured in the springtime when they have a good taste; in later months the roots take on a greasy taste and quality.[31] Summer months were devoted in part to harvesting fruits and berries and digging roots.[32] Prairie turnips are a root shaped like a turnip and available in the spring and summer.[33] Chokecherry, currant, elderberry, grapes, hackberry, plum, and persimmon were gathered and eaten.[34] Lambsquarter's, much like Indian cabbage, pokeweed, and prairie clover, was also available in the summer months.[35] Prickly pear became ripe in late fall. The fruit of the tuna was "much prized by the Indians," who also used the leaves as a mordant for painting on buckskin.[36] Fall and early winter offered nuts, button snakeroot, hazel bush, and bush morning glory as a last-resort food.[37]

Food preparations depended on women's knowledge of dressing the meat of buffalo, antelope, deer, and small game, which was combined with fruits and berries not immediately consumed to create preserved foods. Women dried strips of flesh of buffalo and other large game on racks, pounded the dried meat into a finely textured meal, and mixed it with berries to form pemmican. Pemmican was stored in rawhide parfleches, also manufactured by women, for fall and winter subsistence. The bark of cottonwood trees was stripped and eaten for its pleasant nutty flavor.[38] Women mixed fruits and berries with a cornmeal paste for immediate consumption, and also dried them to be eaten in later months. The leaves of various plants were dried and stored for making teas, some medicinal, some simply beverage. It was possible to preserve seeds and nuts for winter use as well. Supplies of foods rarely lasted until mid-spring when fresh resources became available. Women's plant knowledge in combination with men's hunting knowledge carried the bands through the lean months of late winter and early spring.

Plants were also a critical resource in Kiowa medicine and healing. Women relied on a diverse array of flora for treating special ailments and injuries. Beardtongue root, black raspberry root, and buffalo gourd root teas cured stomachache and diarrhea and induced vomiting.[39] Purple prairie clover tea had a constipating effect.[40] A number of plants were used for lung disorders and coughs, including prairie willow, purple coneflower, soapweed, and white sage.[41] Crane's bill was used to treat toothache.[42] Bee balm soothed insect bites and stings.[43] Gay-feather, ground cherry, ragweed, and wavy-leafed thistle dressed and healed wounds, sores, and burns.[44] The latex of silvery wormwood was helpful in dressing open wounds.[45] Chinaberry tree produced a latexlike substance and a healing agent for treating wounds.[46] Women's knowledge of the medicinal properties of certain native plants indicates their vital role in maintaining the health and well-being of their families.

Women's procurement practices depended upon a comprehensive knowledge of plant identification, location, growing cycles, uses, and appropriate methods of preparation and preservation. The successful exploitation of plants demanded that women follow their cycles of production or lose important resources. Prairie potatoes could be seen briefly in the spring before their stems blew off and they were nearly impossible to find. And their safe and optimal use required that women understand their properties so they could be processed and preserved appropriately. Acorns, for instance, are toxic if they are not leached.[47]

Men also collected the plants that went into making hunting equipment, veterinary medicine, healing, and ceremonies. Albers' discussion of horse care indicates that Plains men possessed a broad knowledge of plant medicine relevant to the care of their horses. They knew the locations that offered the best pasturage (little bluestem grasses and Indian grass) and healed horses' sore backs and festering sores (American licorice), coughs (fetid marigold), diarrhea (broom snakeweed), and distemper (purple coneflower).[48] Kiowa men possessed knowledge of trees particularly useful for materials that went into the production of bows, arrows, clubs, drumsticks, walking sticks, shield stands, tipi poles, stays, and arbors. Women's knowledge of trees aided them in the manufacture of cradleboard frames, drying racks, cooking and eating utensils, and saddles. They also were the primary gatherers for firewood. Both possessed knowledge of dyes, used by men, for example, for marking arrows, painting shields, and coloring bows.

Though plants were critical resources to the Kiowa, bison and game were the major foci of subsistence for both men and women, although at different points in the production cycle. The meat of large ungulates, especially buffalo, was a staple in Kiowa diets. Men formed parties to carry out the arduous work of hunting buffalo. The arrival of the horse dramatically changed transportation among Plains Indians, to particular affect in the hunting of buffalo. Previously men hunted on foot, employing tactics like driving the animal into an area without exit, such as a canyon. Another method involved a coordinated effort to direct stampeding groups of bison over cliffs. The horse and rifle, however, had transformed the buffalo hunt into a more effective, but still dangerous operation. The horse injected flexibility into the hunt, allowing hunters to descend rapidly on resting herds before they stampeded and became lost in the flying dust, ending the hunt. Once the buffalo had been killed, women devoted themselves to slaughtering the animals and packing the meat.[49] Horses could drag up to six hundred pounds of buffalo meat wrapped in skins secured on a travois. Back at camp, women quickly concentrated their energies on processing the meat.

Women processed a hide in various ways depending on whether it would be transformed into a robe, tipi cover, parfleche, shield, drumhead, or clothing. Kiowa women used different methods for winter and summer robes. The work took several days and numerous steps to produce a high-quality finished product. Women usually worked with the hides in pairs, pooling their labor and expertise. Alice Marriott's field notes contain descriptions of women's work with buffalo hides that illustrate the emphasis on women's expertise, cooperation, and knowledge.[50]

Winter hides were staked flat to the ground, stretching them if possible, as soon as they were brought in. A toothed scraper of metal or bone was used to remove all the meat. Frequently two women worked together on this part of the work. The hide was left staked to dry. When it was quite dry it was removed from the stakes and scraped again with a smooth blade. Brains were boiled, mashed to a fine paste, sprinkled on the inner surface of the hide, and rubbed well into it. The hide was dried again for four or five days. Then it was sprinkled with warm water, gathered into a heap, and trampled, so it became thoroughly moist. It was left bunched overnight. In the morning it was hung from a vertical frame outside the tipi, so that the fur might dry. The inner surface was thoroughly rubbed with a flat stone. A large rawhide or sinew strip was hung from the top of the frame and fastened securely to the ground, and the hide drawn back and forth across it. When finished, the inner side of the hide was white and smooth, the hair clean and soft from brushing. Such hides, often painted, were worn as robes and were highly valued.

Summer hides were used for tipis. The initial steps in their preparation were the same, but after the hide dried the first time, it was removed from the stakes, and the hair was scraped off. After being rubbed on both sides with brains and soaked with warm water, the hide was tied to a pole and twisted with both hands until it knotted. It was then hung from the vertical frame and scraped with a sharp stone before being pulled back and forth around the rope. A soft hide was proof of the skill of the tanner.

Some items required special handling. For example, when the skin was intended for the production of moccasins, it was processed in the usual way, but was rubbed with tallow instead of with brains. Tallow stiffened the hide and made it waterproof. Hides were also smoked by laying them on a heap of sticks that covered a fire of rotten wood. Painting involved ground earths mixed with water, or plant juices. After drawing the design with coal on the object, the artist applied the color with a small, sharpened bone dipped in paint.

Kiowa women are perfect examples of the mutual dependence and cooperative labor that characterized Kiowa society. Women's construction of tipis is a study in shared work, reputation making, and cementing social ties. Alice Marriott's notes are worth quoting in full:

> The woman who can fit the hides together is called that—ekomk'upd'a. She must cut all the hides so as to get that flare. She starts cutting at the top of the back. Then she builds the rest to fit that piece.
>
> While the top is still lying on the ground, there is all the sinew they need and a big pile of pounded meat lying beside it. The

older women wait while she cuts the tipi on down. The hides are tide [sic] together along their edges, and the other women sit at intervals along them and sew them up.

The woman who does the cutting takes the biggest piece and lays it out to make the flaps. As she cuts the hides, she pins them together for the other women to sew. She fastens them with little pieces of sinew. A woman sews from one pinned place to the next. They sew in relays. They can get a tipi finished before sundown. The sewing is all even. The water doesn't come through, either.

The women sew the hides on one side and then turn and sew them on the other. They cut the smoke flaps last and fit them in. That's the most difficult job. The one that supervises must do that herself. The one that supervises must be someone else; not the woman that owns the tipi. Even if she is good, she must not do it, but must invite someone else.

At sundown, when they finish, the woman in charge takes this pounded meat. It is good, and it is still damp and is mixed with fruit. She gives it to each woman where they sit sewing. Then they eat it.

There were very, very few who could cut tipis. The cutter ties the holes for the sticks and then puts the sticks through. She does this after the tipi is up.[51]

When Marriott's source was age fifteen, her mother arranged to have skilled women make the first of two hide tipis for her. They were made in the way she described to Marriott. Each required twenty hides, "all soft-tanned," "all the same size." She watched the ten women who made her first tipi, which she would not move into right away because it was so new.[52]

Tipi making required collaboration and organization that flowed from the cutting and pinning skills of the expert woman. Other women followed the lead of Marriott's source because of her known expertise. Ten women working together accomplished in a day the work one woman could only perform over many days. But the reason for this seems to have been more than work, time, and efficiency. As the woman who described tipi making pointed out, even if the woman who would eventually occupy the tipi possessed similar levels of talent, she put the tipi making into the hands of another accomplished woman. Although the tipi involved the work of many women, the lead woman added the tipi to her personal tipi count and consequently to her prestige and status. Generosity, criticism, and respect flowed in all directions among the talented women, reinforcing social bonds and social values of mutual interdependence.

Kiowa women's social convention of numbering the dresses and tipis they make by hatch marks on a stick are comparable to the well-known male practice of recording honored deeds through pictograph painting on buffalo hides.[53] These gendered forms created a permanent and public community record of men and women's achievements. Keeping count of dresses and tipis also demonstrated ways in which women valued work, measured achievement, and asserted their self-worth.[54] Each notch that represented the production of a tipi reinforced ideas of cooperation, collaboration, and respect, the social glue of the Kiowa women's world. Also, their participation in the nineteenth-century Kiowa Industrious Women's Society encouraged cooperation and rewarded the accomplishments of its members, who consisted of five or six women in middle years reputed to be the best hide tanners and cutters in the tribe. Like some men's societies, it passed out of existence, and little is known about it.[55] In Kiowa society, as suggested in Alice Marriott's extensive field notes, women gained respect and status in their families and among their peers not only through their success in provisioning their own households and families with food, clothing, and shelter, but also through their varied efforts to display and share their productive knowledge, skills, and accomplishments within wider community circles. Bernard Mishkin compiled a list of "The Most Famous Women" from his 1935 fieldwork among the Kiowas in Oklahoma.[56] Of the twenty-one women included in his list thirteen were famous for proficiency in women's crafts, five famous for good looks, and three famous for women's sports, thus demonstrating the linkage between expertise, skill, and status among Kiowa women.

The socialization of girls and young women focused on the realm of work, bearing, and reputation. Young girls learned the arts of maintaining camp, clothing production, beadwork, and procurement through play and practice under their relatives' watch. Their play life as young children included young boy relatives and friends. Together, they explored their environment, played games, and shared adventures, until the age when it was no longer appropriate for such close relations. At the time of young adulthood, boys and girls were segregated in many of their activities, and certain taboos, such as being alone together in the family tipi, were imposed. Until that time, however, young girls and boys were permitted to have shared experiences that contributed to their early education in the work, social practices, and social values of the Kiowas.

The early life of a young Kiowa woman emphasized the training in increasingly specialized work, much of which has already been described, and in the maintaining of proper comportment to ensure her reputation. Although Kiowa women had the option of marrying outside the social rank of their families, marrying a man who was competent in his role as provider was a paramount priority. A woman's success in this regard depended, in part, on her own competency in skillful work. The Kiowa woman played an important and complicated role in her husband's good reputation. Her camp, preparedness in receiving his relatives and friends, comportment during his absences and so on, if done well, made her reputation and enhanced his.

Conversely, her husband's hunting, capturing, and warring competency enhanced her material life and social capital. His success increased the means by which she could receive relatives and friends in appropriate ways and allowed her to redistribute some of her family's material goods to relatives. A husband who lacked competency and success in such endeavors undermined his wife's standing, but more seriously, produced deprivation. A Kiowa women's song speaks to this interdependence:

> I envy those who are married,
> They have their racks of meat hanging
> And they always have plenty to eat.
> I have no one to get me meat.
> Oh, how I envy those who are married.[57]

The division of labor between Plains men and women has been portrayed by scholars as uneven, but their organization of work allowed them to gain social capital from their respective competencies and successes. Women's processing of hides and meat, as one specific example, realized the value of men's hunting, while men's trade with others realized the value of women's hide production. Women's work transformed raw buffalo material into food, manufactures, and robes, both for Kiowa consumption and for trade. Men's trading activities placed the hides into the circulation of goods that linked the Kiowa and mercantile economies, providing them with access to guns and other goods. The valuation of men and women's work changed with disruptions to the southern Plains economy, the coming of the reservation system, loss of buffalo, and rapidly changing technological and economic conditions. As later chapters show, the valuation of men and women's work was not only economic, but became infused with political meaning as American colonialism became an increasingly successful dominant force in Kiowa lives.

Like women, men achieved repute and honor for the labors they typically undertook. Skill in hunting and craftsmanship brought reward to men, but it was horse raiding and warfare that brought them the most honor and acclaim. Ethnographic sources describe the conditions and terms for achievement, respect, honor, and prestige in Kiowa society through work in much greater depth for men than for women. What is presented next on male status acquisition reflects this unfortunate disparity.

All men hunted, from young boys to the oldest of males, but at the extreme ends of the age spectrum the children and elders tended to concentrate their efforts on small game. D'*ogudle*, young men aged eighteen to thirty, constituted the bulk of labor for the hunting of bison and other large ungulates. They also contributed most of the labor for raiding and revenge taking, dangerous work that required much skill and discipline. Reflecting on earlier times, a Kiowa woman observed, "Parents, friends, relatives held the young man dear because his life was uncertain. He may be killed at any time. For that reason they value him."[58]

Though hunting and raiding constituted obvious economic and political practices, they also established arenas in which men built their reputations. Rules governed the acquisition of honors, the very highest of which was being first to count coup on an enemy. A man's performance in the practice of raiding, hunting, and revenge was the basis of other men's assessments of his talent and character. Those assessments traveled back to the band's camp and became his reputation and identity as a *sa(n)k'iahi*, a good, capable worker, a man who can handle horses, a good hunter and fighter.[59] A man's honors accumulated into a permanent history preserved in the band's oral history and through pictographic paintings on personal buffalo robes.

Raiding, revenge, and war parties offered opportunities for men to apply the principle of balancing individualistic quests for honors and submission of ego to the welfare of the group.[60] This art of balance was dramatically evident in the discipline of the Qoichegau military society.[61] Composed of ten sash wearers, ten assistants, retired members, and young "colts," Qoichegau members were distinguished by the practice of being the first warriors into battle and the last to retreat.[62] Society members involved in raiding or revenge parties might sacrifice their lives if necessary when it appeared enemies might overtake the group. In such cases, Qoichegau society obligated members to stake themselves down (by an arrow shot through the sash) and continue fighting, risking death, to cover the other warriors' retreat.[63] Even common warriors outside the ranks of Qoichegau might acquire comparable honors by voluntarily breaking away from the escaping group, diverting the enemy, and protecting the retreat of the others. Thus, the highest honor an individual warrior could earn involved acts of self-sacrifice for the benefit of other men and women.

A mature man's reputation and status in Kiowa society were materialized in horse wealth. A young man's early efforts in reputation building were determined to some degree by the material circumstances of his family of origin and extended kin. Kiowa society was composed of four ranks ranging from *ongop*, or the strongest and most esteemed families, to the lowest rank of the unproductive and poor.[64] Young men of *ongop* families enjoyed material advantages that aided their early reputation-building efforts, such as possession of large horse herds, an expectation of that rank.[65] A young man could count on a share of the family's herd to help establish himself. Sons of *ongop* families, with family support and inherited horse wealth, were free from the labor of accumulating horses and could therefore devote themselves to the acquisition of more socially valuable honors through war and revenge parties. A son of a less-well-off family without inherited horse wealth was relatively disadvantaged. Ambitious young men whose families were not *ongop* rank faced the dual burden of acquiring horses through raiding in addition to accumulating honors through acts of skill and courage.[66] Kiowa emphasis on reputation and its connection to status and rank required individualistic achievement, but did not overlook the benefit and necessity of balancing that individualism with obligations to social groups, strong character, and dignified bearing.

Young Kiowa boys were initiated into the realm of male relations through Kiowa military societies. There have been eight military societies recorded since the late eighteenth and early nineteenth centuries, with some falling away over time. The most recent military society, Ohomo, emerged in 1884.[67] The sodalities were also open to young people who assumed defined roles through which they learned proper conduct and social values. Polahyup (Rabbits) was a children's society from which young boys were then invited to join adult military societies.[68] Adult societies offered special roles as assistants to the leader (aljoqi) for exceptional boys.[69] Aujoqi (those who keep things handy) and ijeqi (distributors or rationers, in reference to serving at shared meals) were usually favored boys (audetalyi) of high-ranking families. A talisan (boy who can walk, or little boy), recruited at age seven or eight, was assigned various responsibilities, including maintaining the fire, serving food, heating the dance drum, carrying messages, and providing general assistance to the military society leader. The boys held their positions until age seventeen. In the intervening years, a boy's identity had

evolved from that of a little boy to a *tali* (boy) to a *d'ogudlsan* (old boy).
Thus began a young Kiowa boy's education in balancing his investments
in individualistic achievement with those to larger social groups.[70]

Boys and girls' education involved observation, membership in societies, and interactive pedagogical activities with relatives. Whether
being taught how to identify a buffalo's organs during the slaughter,
training horses for specialized work, understanding the fine points of
hunting, or learning any skill, boys becoming men were dependent on
their kinship networks.[71]

Men and women's systems of knowledge, education, and recognition
turned on different kinds of activities. But, overall, women and men's
activities were complementary in the prereservation economy. The
work was differentiated but in ways that established a necessary inter-
dependency between the sexes that benefited the entire community. As
camp owners, women were responsible for the upkeep, construction,
and maintenance of shelter; procurement of plant resources; coordi-
nation of food preparation activity; and manufacture and repair of gar-
ments. Men hunted, determined the movements of the camps, scouted
the whereabouts of game and other resources, initiated relationships
with outsiders, and defended their communities from enemies. Each
kind of focus and expertise, that is, attention both to the internal work-
ings of the camp and to its placement in a wider environment, determined the safety and well-being of Kiowa bands throughout the year.
When camps moved, as they frequently did, the disassembling of tipis
required impressive managerial skills on the part of women who organized poles, skins, all supplies, robes, the elderly, and small children
for travel to a new location on horses and travois. Equally, mapping out
the routes of travel, determining opportunities for procurement and
trade, scouting out safe and habitable sites, and spotting the presence
of enemies demanded expertise on the part of men. Together, the different yet complementary responsibilities of men and women created
a balance. This fostered a wider pattern of cooperation that facilitated
the productivity of the entire community.

Nineteenth-century Kiowa self-identification was located in family,
band, social rank, and tribe. Kinship was central to the way in which

Kiowas thought about themselves in relation to others, and to the reinforcement of social ties. Bilateral descent, in contrast to descent
through mother's or father's line, allowed an individual to maintain
strong ties to both sides of her family. All children of parents and their
siblings were brothers and sisters. Mother and mother's sister, father
and father's brother, mother and mother's brother, and father and father's sister had separate kinship terms. Some kin relationships had
specific protocols and were expected to be especially strong. For example, brothers and sisters treated one another with respect, and after
reaching age ten, they did not spend as much time together as when
they were younger; a man was close to his sister's husband; sisters-in-
law were also close. Frequently, a man married the sisters of his first
wife. Sororal polygyny and arranged marriages contributed to reinforcing and extending kinship lines.[72]

Kindreds (topadoga) were the fundamental units of Kiowa society.
They were comprised of extended family groups consisting of a leader,
usually the oldest of a group of brothers, his own brothers, his sisters
and their spouses, his parents, the brothers of his mother's father, and
his sons and daughters with their families.[73] The kindred formed the
nucleus of the Kiowa bands, joined by persons from unrelated "poor"
people from the fourth and lowest rank and a following of non-kin
from other lower ranks of Kiowa society. Topadoga ranged in size from
twelve to fifty tipis, and families moved between several bands as a result of disagreements or to visit with other relatives. Thus, residence
groups were fluid, allowing individuals and families to move from one
to another. Consequently, mobility preserved social harmony when
disputes arose and broadened access to resources.

Households were equally varied. Many were built around monog-
amous unions, consisting of the couple, their offspring, and elderly
parents and unmarried siblings. Some were polygynous; the additional wives usually include the sisters of first wives. Kiowa language,
not to mention the historical record, evidences the existence of senior-
ity among wives. At'ontaiade is "first wife," a'yogutaade is "second wife
during the life of first," and oyoytade is "second wife; he married again
after the death of first," and so on.[74] The practice of men taking mul-

tiple wives required young women to learn the rules of this particular
social arrangement. Domestic abuse was not unknown, but household
harmony was not normally achieved through coercion. Equally, men
had to learn the art of engaging with multiple wives in order to maintain peace and productive relations. The most obvious benefit of polygynous practices to women was the potential for distributing work,
sharing responsibility for children, and pooling knowledge and expertise. Jealousy was not an uncommon occurrence, but could not be permitted to go unattended if it led to abuse by the first wife of another
wife. Relatives might step in to resolve the conflict. Polygyny increased
men's advantages economically and socially. Multiple wives increased
the chances of producing children who would survive into adulthood.
The wives constituted a labor pool that could carry out more work than
one wife could successfully complete. If they were not sisters, multiple
wives also extended the husband's kinship network.

During the reservation and postreservation period, loss of resources,
market changes, federal Indian policy, and the civilization program
eroded the institution of polygyny. Following the Kiowas' entry into the
extended market for buffalo hides, multiple wives became an important labor pool that processed hides for the Indian traders. The work
of processing hides demanded more of women's time as the demand
for hides increased until the buffalo extermination was completed.
The Code and Court of Indian Offenses, created originally in 1883 and
established on the Kiowa reservation in 1888, outlawed polygyny, although Kiowa men continued to take multiple wives.[75] The pressure to
end this social practice continued as land allotment, Christianization,
and boarding school education eliminated it altogether after the turn
of the century.

Though Kiowa communities were built on principles that worked
toward maintaining peace and cooperation, they were not egalitarian.
There were important differences in the wealth and standing of families and bands. Social rank was determined by birth, but was not necessarily unchangeable. Kiowa society was organized into four ranks
whose membership was determined by personal attributes, kin relations, military prowess, and economic success. The hierarchy was fluid

and shaded in demarcation. *Ongop* rank was synonymous with "fine, distinguished, perfect, best" persons. Members exhibited fine bearing, generosity, martial achievements, and enough property to distribute among others. The main requirement was a distinguished war record. The second grade was *ondeigupa*, who had similar requisites, absent only the war deeds. Usually nonmilitary specialists such as herders, artists, and hunters fell into this category. *Koon* lacked military achievements and economic independence but were seen as valued people. Occasionally, the phrase "They will always be here" marked their position in the band. Finally, *dapom*, the lowest class, lacked honesty and industry, and its members were marginalized. Men of the lower grades could move up the ranks through military and raiding activities that increased their horse herds and enhanced their reputations. *Ongop* tended toward exclusivity, however, with its membership restricted to relatives. Family membership did not automatically admit a warrior into *ongop*, however. The exclusion of warriors of lesser ranks tended to be the result of their concentration of energies on acquiring horses rather than accruing military achievements. Thus, they might acquire reputations for economic success, but continue to lack the required honors.[76]

Scholars and hobbyists have shown a preoccupation with the so-called war culture or warrior culture of Plains Indians, which obscures a more fundamental characteristic of Kiowa life. Kinship and other kinds of relationships forged across kinship lines and band affiliation were significant to Kiowa unity because they reinforced interdependence between the individual and the collective. Military societies, then and now, played an important role in cementing relationships. Kiowa males, regardless of war record or social rank, belonged to a society. The societies, including the women's industrious society, were based on the institution of kom or "blood-brothers."[77] Kom relationships were lifelong friendships between Kiowas. The men's societies were active principally during the summer Sun Dance when all the bands congregated. The societies were in charge of policing the communal buffalo hunt to prevent individuals from taking more buffalo than their share and thereby depriving others. The purpose of Kiowa sodalities was to ensure an organized buffalo hunt and thus the security of the entire tribe.

The conceptualization of Kiowa humanity is brought to the foreground here in a pointed way because it has been so obscured by the image of Kiowas as obsessed with war. Without attention to the questions of what constituted a good Kiowa life, we simply cannot see their humanity, and we build our histories on nineteenth-century stereotypes. Native peoples can claim as a part of their history the existence of "brilliant plans for living" that interwove the social, political, and economic habits of mind, spirit, and daily life into a cohesive whole. Gender in the Kiowas' plan for living exhibits the mutual reinforcement of men and women's work, while avoiding the patterns of patriarchy found in Western society. Women not only managed the camps but owned them as well. Men and women rejected interference in their respective areas of work by the other gender. The activities of women who traveled with revenge and war parties, in addition to economic practices and ceremonial life, show that gender was a flexible dividing line. The realm of work appears to illustrate best the interdependence that was an organizing principle in relations between men and women.

After the onset of American domination, the attack on Kiowa humanity is evident in the area of gendered relations. The civilization program included the imposition of patriarchal patterns and practices, which in combination with conditions of poverty, lost economic roles, and criminalization of Kiowa cultural practices, undermined the old ethic of interdependence between men and women. The tragedy was more than a question of women's loss of status, but the erasure of a principle that made Kiowa and tribal life a "brilliant plan for living."

Chapter 3. **Values of the State and U.S. Indian Policy**

O n October 21, 1867, the United States and Kiowa, Comanche, and Apache tribes entered into a treaty that called for peace and established a reservation carved out of lands in southern Indian Territory.[1] In exchange for the tribes' concessions on the construction of roads, railways, and military posts, the United States government promised to pay an annuity.

A commission of U.S. government and military representatives led by Nathaniel G. Taylor, Commissioner of Indian Affairs for the Department of Interior, met the tribes at the site of the peace council camp in the Medicine River Valley, about three miles above the town of Medicine Lodge, Kansas.[2] The commissioners had come from meeting with the Oglala and Brulés Sioux and others in the north. They had set out from Omaha in late September for Medicine Lodge Creek. After meeting the military contingent at Ellis, Kansas, they traveled south via Old Fort Ellsworth, Fort Harker, and Fort Larned. From there, they crossed the Arkansas River at Big Bend. They camped and watered their animals at Walnut Creek, Cherry Creek, and Rattlesnake Creek, reportedly the center of the buffalo range at that time. Finally, the large party descended into the Medicine Lodge Valley where they sited Indian camps. The meeting of the Americans and southern Plains tribes resulted in the Treaty of Medicine Lodge Creek and the Kiowa, Comanche, and Apache reservation.

The treaty is an entry point into a study of American Indian–U.S. relations in a colonial context.[3] The Kiowas and other tribes treated with the Americans and fought them on the battlefield, but they were far removed from the most significant work of the state, which tribal leaders well understood. American treaty promises, including the provision of rations and annuities critical to the Kiowas' transition from a broken economy to the reservation system, were contingent on the work that took place in distant Washington. However, the United States Congress, the Departments of the Interior and War, and the Executive Office took steps that impeded the fulfillment of those promises. The state was a major agent in the Native genocide that we lump under such terms such *colonialism, expansion,* and *hegemony.* Behind such terms is a system that determined Kiowa, Comanche, and Apache reservation conditions and rationalized a federal Indian policy that nearly rendered American Indians within the United States extinct.

Both houses of the legislative branch played central roles in shaping the conditions of local Indian reservations. Specifically, the Senate confirmed treaties with Indian tribes, and the House of Representatives passed legislation containing appropriations to cover U.S. obligations defined in the treaties. Both houses were involved in the work of arriving at final appropriations figures. Appropriations legislation, however, did not emerge from a vacuum, as the debates in which appropriations were situated reveal. The debates put the state's intentions in the context of colonial ideology and the language of genocide.

On the surface, the central issues of the 1860s that bogged down the work of the legislators included questions about which house possessed the authority to create treaty commissions and approve funding for them, the transfer of responsibility for Indian affairs back to the War Department, and the implications of treaties already in existence for the future of the federal budget. House and Senate discussions over seemingly pragmatic colonial housekeeping matters were accompanied by the mission to civilize Indians and destroy tribalism. The floor debates also contained ideological digressions into large questions about continuing to treat with Indians, the pros and cons of providing Indians annuities and rations, and Indian land title.

The exchanges among legislators show the systemic goal of keeping Indians on an abstract and real trajectory to economic and political marginalization.[4] The House and Senate debates show that compensation for ceded Indian land outlined in treaties metamorphosed into state assistance for poor Indians. Native persistence in tribal culture explained their failure to achieve civilization and material improvement. The language of anti-tribalism and Indian failure justified appropriation reductions and tied the work of Washington lawmakers to the misery of the local reservation. A study of federal Indian appropriations produced from 1860 to 1910 in the context of the legislative debates illuminates the United States government's role in depriving American Indians of the means to exist (see appendix A). Federal lawmakers' actions and inactions helped form local conditions that enabled genocide.

The Kiowas and the United States brought their respective histories and agendas to the Medicine Lodge Creek meeting grounds just over the Kansas line in 1867. The Kiowas brought decades of experience in southern Plains relations and diplomacy, political and economic autonomy, and significant status as one of the major tribes of the region. But recurrent disease, conflicts with intruders, and the loss of Dohausen, who had provided extraordinary leadership before his death in 1866, had also challenged the Kiowas' resources. More than anything, the Kiowas wanted peace, protection from white intruders, the removal of soldiers from their area, and permission to continue hunting. The Americans brought a vision of empire and an ideology. Accompanying U.S. colonial ambitions were policies aimed at taking Native lands and creating reservations, a politicized bureaucracy that insinuated itself into tribal affairs, and an ideology that rationalized policies and laws designed to destroy Native people. The U.S. government wanted to accomplish two incompatible goals: to avoid an all-out Indian war of extermination to protect its international image and to acquire Indian land and other resources through treaties while simultaneously undermining tribal autonomy. The Americans approached the treaty table with insincere declarations of respect for tribes' political status and of desire for peace. In reality, the Americans treated with tribes because they lacked the resources and the will to wage a war that would clear the lands of Indian people.

Relations between the Kiowas, Apaches, and Comanches and the United States evolved in the context of sweeping geopolitical changes in the southwest, including the separation of Mexico from Spain, of Texas from Mexico, and the admission of Texas to the Union, all in the first half of the nineteenth century.[5] The Kiowas, Apaches, and Comanches confronted these shifts while keeping track of relations with the removed southeastern tribes who occupied much of Indian Territory and with the numerous friendly tribes and enemies surrounding them. The complicated web of external relations conditioned the tribes to adaptation, preservation of their trade interests, and diplomatic acuity. The Americans, the most recent newcomers, were just one group of many with whom the Kiowas, Apaches, and Comanches dealt, and the tribes' long experience with outsiders had shaped their political agility and endurance. Combined with the tribes' successful adaptation to the challenging southern Plains environment, this diplomatic deftness made them a formidable obstruction to American expansion.

As noted in chapter 2, the Kiowas migrated to the southern Plains in the late eighteenth century, responding in part to the pressures of shifting tribal territories in the northern Plains and the pull of year-round grazing for their horses. Seeking allies, they negotiated an introduction to the Spaniards of Texas through the Skidi Pawnee. In 1800, the Kiowas, as part of a large group, explored northern New Mexico, conducting raids and making their presence known. Subsequently, the Norteños—a name the Spanish assigned to tribes north of them, including the Kiowas—sent an emissary to Taos carrying three crosses. A delegation of twenty-three Norteños followed, conveying their desire to camp on the Arkansas River and to trade at Taos. In doing so, the Kiowas and other Norteños encroached on a longstanding relationship between the Spaniards and the jealous Comanches. The Kiowas unleashed a preemptive attack on the Comanches, thus failing in their initial overture to the Spanish.

The Spanish dispatched a representative to explore the possibility of a friendly relationship with the Norteños through the Kiowas. The Kiowas accepted the invitation and promised to bring ten other tribes to make peace with the Spanish. After preliminary exchanges of representatives, peace was in the offing. The final hurdle the Spanish faced was mending relations between the Kiowas and Comanches, but the tribes themselves had reached an agreement in 1806.

The Mexican War of Independence and the 1824 Mexican constitution complicated the tribes' relations with Mexico.[6] The constitution and the principle of federalism put the Mexican states and territories in the position of handling their Indian relations, but not entirely independently. New Mexico's required consultation with the central government led the Indians to question the authority of the representatives who negotiated with them. Consequently, the area between the Comanche and Kiowa territory and that controlled by Mexicans remained an unstable borderland. Comanche and Kiowa raiding reached far into Mexican territory, with minimal consequences to the tribes. The Mexicans sought and achieved a peace with the Comanches and Kiowas, in 1826. When New Mexico acquired department status in 1836, it gained more autonomy and direct responsibility for its Indian relations. During the period of Governor Amijos's administration, 1837–43 and 1845–46, New Mexico's Indian policy mimicked the gifting policy of the Spaniards. Santa Fe was a source of vermillion, corn, mirrors, knives, buttons, cloth, and other manufactured items that the Indians prized.

The Kiowas' political acumen established the tribe's place in a complex network of relations on the southern Plains. Exchanges of spoken promises predated recorded treaties with the United States. Certain values made this delicate process possible, including mutual respect for other parties' autonomy and sovereignty, conflict resolution, and respect for established practices of interaction, combined with traits of flexibility and opportunism. The Americans' racism and unwillingness to recognize these values blinded them to the diplomatic finesse required to negotiate the southern Plains world of competing sovereign interests. The Kiowas' early history on the southern Plains indicates a sophistication that was essential to successful conduct of relations in that world. Their command of southern Plains politics contrasted starkly with American settlers' imaginative portrayals of irrational, warring savages.

These developments coincided with a nationalist program of expanding power over the Great Plains. Territorial acquisitions fed the momentum of American migration, carrying great numbers of the hopeful, desperate, and adventurous to promising opportunities in the West. The first mass movement of Americans began at Independence, Missouri; traversed an overland route across the Plains; and stopped at Willamette Valley, Oregon.[7] By 1848, gold had been discovered in California, and 14,000 people had traveled over the Oregon Trail. When California achieved statehood in 1850, its population stood at 93,000.[8] The population of Oregon Territory had reached 13,000 and Utah Territory 11,000. Within a decade the population of California grew by another 287,000 Americans, and San Francisco, Los Angeles, and Sacramento rapidly grew into major population centers. By 1850, two million people had crossed the Mississippi into Indian-occupied territories. Business interests seeking to expand U.S. commerce pressed for communication and transportation links across the Great Plains. The result was a network of trails and railway lines, including the Santa Fe Trail, laid out in 1822, that cut across Kansas, through the northwestern corner of Indian Territory, and into New Mexico, crossing over the territory of the Kiowa, Apache, and Comanche Indians.

Federal Indian policy and law, shaped by lawmakers and bureaucrats who collaborated in westward expansion, provided the means to clear Indians from the path of American settlers, trails, and railroads. David E. Wilkins's river metaphor is useful for conceptualizing the tangle of sources that contributed to the formation of federal Indian policy and law. Wilkins's river is federal Indian policy and law, fed by streams of legislation, departmental policies, executive orders, and court decisions originating in various branches of the U.S. government.[9] The framers of the United States Constitution provided very little to work with in terms of guiding U.S.–Indian relations. Article I, Section 8, of the Constitution commonly referred to as the commerce clause, "stipulates the power of the Congress To regulate Commerce with foreign Nations, and among the several States, and with the Indian Tribes." Article II, Section 2, which describes the powers of the president as commander in chief of the army, navy, and state militias, states, "He shall have Power, by and with the Advice and Consent of the Senate, to make Treaties, provided two-thirds of the Senators present concur."

A trilogy of Supreme Court cases, including *Cherokee v. Georgia* and *Worcester v. Georgia*, produced landmark decisions written by Chief Justice John Marshall.[10] The Marshall decisions defined U.S.–Indian relations that both recognized tribal sovereignty and designated Indians as domestic dependent wards of the state. Between the Marshall decisions and *ex parte Crow Dog* in 1882 a small number of cases were heard in territorial and state courts, but they failed to form a coherent unified body of law.[11] Meanwhile, the Department of Interior's Bureau of Indian Affairs opportunistically filled the void, enhancing its role in U.S.–Indian relations. Simultaneously, federal Indian policy became more militarized as the Americans focused on the Great Plains, where numerous Plains tribes effected a barrier to westward expansion.

The growing settler society of the mid-nineteenth century introduced a source of constant conflict for the tribes. The settlers' close proximity to the Indians ensured disagreements, charges, and countercharges of thievery and aggressive acts. Texas statehood presented settlers with a higher authority on which to press their claims. They demanded government protection against Indian depredations, while carrying out depredations of their own against Indians.

Following a period of erratic but destabilizing conflicts, the United States met with some northern Plains tribes in 1851 and entered into the first Treaty of Fort Laramie. The United States sought the tribes' agreement to remain within their respective territories in order to achieve peace among Indians and between Indians and Americans. U.S. conflict with the Sioux tribes continued during the American Civil War and following the second Treaty of Fort Laramie in 1868, in which the United States agreed to abandon the Bozeman Trail. The Sioux and other Plains tribes continued to fight the United States well into the 1870s. Indian resistance to the United States was not completely over. It took the United States Army and two Chiricahua Apache scouts to capture the elusive leader Geronimo in 1886.

Lt. Gen. William Tecumseh Sherman made an explicit connection between U.S. Indian policy and law, the treaties signed with the Great Plains tribes in the 1850s and 1860s, westward expansion, and American empire. By assigning the Sioux to territory north of the Platte

River and the Arapahos, Cheyennes, Comanches, Kiowas, and Apaches to lands south of the Arkansas River and east and west of certain lines, Sherman asserted, "This will leave for our people exclusively the use of the wide belt east and west, between the Platte and the Arkansas, in which lie the two great railroads over which passes the bulk of the travel to the mountain territories."[12]

The conflicts of this period produced violence that shocked some Americans, including the slaughter of the Cheyenne leader Black Kettle's peaceful camp in the Sand Creek Massacre. Some Americans called for peaceful relations with Indians and avoidance of further embarrassing episodes like Sand Creek. Throughout the 1860s the United States' Indian policy began to take the shape that would later become known as Grant's Peace Policy. Even before Ulysses S. Grant assumed the U.S. presidency in 1869, federal Indian policy had come to center on the goal of civilizing, Christianizing, and humanizing Indians. In March 1869, Grant consented to the establishment of the Board of Indian Commissioners, which—in the language of the law if not in practice—shared joint control with the Department of Interior over the disbursement of Indian appropriations. The intention was to reform the Bureau of Indian Affairs and drive out corruption. Another important change in the structure of Indian policy was the division of Indian agencies among various Protestant church organizations, whose respective missionary boards nominated agents and employees for the agencies. The Quakers quickly organized and met the president. The Orthodox Friends assumed responsibility for the Central Superintendency, whose district included the Kiowa, Comanche, and Apache reservation. Lawrie Tatum was assigned as Indian agent to the reservation in 1869.[13]

Although Grant's Peace Policy was not formally organized and instituted at the time of the Treaty of Medicine Lodge Creek in 1867, the tide of policy had already shifted to one that claimed a civilizing, Christianizing, humanizing mission. The Americans' stated intentions to humanize Native people only underscored the subaltern status assigned to them. Combined with the Jacksonian assertion of tribal powerlessness as grounds for abandoning diplomacy, Indian policy continued its trend toward mass land seizures and a coercive reservation system through treaty making. Tribalism emerged as a consistent theme of colonial discourse and is evident in the treaties, congressional debates, and appropriations bills of the mid-to late-nineteenth century. All tribes, whether or not they held treaties with the U.S. government, experienced the consequences of a policy bent on eradicating all aspects of tribal life.

The Treaty of Medicine Lodge Creek was the fourth in a series of agreements, the first of which had been the 1837 Treaty with the Kiowa, Kataka, and Tawakaro Nations of Indians. Treaty history between 1837 and 1867 illustrates the progressive erosion of the Kiowas' autonomy. The first official contact between the United States and the Kiowas and other tribes occurred with the expedition of the First Dragoons led by Henry Leavenworth in 1834. The Kiowas departed the negotiations prior to the 1835 treaty of peace eventually signed by the Comanche and Wichita tribes. Two years later, the Kiowas, Apaches, and Tawakoni traveled to Fort Gibson in Indian Territory and signed their first treaty with the United States on May 26, 1837.[14] The 1837 treaty established peace between the United States and the tribes, peace among the tribes, free passage for U.S. citizens through the tribes' territory, the Indians' hunting and trapping rights "in the Great Prairie west of the Cross Timbers to the western limits of the United States," and distribution of gifts. The treaty also confirmed that the United States recognized tribal law over such Indian-on-Indian crimes as murder and theft of stock in the stipulation that "other tribes shall interpose their good offices to remove such difficulties." The United States also agreed that the tribes entering into this treaty would "in no respect interrupt their friendly relations with the Republics of Mexico and Texas." In sum, the United States explicitly recognized the existence and force of tribal law, the self-regulation of intertribal affairs, and the tribes' ability to negotiate relations with other external sovereign governments.

With the expansion of American territorial acquisitions, the discovery of gold in 1849, and growth in the settler population, the Kiowas, Comanches, and Apaches were back at the treaty table with the United

States, eventually signing the 1853 Treaty of Fort Atkinson.[15] The treaty terms show how the Americans' recognition of the tribes' political autonomy had shifted. The new treaty departed from the United States' 1837 position of noninterference with the tribes' external relations, now prohibiting warlike incursions into Mexico. Violations were punishable by the complete or partial withholding of annuities, worth $18,000 per year. The tribes also conceded rights to the U.S. to build roads, highways, and military posts. In less than twenty years, the Kiowas had lost authority to conduct affairs with governments other than the United States, and were threatened with the loss of goods previously promised them. The treaty ignored earlier references to tribal law and Indian control over intertribal relations.

These marked changes in treaty language were rooted in American expansion and in Texas statehood. American troops had entered the southern Plains and southwestern region as a result of the war with Mexico, raising the American presence in the area. The Treaty of Guadalupe Hidalgo in 1848 brought all lands north of the Rio Grande and Gila River into U.S. possession, extending American control all the way to the Pacific. The United States had begun to encircle the Kiowas physically and politically, cutting off contact with external governments and undermining their claims to autonomy. Territorial acquisitions, the gold rush, and a burgeoning settler society seemed to affirm the expansionist promise of Manifest Destiny. The Kiowas and other Plains tribes were the only remaining obstacles to realizing an American empire.

The diminution of Kiowa standing in a community of sovereign nations continued with the 1865 U.S. "Treaty with the Comanches and Kiowas."[16] Article 1 attempted to replace tribal law with the American legal system. The treaty stipulated that henceforth Indian-on-Indian crimes were to be reported to the Indian agent, verified by affidavit, and resolved by the agent. The treaty also called for the unprecedented imposition of a regular census, ostensibly to predict goods needed for distribution among the tribes. Censuses reinforced the United States' ability to control Indian populations. They named individuals, mapped kinship relations, broke down individual and family anonymity, quantified measures of civilization, and calculated ratios of goods to people. Census taking proved to be an imprecise practice. Inadequate agency personnel and Native noncompliance made it difficult if not impossible to make truly accurate counts even after the reservation was established.

The 1867 Treaty of Medicine Lodge Creek demonstrated the progress the United States had made as a colonial power. The treaty was similar in several ways to previous pacts. The Americans sought the tribes' peace and cooperation with U.S. plans for building railroads, military posts, and reservations, to which the Indians would be confined unless hunting off reservation with the agent's permission. In return, the U.S. government promised annuities and cooperation in protecting the Indians from intruders. The principle article of the treaty focused on the reservation in Indian Territory that the Kiowas, Comanches, and Apaches would hold in common. The Medicine Lodge Creek Treaty described the boundaries in painstaking cartographic detail:

> The United States agrees that [the] following district of country, to wit: commencing at a point where the Washita River crosses the 98th meridian, west from Greenwich; thence up the Washita River, in the middle of the main channel thereof, to a point thirty miles, by river, west of Fort Cobb, as now established; thence, due west to the north fork of Red River, provided said lines said river east of the one hundredth meridian of west longitude; if not, then only to said meridian-line, and thence south, on said meridian-line, to the said north fork of Red River; thence down said north fork, in the middle of the main channel thereof, from the point where it may be first intersected by the lines described, to the main Red River; thence down said river, in the middle of the main channel thereof to its intersection with the ninety-eight meridian of longitude west from Greenwich; thence north, on said meridian-line, to the place of beginning. . .

The reservation was carved out of the Leased District in southwestern Indian Territory, lands formerly held by the removed Choctaw and Chickasaw tribes, the southern border of which lay adjacent to the northern border of Texas along the Red River. The land was arid, broken by the jutting Wichita Mountains and by numerous creeks and streams. Located within a larger territory once dominated by the Kiowas, Comanches, and Apaches, the reservation dramatically reduced their land and resources, but was an environment familiar to the Indians.

The treaty talks had been preceded by passage of a federal bill to create the peace commission that would meet with the tribes now waging war against the United States or committing depredations. Senate bill No.136 passed on July 18, 1867, and was approved in the House of Representatives on July 20 with amendments.[17] The bill authorized the president to appoint a commission, which included Commissioner of Indian Affairs N. G. Taylor, the chairmen of the Committees on Indian Affairs of both the House and Senate, and three army officers. They were sent to reconcile differences between the United States and the Plains tribes and conclude a treaty to protect the great railroad projects that would connect the east and west coasts.

The law to create the peace commission arose from a debate that illuminated a policy fraught with disunity, racism, and anti-tribal sentiments. In fact, the decade of the 1860s up to 1871 was the worst possible time to be completing any business in the realm of Indian affairs. The creation of the commission, ratification of earlier treaties, and passage of appropriations bills to fund treaties repeatedly became lost in debates. Lawmakers argued over treaty making, corruption, and incompetence in the Indian Bureau; a divisive proposal to transfer responsibilities for Indian Affairs to the Department of War; and whether Indians should receive annuities at all. Protracted exchanges delayed appropriation bill after appropriation bill. Some lawmakers wanted to put aside the bills before them and attend to sweeping reforms that would fix the broken system of Indian policy and service. Others argued vigorously for postponing the reformist discussion in order to fund the agencies and head off Indian retaliation against the government.

Throughout these prolonged exchanges among U.S. lawmakers, several things became clear. Legislators had ceased seeing Native tribes as sovereign or powerful.[18] The belief that Indians never rightly possessed land and that the United States need not treat with tribes over land cessions replaced the old arguments that peace was preferable to a war. But while congressmen debated questions of land, military solutions, and diplomacy, the United States continued to sign treaties with tribes of the Great Plains and Southwest. Whereas Americans understood earlier treaties as instruments that formalized agreements of Indian land cessions for compensation, the perception of Indian land title, right to sell, and compensation had changed drastically by the 1860s. The treaties that the peace commission of 1867 negotiated were intended to prevent war while acquiring huge tracts of Indian lands for nearly nothing. Many legislators had ceased acknowledging even usufructory indigenous land rights. Treaties based on peace over recognition of tribal territorial holdings allowed legislators to rationalize the pittances exchanged for Indian lands. Legislators saw a never-ending drain on the national treasury stretching out before them. The civilization program, in the opinion of more than a few, was doomed to failure. They saw appropriations not as payments for massive land cessions, but as handouts to a broken people they no longer needed to fear or respect. Protracted exchanges in both houses revealed the hubris of empire, which consigned Indian people to suffer indignities, starvation, and illness.[19]

Throughout the 1860s irregularities had crept into the authorization process, raising debates within and between the two houses of Congress to a shrill pitch by the time President Ulysses S. Grant proposed a peace commission to treat with the Kiowas. Appropriations, like treaties, were acts of law, but required sufficient funding if the United States were to meet its treaty obligations. In March 1867, a specific case of inadequate appropriations prompted a Senate debate on procedures for treating with tribes, U.S.–Indian relations, presidential power to enter into treaties with tribes, and the continuation of treaty making.[20] The Senate had before it House amendments to Senate bill No. 83 making appropriations for deficiencies in the original appropriations for treaty-making expenses. The debate on the Senate floor that ensued on March 27 revealed that both houses felt burdened by the presidential power to enter in treaties with Indian tribes. The Senate, whose constitutional role is limited to treaty ratification, went so far as to vote a prohibition against treaty talks without prior congressional authorization and an appropriation bill. In doing so, the Congress fell back on its original practice: not allowing any treaty to be made with Indian tribes without a proposal submission to Congress and an appropriation passed in advance to fund the negotiations. Despite Sen. Charles Buckalew's (Pennsylvania) protest that the measure attempts "to take away from the Executive a power which no one can question," it passed.[21] In July the bill was repealed. The prolonged exchange foreshadowed the end of treaty making in 1871.

The lawmakers unanimously acknowledged that it had been the custom to treat with Indians for cessions of large tracts of land held by them. Some argued that, given that treaties were made between sovereign nations, the policy of treating with tribes had been a disastrous mistake.[22] In this view, Indians were not sovereign and had never owned the land: "No man has a right to own the land who will not work it."[23] As for the scandalously small price paid to Indians for such land, "Those lands as they are, become more valuable . . . by the settlement of whites," said Sen. Alexander Ramsey of Minnesota.[24] There was no impropriety in paying a small amount of money for the Indians' mere possessory right in return for the government's care and protection. The time had come for occupying the Indian lands under the authority of acts of Congress at will. Rep. Benjamin Butler of Massachusetts argued that "In the treaties made by the peace commission there has been no cession of land, because these Indians were roaming Indians who did not seem to have any fixed habitations or lands they could claim as their own except possessio pedis."[25] Butler summed up the sentiments of his colleagues when he spoke in a vein reminiscent of Andrew Jackson's views on treaties in an earlier era. "They were then strong, and we were weak. Since that time we have become strong, and they have become weak. We deal with them as wards of the State."

The dispossession of Indians was far more than an issue of land. Rather, the issue was framed as a struggle between "civilization and an unproducing, revolting barbarism."[26] The "white man [was] instinctively possessed with the desire for conquest and development," while Indians were stimulated by the instinct of self-preservation.[27] Lawmakers were quick to attribute their restraint from physical exter- mination of Indians to the fact that the white man was fighting not to eliminate the Indian but "for the fulfillment of a destiny," as Sen. Edmund Ross (Kansas), promoter and director of the Atchison, Topeka & Santa Fe Railroad in the 1860s, put it. "It [was] idle to talk about extermination," Ross continued; "the humanity of the age [forbade the legislators] to entertain such a proposition."[28] Even the sanctified mandate of Manifest Destiny was insufficient grounds to unleash the forces of ethnic cleansing by the direct means of extermination, an act that would nullify any American claims to expansion with honor.

Quoting Gen. John Pope, whose long experience on the Plains in- vested his words with authority easterners could not claim, others noted that treaties were not kept anyway. If the frontier was impossible to control, and treaty promises could not be kept, what was the point of making them? Rep. James Augustus Johnson of California, in a House debate on the creation of the 1867 peace commission, expressed a rare counterpoint to the prevailing sentiment. He protested the argument that treaties could not hold on the frontier environment as an affront to the reputation of the United States. "It is idle . . . and disparaging the power of the Government to assert for a moment that it is not in its power to enforce obedience upon the part of its citizens to all these treaties."[29] He foresaw "great damage to the reputation of the United States if it cannot protect three or four hundred thousand Indians in their possessions of land which God and nature gave them in the be- ginning of their existence." His was a minority view.

For each argument for the provision of annuities there was a coun- tervailing argument. In response to the position that the United States government ought to provide annuities to facilitate the Indians' eco- nomic transformation, others argued that if annuities were given at all they should be done so sparingly.[30] To do otherwise would be unfair to frontier whites whose frontier lives were meager and economically marginal. Some posited that annuities were a necessity if the Indians were to become civilized while others countered that the Indians were incapable of civilization and rejected the goods, or worse, were prone to laziness.[31] The optimistic view that annuities were a temporary measure was opposed on the basis that providing annuities was to step on to the slippery slope of endless demand for goods. Many voiced concern that appropriations for annuities were wasted in that the corruption of the Indian Service and Indian traders prevented goods from ever reaching the Indians. The most significant debate over annuities revealed the competing ideas that annuities either facilitated war by strengthening the Indian belligerents, or prevented war by pacification and reinforcement of cooperation of friendly Indians.[32] This last argument would play a direct hand in the local management of Department of Interior disbursements of appropriations and management of Indian rations and annuities.

Some members of Congress exploited arguments about corruption and other failures of Indian policy to advance a case for returning the Bureau of Indian Affairs to the War Department, which had relinquished Indian policy in 1849. In 1868, Rep. James Garfield of Ohio, an ardent proponent of the transfer (from the Bureau of Indian Affairs to the Department of War) introduced House bill No. 1482 from the Committee on Military Affairs to restore the Bureau of Indian Affairs to the Department of War.[33] Two years earlier, the same bill had passed the House of Representatives by a large majority but failed in the Senate. Supporters argued that the measure would remedy the problem of rampant corruption thought to pervade the Bureau of Indian Affairs. Placing the bureau under the authority of the War Department, Garfield argued, "where all the officers are subject to military law and to the jurisdiction of courts-martial," would ensure proper conduct and "remove one of the most tempting opportunities for corruption known to our Government." This rosy view did not convince others who noted the benefits the War Department had gained from Indian conflicts. The transfer never took place, but the War Department played a significant role in an increasingly militarized policy that helped make reputations for many men.

The debates show the anti-tribal, anti-sovereignty context in which appropriations were hammered out. Records of the actual appropriations show how attitudes toward Native people and Indian relations were instrumental in shaping the material conditions of reservation life and the Kiowa response. How can documents capture a moment when a people's economy has been broken and they find themselves thrust into a system that forces dependency on government rations and annuity goods? What are we really looking at when we talk about the reservation, rations, annuities, the civilization program, assimilation, and transformation? The existing records are imprecise, sometimes even contradictory, so my analysis cannot provide a complete picture. But it does document how inadequate the appropriations were at the outset, only to be diminished further as the funds traveled from the Department of Interior to Indian Territory (now known as Oklahoma). With this in mind, we can conclude that if the Kiowas possessed nothing more than the government goods they actually received, Kiowas would no longer be in existence today. Kiowas found ways to respond to their dire circumstances, but their capacity to adapt does not make the appropriation system of the late nineteenth century any less disgraceful.

The analysis prepared for this book focused on all recorded appropriations marked for the Kiowa agency under the Central Superintendency (see table 1 and figure 1; see appendix A for the sources of the appropriations data).

This data provides answers to one simple, key question: How much funding was the U.S. government providing for the Kiowas' subsistence in goods and rations from 1860 to 1910? Remembering that the Kiowas in this period were being confined to territory south of the Arkansas River, then confined to a reservation, and ultimately losing even more land through the General Allotment Act of 1887, the necessity of these goods and rations to Kiowa subsistence grew out of want. Anecdotal accounts of starvation are available, and cited in this book, but data provides a more detailed picture over time.

The appropriations are organized by fiscal year and by recipient tribes who had signed a treaty or treaties. Following the ratification of the Treaty of Medicine Lodge Creek in August 1868, appropriations were passed to fund, for the most part, the United States' obligations

TABLE 1 Estimated Annual Expenditures Per Per Capita (Kiowa) 1860–1910

FY	Expend To*	$ Expenditure[1]	$ "Real" Expend[2]	% of Approp	Est Pop	$ Per Cap	Total Kiowa PC	2005 $[9]
1860	KCA	23,618.73	20,153.24					
1861	KCA	16,707.75	10,666.76					
1862	KCA	4,040.46	4,040.46					
1863[3]	KCA	30,994.48	27,318.14					
1864	KCA	21,251.71						
1865	KCA	8,583.88	6,434.18					
1866	KCA	29,810.11	16,648.47					
1867	KCA	9,714.65	54,781.49		4,000	2.43		
	KC	67,321.01			3,675	18.32	20.75	272.31
1868	KCA	18,741.56	25,807.02		4,000	4.69		
	KC	25,184.91			3,675	6.85	11.54	157.65
1869	KCA	136,822.00	108,390.95		4,868	28.11	28.70	408.80
	KC	2,687.01			4,572	0.59		
1870	KCA	56,410.80	24,639.49		4,938	11.42	11.42	169.92
1871	KCA	53,553.07			4,635	11.55		
	KCA; C&A	203,126.70			8,035	25.28	36.83	585.27
1872	KCA	50,204.04			5,046	9.95		
	KCA; C&A	208,436.65			8,446	24.68	34.63	550.31
1873	KCA	68,544.91			4,635	14.79		
	KCA; A; W	198,962.69			8,135	24.46	39.25	636.72
1874	KCA	58,557.47	218,225.08	64%	5,002	11.71		
	KCA; C&A; W	194,891.20			10,318	18.89	30.60	521.76
1875	KCA	63,156.98	300,290.24	82%	2,965	21.30		
	KCA; C&A; W	276,388.67			8,380	32.98	54.28	960.59
1876	KCA; C&A; W	56,869.32	266,876.14	73%	3,180	17.88		
	KCA; C&A; W	250,612.14			8,593	29.16	47.04	851.83
1877	KCA	43,302.80	235,583.04	78%	2,978	14.54		
	KCA; C&A; W	231,285.17			9,292	24.89	39.43	731.02
1878	KCA; C&A; W	33,356.34	228,899.25	78%	2,939	11.35		
	KCA; C&A; W	216,306.15			9,328	23.19	34.54	672.38
1879	KCA	50,912.37	266,131.07	91%	2,939	17.32		
	KCA; C&A; W	239,897.51			10,248	23.41	40.73	792.88
1880	KCA	36,373.26	296,481.49	87%	3,637	10.00		
	KCA; C&A; W	290,000.00			11,029	26.29	36.29	689.21
1881	KCA	51,509.90	314,396.43	88%	2,875	17.92		
	KCA; C&A; W	205,000.00			10,612	28.74	46.66	886.16

Year								
1882	KCA	52,503.82			2,906	18.07		
	KCA; C&A; W	472,368.27	91%	487,092.34	10,783	43.81	61.88	1,175.22
1883	KCA	52,015.66			2,888	18.01		
	KCA; C&A; W	348,581.98	94%	377,344.64	10,677	32.65	50.66	975.91
1884	KCA	52,700.00			2,858	18.44		
	KCA; C&A; W	404,233.75	87%	402,797.78	10,398	38.88	57.32	1,134.74
1885	KCA	47,065.06			2,864	16.43		
	KCA; C&A; W	388,296.34	86%	375,869.26	7,746	50.13	66.56	1,340.38
1886	KCA	15,152.71			2,889	5.24		
	KCA; C&A; W	373,011.80	82%	346,671.45	7,616	48.98	54.22	1,120.87
1887	KCA	25,511.51			2,909	8.77		
	KCA; C&A; W	306,376.76	74%	270,573.86	7,349	41.69	50.46	1,033.99
1888	KCA	17,000.75			2,797	6.08		
	KCA; C&A; W	290,304.57	64%	223,096.50	7,428	39.08	45.16	925.38
1889	KCA	18,083.06			2,837	6.37		
	KCA; C&A; W	261,779.55	58%	188,637.56	6,934	37.75	44.12	928.51
1890	KCA	18,112.06			2,837	6.38		
	KCA; C&A; W	250,000.00	47%	187,341.30	7,686	32.53	38.91	633.89
1891	KCA	18,200.00			2,880	6.32		
	KCA; C&A; W	224,397.23	72%	208,048.36	7,435	30.18	36.50	782.24
1892	KCA	48,027.56			2,669	17.99		
	KCA; C&A; W	232,655.88	51%	147,258.92	6,992	33.27	51.26	1,098.56
1893	KCA	18,200.00			2,636	6.90		
	KCAW	121,655.05	53%	91,599.32	3,722	32.69	39.59	856.32
1894	KCA	54,857.26			2,635	20.82		
	KCAW	122,244.02			3,722	32.84	53.66	1,216.99
1895	KCA	16,351.48			2,635	6.21		
	KCAW	109,364.66	58%	92,135.33	3,721	29.39	35.60	823.38
1896	KCA	48,728.14			2,663	18.26		
	KCAW	116,497.55			3,782	30.60	49.06	1,134.69
1897	KCA	51,540.17			2,828	18.22		
	KCAW	92,126.43			3,786	24.33	42.55	993.97
1898	KCA	55,478.52			2,872	19.32		
	KCAW	82,051.75			3,828	21.43	40.75	1,134.69
1899	KCA	85,958.19			2,740	31.37		
	KCAW	85,647.49			3,696	23.17	54.54	1,274.05
1900[4]	KCA	8,229.81			2,808	2.93		
	KCAW	80,206.89			3,296	24.33	27.36	636.79

(continued)

TABLE 1 Estimated Annual Expenditures Per Capita (Kiowa) 1860–1910 (cont.)

FY	Expend To*	$ Expenditure[1]	$ "Real" Expend[2]	% of Approp	Est Pop	$ Per Cap	Total Kiowa PC	2005 $[9]
1901 [5]	KCA	25,355.28			2,685	9.44		
	KCAW	54,106.74			3,626	14.92	24.36	563.42
1902 [6]	KCA	14,639.90			2,705	5.41		
	KCAW	43,167.20			3,301	13.08	18.49	423.46
1903	KCA	118.41			2,729	0.04		
	KCAW	5,907.32			3,162	1.87	1.91	43.32
1904	KCAW	28,499.88			3,141	9.07	9.07	199.88
1905	KCAW	23,474.01			3,183	7.37	7.37	160.90
1906	KCAW	22,694.20			3,223	7.04	7.04	155.15
1907	KCAW	22,828.69			3,275	6.97	6.97	150.76
1908	KCAW	23,918.09			3,331	7.18	7.18	148.43
1909 [7]	KCAW	19,970.45			3,362	5.94	5.94	127.30
1910 [8]	KCAW	22,420.38			3,122	7.18	7.18	147.13

* KCA= Kiowa, Comanche, Apache; C&A=Cheyenne, Arapahoe; W=Wichita

1. Expenditure figures do not include unexpended, unaccounted for, or "in the hands of agents" monies.

2. "Real Expenditure" is an unscientific name for monies that are dedicated to rations and annuity goods, that is, government commodities purchased for the Indians' welfare. This figure has been calculated by two methods, depending on the availability of data. The "Real Expenditure" figures for 1860–1870 have been calculated by subtracting personnel salaries. The figures for 1874–1895 are the sum of line items in agency ledgers devoted to commodities. The absence of figures for "Real Expenditures" reflects a lack of sufficient data.

3. In 1863, 1864, and 1866, sums were also expended for opening communication with "Comanches, Apaches, &c." ($8, 362 in 1863 and $1,673.50 in 1866) and "for the purchase and transportation of provisions and presents, and expenses in negotiating treaty with Kiowas and Comanches" ($15,000 in 1864). It is probable that the Kiowas received some portion of these sums.

4. The Annual Report of the Commissioner of Indian Affairs, 1900 indicates that an additional $76,000 was paid to the Apaches, Kiowas, and Comanches as a result of a treaty ratification.

5. In FY 1901 and FY 1902, allotment payments were also made to these tribes (not included in these totals): $19,444.95 in 1901 and $51,446.86 in 1902.

6. Trust funds were set up for these tribes around this time. The Indian Appropriations Bill for 1902 indicates that $1.5 million was possibly deposited in FY 1902 in order to establish the "Apache, Kiowa, and Comanche Fund." The following deposits/accruals to this fund are as follows:

1903=$279,700

1904=$59,800

1905=$400

1906=$281,350

1907=$193,350 (plus $235.33 to the "Apache, Kiowa, and Comanche 4% fund")

1908=($69,457.20 to the 4% fund)

1909=$376,343.88 (plus $61,017 to the 4% fund)

1910=$75,030 (plus $302,636.12 to the 4% fund)

7. The Annual Report of the Commissioner of Indian Affairs, 1909 indicates that $349,437.03 was possibly disbursed in FY 1909 to the Apaches, Kiowas, and Comanches from the "Apache, Kiowa, and Comanche 4% fund."

8. The Annual Report of the Commissioner of Indian Affairs, 1910 indicates that a sum of $500,000 was possibly disbursed in FY 1910 to the Kiowas, Comanches, and Apaches from "funds already placed to the credit of the Indians."

9. Based on CPI (Consumer Price Index).

under the terms of that treaty. For some early years, the treaty signed in 1853 governed the calculation of appropriations until the treaty obligations expired. For this analysis, separation of funds according to treaty was not attempted, and may not even be possible. Ignoring that fine point does not undermine the purpose of the study: identifying the Kiowas' resources under changing conditions that included a destroyed economy, reduced land base, and compensation for ceded lands from the United States government.

Between 1860 and 1873, reports of receipts and expenditures were sent to the House of Representatives under a cover letter from the Department of the Treasury. The annual document *Appropriations for the Indian Department* was the most consistent form in which Indian monies were reported, but it is only available for 1874 to 1895. The document's tabular format stated the appropriation for each individual agency and expenditures broken down by categories, including subsistence and annuities. For the years on either side of this period, information on appropriations and expenditures is available from other branches, but is less consistent and less precise. Between 1860 and 1873 inclusive ledgers did not break out the expenditures into categories at all. There was no annuity payment made in fiscal year 1884. Instead, $30,000 was disbursed for stock for Indians.

The information compiled and presented in the accompanying charts shows the small sum of $25,000 as the annual appropriation to the Kiowas for 1860 to 1866. Fiscal years (FY) 1867 and 1868 appropriations tripled that amount. Despite their presence in the record, other sources state that there were no appropriations for 1867–68. In any event, appropriations remain on the modest side until a sudden jump in 1871, after which there is a steady increase until 1882. After 1882, appropriations slowly taper off, fall precipitously in 1893, and continue to fall, flattening out at $25,000 for the last five years covered here.

In FY 1871 and 1872 the appropriation was extended to the Arapahoe, Cheyenne, and Apache, after which the Wichita were also included. In 1893 the Arapahoe and Cheyenne were omitted from the appropriation, but the Wichita remained until 1910. The inclusion of other tribes under the appropriation did not always translate into an increased ap-

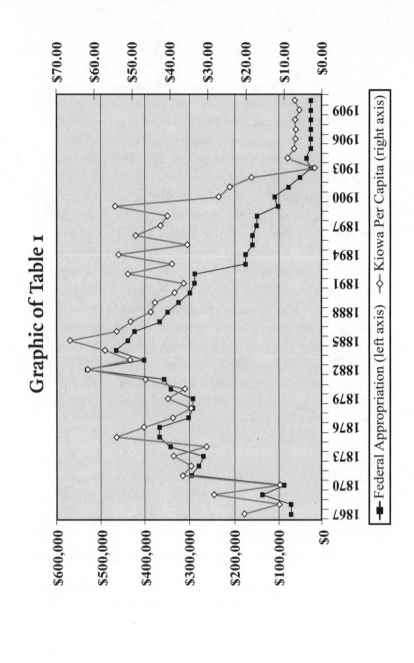

Graphic of Table 1

Federal Appropriation (left axis)   Kiowa Per Capita (right axis)

propriation, as the figure for 1873 illustrates. That year the Wichita were brought in under the $268,700 appropriation, which represented a drop from the previous year's $279,200.

The most significant figures are two: the real expenditure and the per capita figure. Real expenditure is an unscientific designation for monies spent on rations and goods exclusively. This figure was arrived at by two methods. Between 1860 and 1870, real expenditure, rations and goods, was not a separate category. The real expenditure was arrived at by subtracting salaries from the Kiowas' budget. Expenditures were not available for 1871, 1872, and 1873. From 1874 to 1895, the real expenditure figures, specifically, monies spent for annuity goods and subsistence supplies, were arrived at from "Disbursements made from Appropriations for Indian Department." According to the data, the percentage of the expenditure used for "subsistence" and "annuity goods" ranged from over 90 percent to just over 50 percent.

As a percentage of appropriation, the real expenditure fluctuated from its lowest point of 47 percent in 1890 to its highest in 1883, 1882, and 1879, respectively. For the most part, the real expenditure ranged from 70 to 80 percent; overall, roughly 25 percent of the appropriation was spent on goods and services unrelated to subsistence and annuity. Finally, the costs of corruption, undelivered goods, and spoilage cannot be estimated, but the historical literature and other primary sources suggest that those problems were rampant.

The Kiowas did not receive a per capita payment in cash, but a per capita figure is included in appendix A to illustrate the volatility in household income. It was arrived at by dividing the real expenditure by the total population of all the tribes included in the treaties for any given fiscal year (see appendix B for source of population). Because the Kiowas were signers to two 1867 treaties, there are two per capita figures for each Kiowa. The final column in appendix A is the sum of the two per capita figures. Figure 1 best illustrates the volatility in household income from subsistence and annuity goods. Appropriations were unpredictable, requiring Kiowas to devise income-producing measures. The recalculation into 2005 values shows how little the Kiowas were receiving even before corruption and conditions of the goods are taken into account.

As dire as this picture from the official figures of U.S. government documents looks, it does not begin to convey the conditions in which the Kiowas lived. Agency records, correspondence, and other sources detail a life on the ground for the Kiowa people characterized by starvation and extreme poverty. Appropriations might have been made retroactively, but an absent appropriation in any year was devastating. Policies created at the agency level and in Washington DC ensured that the meager appropriations would frequently remain in the coffers of the Indian Bureau, or stored as annuity goods at distant army posts.

What does this say about the values of the state? Throughout the period beginning with the establishment of Plains reservations in the 1859s to *Lone Wolf v. Hitchcock* in 1902, the state repeatedly demonstrated that dominance over Indian peoples was the primary goal of its policies. Indian tribes were an obstruction to national self-interest and commercial expansion. A nation that had been built on a constitutional history appeared uninterested in unifying all people under its flag, instead pursuing hegemonic goals through coercive legalized and militarized means. The state dedicated its policies, legal system, and political power to forcible Indian removals and alienation of resources.

The reservation materialized the state's agenda and political values. The discourse of Indian transformation, however genuine and well intentioned on the part of a few, was as hollow as the government's treaty promises, and transformation and reservation-as-solution demanded the destruction of Indian economies. In the late nineteenth century, dispelling tribalism became a high priority as well. The attack targeted American Indian sovereignty in all its possible meanings, from the political status of tribes to tribal institutions that supported individual human independence and dignity, including family and religion. A state that celebrates independence of individuals imposed a system that stripped Indian people of exactly that.

The way to domination was not a regrettable outcome of progress. It was imperfectly methodical and systematic. The state first reduced the Indians' territory and deprived them of the environment they required to maintain their subsistence. Simultaneously, the state attempted to destroy the exchange relations that contributed to their dynamic economy. Then, having placed Indians on the reservation, the state assumed control over the distribution of capital and commodities, a role it performed poorly. Honoring the terms of treaties, from the perspective of Washington DC, was just another federal program, subject to negotiations, trades, and cuts. Finally, when Indians dared to resist in any way, the state countered with military force. These economic, political, and military interventions were purposeful and coordinated. That Native people seized upon the imperfections and inconsistencies of domination to preserve their independence does not negate the state's intent but rather underscores the nature of the state's intent. The work of young Kiowa men, the subject of the next chapter, illustrates how Native people exploited the imperfections and inconsistencies made necessary by broken treaty promises.

Chapter 4. Young Kiowa Men, Kiowa Social Values, and the Politics of Rations

Throughout the 1850s and well into the 1860s two developments significantly advanced the United States' plan to overcome the Kiowas. First, federal Indian policies became increasingly militarized and the United States Army established a more visible presence on the Plains. Texas and its settlers entered the union presuming entitlement to federal protection from Indian raids. The United States responded to Indian "depredations" against the new Americans by establishing a meager military presence. The U.S. Army carried out sporadic assaults against the Kiowas and Comanches from 1858 through 1860, stepping up the effort following the Civil War.[1] Second, non-Indian hunters and a brisk hide trade had increased pressure on the buffalo population. The consequent depletion of game transformed rations and annuities from an optional supplementary resource into a subsistence necessity.

Kiowa band leaders were in perfect agreement about the problems that lay before them. They saw the Kiowa tribe perched between a diversified economy and strong leadership on the one hand and encroaching intrusions into their territory with potential to undermine their economy and autonomy on the other. The labor of *d'ogudle*, young Kiowa men, became increasingly valuable during the erosive 1860s and early 1870s when local Indian agents and federal policy makers agreed on a strategy of withholding rations to coerce the Kiowas into compliance with the colonial administration. Kiowa leaders from both the reservation and outside bands benefited from the young men's work, claiming powerlessness to control them. The calamity created by the rations situation inside the reservation resulted in cooperative intergenerational strategies between Kiowas on either side of the reservation boundary. Later, the leadership would part on the question of peace or a military response to the United States. Until then, young men continued to fill their traditional work of "bringing home the meat." The young men's continued raids, which blunted the impact of the Kiowas' drastically reduced resources, were represented officially by the U.S. and in popular accounts as "depredations," another case of state criminalization of tribal practices that the reservation system itself had made even more necessary. Young Kiowa men's raids, revenge parties, and inevitable clashes with settlers, intensifying as U.S. colonial policies developed into draconian measures, were situated in the context of Kiowa socialization and economy, and thus constitute subjects for a study in Kiowa social values.

Food was the prevailing reason for contact between the Kiowas and the reservation agent, but there was never enough. Women continued to procure plants and to process game and men to hunt, but a hostile military presence, depleted game, and limited hunting grounds pressed the Indians toward increasing reliance on government commodities. Dohausen's talk at the 1865 treaty signing reveals the great changes he had observed since his 1854 complaint about U.S. relations with Indians. "Great Father," Dohausen pointedly argued, "is always promising to do something for him, but never does anything."[2] The leader spoke to the troubles with the Americans, addressing them directly:

> I wish you to leave my country alone. The Santa Fe road is open, and will not be disturbed. The rest of the country I want let alone. I want to tell you again and again to throw away the soldiers, and I will get all badness out of my heart, so that we can all travel kindly together. I want you to listen to my talk, and take away the soldiers. Keep my talk in your heart, and get rid of the soldiers. I don't like to see them. I wish you to do as the Great Father of Washington wishes you to do; just leave the white folks behind, and take the goods to the Salt Plains for the Indians. Before this half the goods have been stolen by the white men; I want the goods taken to the Salt Plains.

While the lack of food created a reason for conflict between the Kiowas and whites, tensions increased as the United States' Indian policy evolved into a military occupation of Kiowa territory.

A number of Kiowa leaders, including Stumbling Bear, took up Dohausen's challenge to the U.S. government in 1866. They also complained about the distribution of goods that Dohausen had charged were stolen before they reached the Indians. Speaking for the men, Stumbling Bear accused Agent Jesse Leavenworth, agent for the Kiowas, Comanches, and Apaches, of manipulating the annuities system to his personal advantage, thereby forcing the Kiowas to trade mules, horses, hides, and other goods for the rations promised them in an earlier treaty. Stumbling Bear reportedly set forth their grievances:

> Those goods that he trade with us, is Indian goods. We know it. Indian goods and trade goods are not alike. The only way we can get our goods is to give him our ponies, our robes and our furs. He kept them from us. The Great Father sent them to us. He thinks his time will be short and he wants to make a good bargain. But it is a better way to trade our own goods than take them by force. The braves that bring him most horses get most goods. More than one third of our tribe gets none at all, for they have not any to give. They are poor. We hope the Great Father will send some one to see he can't steel [sic] from us.[3]

At first glance, Stumbling Bear's description merely confirms the known practices of Indian agents, who were exploitive political appointees lining their pockets at the expense of their charges, the practice Stumbling Bear called making a good bargain. The leader, however, told more than a tale of corruption. Importantly, Stumbling Bear's statement provided a significant partial description, from a Kiowa perspective, of the Kiowas' response to their dire circumstances. Instead of employing force, a rational option considering the meager U.S. military presence, the Kiowas fell back on established patterns including procurement and trade. Stumbling Bear's "braves," a gloss for young men, obtained the horses and mules Kiowa leaders traded to Leavenworth. According to colonial logic, Kiowa procurement of horses was a criminalized practice of "depredation." Stumbling Bear, like Dohausen, used oratory to put the practice of procurement in context as a rational Kiowa practice and response to the consequences of United States policy.

The young men's practices were consistent with their traditional work of obtaining horses and mules, trading buffalo hides for guns and goods, and hunting. Women's labor, although not mentioned by Stumbling Bear, had produced the buffalo robes and other furs. "Poor" Kiowas' inability to participate in the trade raises questions about the impact of this breakdown on the tribe's social organization. Kiowa ranked society had always included less-well-off and poor people, but they were usually attached to bands and were included in the circulation of goods. Stumbling Bear's description raises more lacunae than it provides answers, such as specific information about the young men, their identities, and the details of interaction between them and reservation Kiowas. However, his complaint nevertheless offers a new and valuable entry point for exploring the Kiowas' reservation experiences and their connections to Washington policies.[4]

Stumbling Bear was a firsthand witness to the Kiowas' experience in the 1860s. He was a prominent leader, definitively described as a member of the reservation people.[5] His representation of the Kiowas' response to hardships is significant because it contextualizes outside bands' and young men's behaviors within Kiowa social ideals, and in doing so counters the U.S. representation of Kiowas as chaotic warriors. By this time Dohausen, the most respected leader, was ill and would soon die, and the remaining headmen were left without the kind of leadership Dohausen had given them. Stumbling Bear shows that the pressure to accept a reservation did not vitiate cooperation between off-and on-reservation groups as the first response in this new early reservation period. Scholarly interpretations of the competitive factions split between off-and on-reservation groups have oversimplified the Kiowa situation. In the final analysis, the military conflict thesis that dominates historical interpretations of the period has been an overdetermining factor in understanding the Kiowas' experience.

Stumbling Bear's unambiguous identification with the reservation people suggests a motivation to put the young men in a correct context. The headman defended the actions, "depredations" in American terms, of the "braves"—whom the American record had already defined as outlaws—as a Kiowa reaction to crisis rather than the work of opposing groups. Stumbling Bear framed the problems as being common to all Kiowas.

It is worth taking the time to consider the vocabulary that scholars have used to describe disagreement within tribes that are confronting multiple crises created by colonialism. For example, Jerrold E. Levy's oft-cited dissertation on Kiowa political and social organization argues that during the reservation period the Kiowas divided into factions over how best to deal with the United States: war or compliance? In critiquing the faction model common to numerous histories, we must first recognize that the question of war or compliance never existed in isolation. Rather, it was situated in the multiple consequences of a broad policy of coercive colonialism bearing down on the Kiowas and others in various forms. Tribal leadership therefore had to respond to many demands and crises arising out of colonial policies, war being only one. For example, throughout the 1860s, Kiowa headmen faced challenges in keeping their people south of the Arkansas River, in following the buffalo herds in a constricted land base, in responding to an increasingly militarized American policy, and in resolving conflict arising from growing numbers of white intruders in their country. Second, the faction model frequently is discursively organized around colonial dualisms: progressive and traditional, civilized and uncivilized, peaceful and warring. The use of black-and-white dualisms should raise immediate questions given that Plains Indian politics, contextualized within notions of band organization and police societies, is fluid and flexible. Third, using Levy again to illustrate a point, paying attention to specified historical locations is critical when examining disagreements within tribal leadership. When observed over time, factionalism, at least in the Kiowa case, appears to offer limited analytical usefulness. Rather, until 1873–74, the Kiowa bands' interrelations exhibit characteristic autonomy and interband consultation.

This chapter does not seek to refute the notion that the question of war or compliance divided opinion among the Kiowas. Rather, it asserts that until 1873 and 1874 intratribal politics looked more like traditional Kiowa politics than a model of disintegration. Although the Treaty of Medicine Lodge Creek was the conventional marker for the beginning of the reservation period, the United States had been pressuring the Kiowas to accept a reservation for well over a decade. During that time U.S. local representatives began to use rations to manipulate the Kiowas' behavior, with some results. Disruptions to their indigenous regional economy had already led Kiowas to rely on rations for part of their subsistence. As the reservation became a concrete reality for most Kiowas after 1867, the American bureaucracy identified the Kiowas as two populations: the compliant and the outlaws. Stumbling Bear's speech shows us that these artificially marked groups shared concerns about how to feed the bands in the midst of (1) confinement to a much smaller land base; (2) a requirement that they apply for a permit to hunt buffalo off the reservation; (3) the dwindling numbers of buffalo in that area; (4) the smallpox epidemic of 1861 and 1862; and (4) the failure of the United States government, having destroyed the Kiowa economy, to honor its obligations to provide rations and annuities.[6] In 1873 and 1874, statements by Kiowa leaders show dwindling support for the outside bands' open defiance. At that point, evidence suggests a hardening split among the Kiowas.

Stumbling Bear's statement also contests the narrative of Plains Indian violence, menacing "outlaws," "good" reservation Indians, and an increasingly militarized federal Indian policy. "Outlaw" language criminalized Kiowa practices and the work anonymous young men continued to carry out in order to provide the Kiowa people with subsistence in rapidly disintegrating circumstances. Stumbling Bear's brave, similarly anonymous, contradicts connotations of roaming, violent Indians who committed depredations on vulnerable American settlers and "peaceful" Indians. Colonial policies and practices and the cultural context of young Kiowas' socialization placed the men in a new light. Stumbling Bear's braves met the invasion of the state in accordance with the social values instilled in them, rather than as randomly, chaotic savages.

The American characterization of young Kiowa men partook of a stereotype of a warrior's ego-centered desires to avenge, count coup, and accumulate honors. This crude interpretation centers Kiowa manhood in warrior culture, which distorts Kiowa manhood and society. One documented event allows a glimpse into the Kiowas' attitudes toward accomplished young men and puts a different face on the raids and occasional violence. During the spring raids, Setangya (Sitting Bear), a high-ranking, young pipe bearer and son of an off-reservation band leader by the same name, set out with a few followers to raid settlements in Texas.[7] The young Setangya was fatally shot during one of the raids. The others in his party hid his body in Texas, and his father later retrieved it following the May Sun Dance. Setangya the father, a respected Qoichegau warrior, returned with the young man's remains wrapped in a bundle atop a horse he led. Back in his band's camp Setangya built a tipi with a raised platform inside. He hosted a feast in his son's honor and invited all his friends, announcing, "my son calls you to eat." Following the feast, Setangya kept up the practice of leaving food and water for the son he insisted was sleeping, not dead. The son's remains placed atop a horse accompanied Setangya the father whenever he went out on marches. Not until the father's death in 1871 were the young man's remains interred.

Young Setangya's death is included in the Kiowa winter count of 1870–71. He was already a distinguished *d'ogudle* in part because of his patrimony, in part because of his participation in raids and revenge parties. It is striking that the father created a ceremony that memorialized his son's life through feasting, especially given the chronic shortage of food. The connection between the dead young man and feasting also emphasizes the enormity of the loss of a young man rather than the honors he earned as a casualty of raiding. That is, Setangya's choices for his son's funeral situated the young man in the labor of providing meat as part of his responsibilities to the people. The feast associated the young Setangya with values of generosity, reciprocity, respect, and the spiritual realm.

The young Kiowan men's activities were linked to Kiowa spiritual beliefs and practices. Young men, like other segments of Kiowa society, called upon external sources of power to help them succeed as individual warriors and meet obligations. At the center of nineteenth-century Kiowa belief was the concept of *dwdw*, power or spirit force, which inhabited all things—animate and inanimate. *Dwdw* inhabited animals, the earth, sun, moon, and stars.[8] Natural phenomena possessed varying degrees of *dwdw*, with the sun holding the strongest spirit power. Sun, addressed as "grandfather," nurtured the spirit of the buffalo, making this mainstay of Kiowa materiality and diet one of the most powerful animals in spirit terms. Kiowas ceremonially drew on these external sources of power. They kept their connection to the sun and its spirit power through the Sun Dance, which began with a buffalo hunt. Kiowas also availed themselves of the *dwdw* of other animals and inanimate forms for the purpose of gathering curing and war powers. Vision quests were a common means of power seeking among warriors, though *dwdw* might also manifest itself in dreams. The strength of *dwdw* was a matter of degree that depended on the power seeker, source, and context.

Spirit power circulated throughout Kiowa society between warriors and from warrior to animals by various means. *Dwdw* was mediated through the warrior's dream or vision and through a sign painted on his shield, body, and favorite horse. A man might receive the *dwdw* of an older male relative as a gift, or he might borrow another warrior's power temporarily. Some warriors acquired the power of another by exchange or purchase. By painting the body of his horse, a warrior disseminated the protective and strengthening properties of his power to the animal that would carry him into battle or on a revenge party, thereby uniting the warrior and his horse. Kiowa flexibility and opportunism is evident even in the spiritual realm as *dwdw* circulated among men, animals, and objects.

The work of the late Alfred Gell is helpful in seeing the significance of the connections between a young Kiowa man, the realm of spirit power, and the young man's material world.[9] Young Kiowa warriors, to paraphrase Gell, are not simply young men, but young men with horses, body paint, and accouterments of war imbued with spirit power. Except for them the young warrior could not exist. The young man's ceremonial life realized his agency in his material and spiritual worlds simultaneously as their agency was realized in him. Gell's theory of agency embedded in the social relationships of humans and objects is particularly potent in conceptualizing the connections between the ubiquitous Kiowa spirit power *dwdw*, which inhabited the animate and inanimate world and aspiring young warriors who drew on it.

Dwdw was represented in painted signs on animal bodies, shields, and buffalo hides used for tipis and robes. Humans, animals and events merge:

> some men without power also painted war symbols on their horses, and if a man achieved a high war honor riding a painted horse, his design became patented for life. This entitled him to paint the design on his horse prior to battle or the parade before the Sun Dance. Some men painted the right side of their horse red, the left side white; other popular designs consisted of yellow circles representing Sun, zigzag lightning marks on the legs symbolizing thunder, hand imprints and other markings. Another popular practice was to paint bullet scars where his horse had been hit, for it was a high honor to recover from combat-inflicted wounds.[10]

The relationship between a man and horse was grounded in the translation and sharing of power between mutually dependent man and animal. Horses and humans were bound through painted symbols of *dwdw* that were more than mere amulets, but rather materialized the shared power they called upon for the work of procuring and revenge taking.

Horses ridden into situations that required great skill and speed were typically favored horses. Favored horses were experienced in the dangers and demands of raiding or hunting parties, animals on which riders could rely and even entrust their lives. More significantly, a warrior shared power with a favored horse. Nothing attests to the social and psychic bond between a rider and a favored horse more than the common Kiowa practice of slaying the animal in the event of the warrior's death. The slaying ensured the relationship between the horse and rider, that the agency of each was realized and remained unbroken, perpetuating the power they shared.

Training in Kiowa social values provided the glue that held together young Kiowa men, horses, body paint, and accouterments of war. The power of a young man had its genesis in his education and the social values transmitted through his relations with family and older men as role models. Power was not the crude, brute force associated with acts of violence, but rather was interwoven with values of discipline and balance, social responsibility, and the capacity to combine physical strength with internalized rules of warrior behavior. Although *d'ogudle* did not yet possess the status of senior men, they were a labor force for dangerous assignments, and thus possessed a kind of moral authority and political influence acknowledged within the community. Young men embodied Kiowa social principles, the spirit of self-determination and entitlement to Kiowa autonomy on the southern Plains. As a consequence, the recorded interactions between Kiowa young men and American authorities, although mediated through colonial logic of conquest, help us interpret their attitudes toward and reactions to the new order.

On May 5, 1853, Commissioner of Indian Affairs George Manypenny wrote a letter to Thomas Fitzpatrick, one of the commissioners detached to secure a treaty with the southern Plains tribes. The letter instructed him to strike an agreement with the Indians as to reasonable compensation and annual payment in goods and provisions in exchange for the safe passage of citizens through the Kiowa territory and construction of military and other posts along travel lines.[11] These annuities and rations, or provisions, became a permanent source of bad feeling between the Indians and the United States.

On one hand, to say that Indians became dependent on government annuities is an overstatement because they continued to produce food, medicines, and manufactures from old resources. Moreover, the rations and annuities were so inadequate that Indian dependency was impossible. Annuities arrived and were distributed to Indians at the will of the state. Rations of beef, bacon, flour, sugar, coffee, and corn supplanted, but never entirely replaced, a diet of buffalo and other game, various legumes, seeds, tubers, roots, berries, nuts, and fruits. Only some annuities, such as calico, canvas, shoes, umbrellas, kettles, plows, hoes, and a lengthy list of other tools and materials, replaced Kiowa manufactures. Other Kiowas simply dismissed some goods as useless, or radically altered their function. Kiowas had no use for corn, and reports of them abandoning sacks of corn between the agency and their camps are numerous. So obvious was the waste that one officer proposed that "Indian women should be compelled to come in to the Agency, and learn to make lye, hominy, corn bread and corn mush."[12] For many years, the Indians discarded shoes and cut men's trousers at the legs and turned them into leggings and breechcloths in the traditional style. Other annuities, like canvas for tipis, still required women's design and construction skills, previously applied to buffalo hide.

While the rations were insufficient to create dependency, they were increasingly significant to the reservation Kiowas' subsistence during the reservation and allotment period. Constriction of resources as a result of land contraction, the buffalo reduction, and elimination of exchange opportunities coerced Indians into reliance on rations to supplement their subsistence, at the very least. The decimation of the buffalo population in the second half of the nineteenth century, a disaster for the Kiowas and other Indians, was a result of a perfect storm of economic, political, and environmental elements. A number of studies have explored the disaster of the buffalo loss, but Isenberg's is especially helpful in understanding the interplay of complex environmental and social conditions that conspired against the buffalo. The buffalo is an impressive animal in its size and speed, but it had natural predators like the wolf. It was amazingly well adapted to the arid climate of the Plains, but was vulnerable to the cyclical drought that visited the region. Competitors like the horse and cattle impinged on the herds' short grass sources. Railway lines, human migratory roads, and cattle trails constricted the buffalo's movements. Commerce produced a niche for buffalo hides in the American market. American Indians, responding to the hide trade, increased their take of the herds, contributing their own pressures on the migratory beasts.[13]

Nothing, however, had befallen the buffalo before like the American commercial hunting that exploded in the second half of the nineteenth century. Gun technology overcame the buffalo's size and speed as well as the challenge of shooting distance. Humans did the rest. Using hide hunters' estimates of their own productivity, Isenberg estimates that at twenty buffalo per day for a three-month season, and with one thousand hunters on the plains, "they could easily have supplied tanneries with over two million hides every year." The introduction of bovine disease, diminishment of summer breeding groups, and the ever-present drought, competitors, and predators combined with the commercial hunting frenzy to reduce the buffalo herds estimated conservatively at 30 million to 1,000 by 1900.[14] Federal Indian policy's contribution to the destruction of the buffalo took the form of an encouraging discourse on solving the "Indian problem" by depriving them of this critical resource through the activity of the commercial sector and the inactivity of the legislative sector. The United States' elimination of the buffalo to coerce all Indians into compliance with the reservation system took time and was not completed until the mid-1870s.

The displacement of traditional Kiowa goods for Western goods, however, only scratches the surface of colonialism's destructive dynamic. Comestibles and manufactures that the U.S. intended for Indian consumption served purposes beyond the most obvious one of feeding and clothing men, women, and children. They also did the work of colonizing literally from within, determining Indian health, mortality, psychological wellness, and self-determination. Rations and manufactures were an important component of the colonizers' tool kit, creating conditions that promoted the decline in Indian health and autonomy.

The reality of early rations distributions, the locus where Kiowa and American resentments were acted out, contrasted with the detached formality of treaties to illustrate the liminality between dependence on and independence from government commodities. Annuity days were occasions for collision between the Kiowas and the authorities, and revealed the ongoing contest to shape local relations between the Indians and the United States. From the outset, Indian agents attempted to use rations to extend their personal authority over the Indians. Following the 1853 treaty, the Indians habitually met with Agent Robert C. Miller on the Arkansas River to collect their rations. Miller complained that the Kiowas defied his efforts to impose order over the proceedings. As the bands straggled in, Miller announced a halt in the distribution of goods until all were present. The Indians, according to Miller, were "audacious and insolent" and rejected his proposed delay. Kiowas left the meeting and returned with armed young men who threatened to take the goods by force. The Comanche contingent's intervention prevented violence, but the Kiowas claimed the upper hand. The agent reported that "They said they knew their Great Father sent them presents because he feared them; that he was no brave, or he would not talk so much, but would act; would send the soldiers." The taunting represented more than hollow boasting and bravado. In 1853, the Kiowas had reason, and a treaty, to expect rations in exchange for their amity, without American intimidation.[15]

The young men's rebelliousness, translated by the agent as arrogance and a challenge to his authority, stemmed from the detested annuity system and their awareness that they were a valuable labor pool. They formed the core of raiding parties that procured horses, mules, and stock, the currency of the trade system. A later confrontation in 1866, the year of Stumbling Bear's statement to Agent Leavenworth, ended with Kiowa leaders telling the Americans to keep their goods. They reminded the Americans that they had an alternative source of similar goods in their Mexican trade partners that diminished the value of U.S. rations. The young men's confidence was founded in the Kiowa bands' long experience in external trade relations with Mexicans, Americans, and others, through which they had continued to obtain goods and maintain economic and political autonomy from the Americans.

The Americans, according to Thomas Fitzpatrick in 1853, had two options. "Our relations with the wild tribes of the Prairies and Mountains resolve themselves into a simple alternative. The policy must be either an army or an annuity."[16] Fitzpatrick attributed the Indians' confidence to the inefficacy of the limited military presence on the Plains, of which he wrote: "so small is the force usually at the Army's disposal, that they maintain their own position in the country more by the courtesy of the

Indians than from any ability to cope with the numbers that surround them." The Americans reasoned that rations compensated for the lack of an impressive military presence, which "Instead of serving to intimidate the red man [created] a belief in the feebleness of the white man."[17]

While the Americans were weighing the options of rations or war, and following through on neither, the Kiowas had spoken with unity through the voice of Dohausen. It was during this time that Dohausen reacted angrily to the agent's threat to withhold rations and spoke of the Americans' childishness. He affirmed the propriety of his young men's efforts to feed their families and their exhibitions of resistance, while chiding the agent for using food as a weapon. Raids resulting in American loss of "a cup of sugar or coffee" were not for Dohausen a matter of war but a matter of procurement, goods supplied in return for Kiowa tolerance of the American presence in their country, and a reaction to the failures of rations to arrive. The Mexicans had appeared to Dohausen to accept limited acts of violence, a tolerance they might have put aside if they had possessed the resources to stop it. The Americans, however, offended the Kiowas on every front. They failed to keep treaty promises, traveled through Kiowa country killing buffalo, and then resented Kiowa attempts to complete the exchange.

Great measures had to be taken by the United States government to bring the Kiowas to the point of starvation. The Kiowas, like other tribes, were adapted to the Plains environment and boasted a diverse economy of trade, hunting, and procuring. The young Kiowa men's country was not a desert, only arid. Rivers, which comprised 7 percent of the region, supported trees and tall grasses. Outside the river valleys, grama, buffalo grasses, and other plant species adapted to irregular precipitation, aridity, and high winds.[18] Through the eyes of people familiar with the environment, the subtle presence of abundance in this deceptive country was clear in a way that admirers of cultivation could not imagine.

An August 1867 report from an agent in New Mexico about the activities of the Kiowas and Comanches in the west Texas and Panhandle range considered their territory and offered a description of the tribes' resources.[19] Two months before the Medicine Lodge Creek treaty, the agent wrote:

The Comanches and Kiowas, in my opinion, are good Indians. They look upon the officers of the government with respect. These Indians appear rich; they live in a country full of buffaloes and mustang horses. They have about 15,000 horses and 300 or 400 mules. They raise much of their own stock and they have now more than 1,000 cows. They also have Texas cattle without number and almost every day bring in more. Their country is large and fruitful. Almost all kinds of wild fruit can be found; grass is abundant, but wood is scarce. These Indians are good of heart, and desire to leave [sic] at peace with our government. At no time have most of them seen their agent. They know about the government distributing annually presents among the Indians.

Though a majority of Kiowas attempted to follow the path of the Americans' reservation plan, a significant number of Kiowa bands refused to cooperate with territorial constrictions, annuity distributions, and bans on raids. Those who did comply with the Indian agents' orders and those who were already at risk without the security net of the band system were the first to become vulnerable to a policy of withheld rations. The agency administrations of Jesse Leavenworth and of his successor, Lawrie Tatum, relied on withholding rations from the Kiowas, but for different purposes. With the pressures of diminishing buffalo herds and poor rations as a backdrop, Kiowas responded to each agent in similar ways.

Jesse Leavenworth, the first Indian agent of the Kiowa reservation, was the son of military figure Henry Leavenworth and a former army officer himself. More persistently than anyone, Leavenworth argued that the Kiowa and Comanche trade strengthened the Indians' autonomy, creating motivation for raiding and a source of conflict between the tribes and the Americans. Leavenworth sought to cut the Kiowas off from their old trade. Mexicans, both old *comanchero* traders as well as traders with permits, supplied the Indians with ammunition and other goods such as Mexican cloth in exchange for horses. Leavenworth argued that Mexican demand was a main cause of the Indians' raids into Texas, where they stole horses and mules. He recognized that the

Mexicans gave the Kiowas leverage against American authorities and ensured them an alternative to licensed Indian traders, the only traders he recognized as legitimate. The Mexican trade also encouraged the Kiowas' movements beyond the territory of the reservation and his authority. In 1866, Leavenworth unsuccessfully petitioned the governor of Mexico to deny his citizens the required permits to travel among the Indian camps for trade purposes.[20]

Leavenworth devoted himself to regulating trade with the Indians of his agency. In 1865 he wrote to the Commissioner of Indian Affairs in an effort to broaden his authority over trade with the Kiowas, Comanches, and Apaches. He argued that traders with licenses from other agencies should not be allowed to do business with the tribes of his agency because such arrangements threatened to introduce "confusion." Additionally, Leavenworth wanted to license all citizens who might trade with the Indians.[21] A former soldier who had corresponded with Leavenworth credited the agent for the proposal in a letter the soldier wrote to the commissioner to contest the idea of issuing "special permits" to "honest, loyal American citizens."[22] Leavenworth's proposed solutions to his concerns entailed extending his authority over all who might engage in trade with the Indians of his agency, thereby cutting the Kiowas off from their external sources beyond his authority.

Leavenworth's petitions to the governor of Mexico and to the Commissioner of Indian Affairs represented a type of local colonial innovation, encouraged by the agency's distance from Washington and a splintered bureaucracy, to cut Indians off from their old economic independence. Leavenworth and traders knew what was going on in the Plains. News traveled by various means, and Leavenworth was privy to official correspondence, trade news, and news from army personnel. Stumbling Bear's testimony about Leavenworth's practices and the record of his efforts to control the trade unveils Leavenworth's self-interest. While protesting the Indian trade as an obstacle to establishing government control over the Kiowas and Comanches, in practice Leavenworth's quest for control over the trade was an attempt to establish a monopoly on trade using contraband rations.[23]

From 1865 to 1867 Leavenworth had established a pattern of trad-

ing annuity goods for robes and furs with other tribes under his supervision. He and his longtime business partner, William Matheson,
set up a headquarters at Cow Creek Ranch and carried annuities to
the Kiowa camp six miles south of the mouth of Bluff Creek on the
Cimarron River. Following the trade, Leavenworth took the Indians'
ponies, robes, and furs to Leavenworth, Kansas, where he sold them
to a local merchant who was accustomed to moving large quantities of
buffalo robes and pelts. In this way Leavenworth accomplished what
Stumbling Bear called "making a good bargain." Leavenworth realized
profits in the thousands of dollars from the southern Plains economy
that he claimed he wanted dismantled but in fact encouraged by his
own dealings.[24]

Kiowas who complied with the Treaty of Medicine Lodge Creek of
1867 faced chronic food shortages from the outset. The 1867 treaty,
signed in October, was not ratified until the following summer. There
were no appropriations to fund the terms of the treaty for fiscal years
1867 and 1868. Following the treaty, Leavenworth was named agent of
the new Kiowa, Comanche, and Apache reservation, and was charged
to "congregate" the Indians. According to his account, in January
1868 he took some Indians to the Eureka Valley between the Keechei
Hills and the Washita River, about ten miles southeast of Fort Cobb.
He reportedly sent his associate William Matheson ahead with provisions, but the Indians, according to the trader, would not permit him
to get any closer to their location than Cache Creek. Leavenworth and
his clerk Walkley arrived in March and, according to Walkley, found
the Indians "destitute."[25] Rations had been distributed in February
from Matheson's supplies and in March from another trader's stores,
but the cornmeal, corn, salt, and beef rations were small and the beef
poor.[26] With the Kiowa lacking rations or means for trade Leavenworth
then abandoned the agency on May 26, leaving his inexperienced clerk
in charge.[27]

For 1868, agency documents record two distributions of rations,
which Walkley described as "stinted," and three distributions of beef in
April, September, and October.[28] Leavenworth allegedly had arranged
for traders to provide the clerk with food supplies, but the skittish trad-

ers feared that without official receipts bearing Leavenworth's signature they would not be paid. After filling one or two orders, both traders ceased supplying the reservation. The Caddo Indians of a neighboring reservation were in similar circumstances, having been abandoned by their agent without any provisions for rations. When Walkley received the September and October beef issues for his agency, he divided them with the Caddo reservation. Walkley resigned in October without issuing more rations.[29] Meanwhile, C. E. Mix, acting Commissioner of Indian Affairs, found an unexpended balance of $21,311 appropriated under the treaty of 1853, $161 unexpended funds from the treaty of 1865, and $11,173 from the treaty of 1867. Authority to expend these sums in addition to $50,000 from the War Department accompanied Lt. Gen. William T. Sherman's order to General Hazen to proceed to "the frontier" to keep the starving Indians from joining up with the Cheyenne and Arapahoe against the United States. Hazen assumed command briefly in November, pending the arrival of Leavenworth's replacement, and we might presume he distributed food to the Indians.[30]

In December Boone arrived at Fort Arbuckle (some eighty miles distant). The Indians' conditions were such that Hazen, out of concern for Boone's safety, advised him not to proceed to the reservation unless "accompanied by their goods."[31] If a distribution had taken place in November, it must have been inadequate in order to elicit such warnings from Hazen. According to the report of the central superintendent, Thomas Murphy, writing in October 1868, the Indians had not received annuities in 1868 because he had stored the goods at Lawrence, Kansas.[32] Those annuities arrived in January 1869, and Agent Boone distributed them, but it being in the middle of winter when the bands were dispersed, only two groups of Comanches and fifty lodges of Kiowas were present to receive them. The rest of the Indians had left the dire situation for the Plains, where they had a better chance of finding game and feeding themselves. Meanwhile, Sherman had announced in September 1868 that he would "solicit an order from the President declaring all Indians who remain outside of their lawful reservations to be declared 'outlaws,' and commanding all people— soldiers and citizens—to proceed against them as such." Leaving the reservation to hunt or gather food put Kiowas at risk of being shot or of being arrested as outlaws. Sherman also suggested for future policy that Indians be required to obtain an agent's permit to hunt buffalo in the treaty-designated area. Violation of the treaties in any way also put the hunting rights in jeopardy.[33] All of Sherman's recommendations were formalized as federal policy later.

In May 1869, Lawrie Tatum, a Quaker from Iowa, arrived to assume the position of Indian agent for the Kiowas, Comanches, and Apaches. During his first year as agent, Tatum left ample testimony about the shortages of food, inferior rations, and his own frustrations as a representative of the U.S. government with insufficient resources to implement a policy of peace. Tatum's arrival also signaled the elimination of the agency middleman, a role held by Agent Leavenworth and interim Agent Walkley. What this meant for the Kiowas was not clear.

Tatum's immediate energies, not surprising given Hazen's earlier warnings to Agent Boone, were focused on providing food for the Indians of the Kiowa, Comanche, and Apache reservation. Two months after his arrival he wrote to the Commissioner of Indian Affairs complaining that rations were insufficient. By August, Tatum had absented himself from the agency and was gone for two or three months.[34] Military officers attached to the area including the Kiowa, Comanche, and Apache reservation complained that Tatum neglected to name a competent person to take charge of the agency in his absence. Before Tatum left he had refused to issue the rations that had been delivered to him in bulk, stating that he had insufficient assistance to carry out the work. Like Agent Thomas Miller in 1853, Tatum seemed concerned about maintaining control. Was this a result of misplaced fears? Had the situation so deteriorated that orderly distributions became impossible? One cannot know from the sources. However, before his departure, Tatum also granted the reservation people permission to hunt buffalo in the western area of the reservation while he was gone.[35] In the same period he wrote a lengthy letter to the Commissioner of Indian Affairs, Ely S. Parker, in which he expressed alarm over the lack of food.[36] Two seemingly contradictory acts—refusing to issue rations and calling attention to the lack of food—reoccur throughout Tatum's tenure as Indian agent and appear to result from initial frustration with the government and, later, resentment toward the Indians.

Tatum had replied to the commissioner's "Circular Letter to Superintendents and Agents" dated June 12 in which Parker promoted the government's Indian policy of cultural transformation. A Seneca Indian himself, Parker represented a view that the Indian's future rested in rejecting tribalism and embracing assimilation. Parker would later support the 1871 legislation to end treaty making. Tatum wrote: "It is gratifying to me to read the liberal expression that when the Indians locate as desired [quoting from Parker] 'Every assistance practicable, authorized by law will be given to advance them in agricultural pursuits, and the arts of civilized life,' and if this assistance is to be 'in the way of clothing, provisions and agricultural implements.'" Tatum then praised a number of the Indians of his agency who endeavored to grow gardens and remain on the reservation. He expressed optimism that "a large portion of the Indians" wanted to "walk in the 'white man's road.'" Furthermore, "We hear that there are several thousand more now coming in off the plains, and will probably be hear [sic] in a few days, expecting to be fed and clothed"—which, if true, would have created a nightmarish scenario.[37]

If the implications of U.S. success in bringing the Indians under control were lost on the authorities back in Washington, Tatum fully comprehended them. He explained that feeding several thousand Indians could not be done with insufficient rations that are "licked up like the morning dew"; "corn meal . . . that is often so musty that it is unfit to eat, and it makes them sick"; corn that is not ground; short beef supplies; and the exclusion of coffee and sugar. Under the current conditions he had no motivation or means to restrain the Indians' old practices. Tatum appealed for more food, "for humanity's sake" and "to give us a fair chance to civilize the Indians." He revealed other anxieties in his letter to the commissioner. He wrote: "The Indian realizes that the promise of the White men is not kept. He tells us so and we feel the truth of it. It may cost the Government one hundred times as much to half feed the Indians as it would do to give them soldiers rations." Half rations would induce the Indians to war. More ominously he asked, "What they may *do before or after leaving* [the reservation] and what it may cost the Government to get them back to where they are today I will not surmise" (italics mine). Indeed, the Indians were starving, as two leaders would report in September when they came in for rations. They also told Tatum that there was "much sickness among the people" and that "numbers have died."[38]

What the Indians might carry out "before or after leaving the reservation" was Tatum's dread-filled reference to Kiowa and Comanche procuring activities.[39] Bands who remained outside the reservation after the treaty apparently had access to natural resources and plenty of stock. Americans, however, had changed the meaning of a Kiowa economic activity into a criminal practice carried out against Texas settlers and, less frequently, against the agency itself. Tatum possessed, perhaps unwelcome, but full knowledge of raids, past and ongoing. Following the establishment of the agency, authorities had begun to record incidents involving Kiowa and Comanche strikes against American homes and trade businesses. It is recorded that on May 24, 1868, the same day Leavenworth departed, a party of Kiowas and Comanches raided merchant Durfee's store, absconding with nearly $4,000 in goods.[40] The stolen inventory consisted of items that would commonly appear in the Indians' annuity distributions, including cloth and blankets. A month later, the Indians returned to burn the building. A party of Kiowas and Comanches raided another Texas store they frequented. They attacked merchant Shirley's trade post, "plundering his store of a valuable lot of Indian goods. On their return, . . . [t]hey also burnt Shirley's trading house."[41] Given the goods the Indians took, it is likely that they were annuity goods being stored at the trade posts, a common practice at that time. Burning the stores destroyed storage sites that kept the Indians from their goods. From the Indians' perspective, they were only taking what rightfully belonged to them.

Agent Boone, Tatum's predecessor, left an account of the off-reservation bands' raids throughout 1868.[42] According to him, the Kiowas' procurements maintained a steady pace throughout the year. A party of one hundred Indians crossed into Texas in January and absconded with two hundred horses. A smaller party of thirty struck the Cloud Ranch in Montague County of north central Texas in February and took another thirty. Similar small-sized raids occurred in April and May. In June the Indians struck Parker and Wise Counties and escaped with three hundred horses. They took another two hundred in August. A party of two hundred Indians hit Jack County in November and made off with five hundred horses. Other small raids occurred throughout the fall of 1868. These raids occurred while Congress failed to pass an appropriation; goods remained stored at Leavenworth, Kansas; and monies were cobbled together to feed the Indians who had compliantly congregated at Eureka Valley. Though Tatum did not leave a similar re-cord for 1869, Indian depredations claims from Texas documentation evidence that the raiding continued after his arrival.[43]

Agent Lawrie Tatum was in a most unenviable position. As a Quaker, he had been enlisted into a project to clean up the Bureau of Indian Affairs and bring peace and civilization to the Indians. Rations were the primary means by which local agents were to affect stability. The absence of annuities would leave the Indians desperate and, in the U.S. way of thinking, lead them to a war the Americans could not win. As an agent of civilization, Tatum needed rations and annuities to persuade Indians to agriculture and away from tribalism. The situation intensi-fied as Tatum came to believe his safety and that of his employees and the government property for which he was responsible depended on government rations. When Tatum left for Iowa, he removed himself from circumstances in which he had come to see himself as represent-ing the broken "promise of the white men." It appears he chose to ex-tract himself from the potential threat of able-bodied and noncompli-ant *d'ogudle* denied adequate rations. When he did eventually return in late summer, he would find things unchanged. A shortage of rations and beef continued, as did the young men's forays into Texas.

Prior to 1868, Leavenworth and other Americans had interpreted Kiowa raiding practices as an obstruction to U.S. control and to Indian assimilation. Raiding also created fear among settlers, however, and by 1868 the authorities' discourse took on a sharper edge. It represented raids not as stubborn recalcitrance, but as acts of Kiowa militancy, an interpretation that mirrored their own militarized policy. An environment of fear and anxiety fueled the discourse of war. The practice of Indian raids terrified the American settlers in Texas.[44] The best conditions for Kiowa and Comanche raids—a clear night, full moon, well-fed ponies, and an isolated target—allowed a raiding party to strike suddenly, gather up horses and mules, split up into small groups or single-man sorties, and escape with the animals to the Staked Plains. In most documented instances it appears the Indians were more interested in acquiring stock then in harming settlers. The circumstances in which they struck, however, underscored both the settlers' feelings of isolation and vulnerability and their perception of Indian supremacy on the southern Plains. Settlers appealed for government protection, but the inescapable reality of mid-nineteenth-century life on the southern Plains was the continuation of Indian raids. The raids and less frequent acts of violence against settlers seemed to justify the argument that the U.S. War Department should assume management of Indian affairs and pursue military solutions to the "Indian problem."

The white settlement of Texas had complicated an already complex array of intercultural relations in the southern Plains and southwest. Texas settlers, or *tejanos*, were not Americans from the Kiowas' perspective. Even after statehood, the Kiowas continued to think of settlers south of the Red River as *tejanos*. The targeting of Texas horses, mules, and cattle had begun long before statehood. The bitterness of *tejanos*-turned-Americans intensified with each passing raiding season. The numbers of animals—available in depredations claims gathered county by county and recited anecdotally in other official sources —taken out of Texas are impressive. Though depredations claims are problematic because of the conspicuous motivation to inflate the numbers of lost stock, except in a very few cases of suspiciously high claims most of the reported losses seem plausible. Another complication with the depredations claims is that only infrequently are the perpetrators identified by tribe, and even when they are attributions of guilt to specific tribes are unreliable. Nevertheless, the reports give a general picture of the magnitude of the raiding and of the quantities of horses, mules, and cattle being trafficked in the southern Plains.

A condition of anonymity protected the Kiowan young men from identification as individual perpetrators, but it also fueled settlers' images of them as collectively dangerous, uncontrollable, unpredictable, and a threat to relations between the United States and the Kiowas and Comanches. Accounts commonly vilified them as sinister and nearly inhumane perpetrators of thievery, captive taking, and vicious murders on the Texas frontier. The official record leaves an image of frontier chaos and settler hysteria over the threat of Indian raids. As mentioned, however, records of depredations and atrocities suggest that the young men's "crimes," to use the parlance du jour, were grossly exaggerated.

William Tecumseh Sherman was a noisy promoter of the image of Kiowa young men as outlaws. He decried them as perpetrators of violence driving settlers from the western Texas frontier, thus obstructing expansion and prosperity. American ideas about young Kiowa men interwove threads of fear, loathing, and misconception about Plains Indians. Language is a tool of empire; the American representations of young Kiowa men as outlaws and perpetrators of "depredations" and "atrocities" were instrumental to the United States' conquest of the southern Plains. Americans used the interpretation of young Kiowa men to promote the war option, to justify starving the Indians, and to structure an increasingly efficient colonial bureaucracy to control them.

Americans blinded by the race hatred permeating the southern Plains linked Kiowa male status to such violence as murders of settlers, which were accompanied by scalping and other horrors. This interpretation satisfied any doubts about policies involving military solutions and reservation conditions. The military solution was still unavailable because of inadequate American resources and continued Kiowa superiority in the southern Plains. Aware of the cooperation between the off-and on-reservation bands, the authorities targeted the Indians' subsistence to coerce their compliance.[45]

Leavenworth's practice of withholding rations for personal gain metamorphosed under Quaker Agent Lawrie Tatum into punishment for "depredations." From 1870 until the end of his tenure at the agency, Tatum's letters were peppered with reports of his refusing "subsistence or annuity goods to Indians who are off the reservation to the South or West" and distributing only to the Kiowas who more or less permanently remained on the reservation.[46] Tatum's turn to punishment and discipline suggests his growing reliance on coercing a people he initially feared. A pattern of relations emerged among the agent, the reservation Kiowas, and the off-reservation bands: reservation Kiowas received rations from Tatum, but he refused them to off-reservation bands.

The agent complained with frustration, however, that the reservation people shared food with the off-reservation Kiowas. For example, Wo-haw, a member of Satanta's group, received rations during the week of August 21, 1869, for twenty-four people. The rations included 144 pounds of beef, 24 of bacon, 168 of flour, and 168 of coffee. Kiowa veneration of exchange makes it difficult to envision such activities as one sided; it is most likely that reservation Kiowa received goods in return. Summer raiding continued apace, which in combination with an attack on the agency beef pen, prompted Tatum to withhold rations from the reservation recipients.[47] The real expenditure for 1870 was $24,639, about 80 percent of the appropriation for the agency, which would have accomplished the same goal as withholding rations—deprivation. In August 1870, "nearly all the Kiowa chiefs," "except Satank and Big Bow," arrived at the agency with two hundred to three hundred women and children to surrender twenty-eight mules. Tatum boasted that he understood this "to be 28 mules more than was ever recovered from them before." Feeling victorious, he resumed distribution of rations in exchange, and the Indians promised to bring in captives for more.[48]

Rations were unambiguously insufficient. Only two weeks later, the Kiowa food situation compelled Lone Wolf, a reputed war chief, to compose a communication to the Commissioner of Indian Affairs in Washington DC.[49] His letter centered on the unfulfilled promises by the United States authorities to provide food. He complained that two years before Generals Sheridan, Custer, and Hazen had agreed to give money and all the rations, annuities, guns, and ammunition that he and the Kiowas wanted. The treaty, however, had not been fulfilled.

There were never enough rations, especially of coffee and sugar, nor were there sufficient annuity goods. Tatum had punished the Kiowas for the summer raiding and the attack on the beef pen by giving them only half their sugar and coffee rations in September.[50] The agent appears to have abandoned his earlier position that the absence of annuities instigated violence. His new policy was to withhold food to punish and to avert war. He stated: "I did it to punish them, and I thought the punishment would be the most effective by keeping the sugar. I believe it had a very salutary effect upon them. They have not appeared to be nearer conquered since I have been here than they did on that day."[51] It's hard to say if the Indians' appearance was due to being beaten by Tatum's strategy or to starvation. Soon after, Kiowa young men were reported to be raiding in Montague County, indicating that withholding rations to deter them had failed.[52]

In late 1870 there were few rations to share among the bands. Tatum gave the Kiowas permission to hunt buffalo south of the Arkansas in accordance with the treaty, and "encouraged them to go and obtain as many robes as they could, to trade for clothing, as this is the only resource for procuring a supply beyond the small amount furnished by the Government."[53] When the expected shipment of rations failed to appear in December 1870, Agent Tatum departed from Iowa, leaving acting Agent George Smith in charge of the agency's affairs. Col. B. H. Grierson, Tenth Cavalry, reported that during the agent's absence, "the non-arrival of annuities and short rations caused considerable murmuring and dissatisfaction" and that when "the annuities . . . arrived . . . there was considerable complaint with regard to the quantity and division of goods."[54] Two months after Tatum had gone to Iowa, acting Agent Smith warned his superiors that the absence of food would drive off the peaceful Kiowa headmen. Ely Parker wrote a letter dated March 13, 1871, to the Secretary of the Interior to inform him of the shortness of supplies and that the Indians would run out of food by June 30. He blamed the situation on the absence of a provision for subsistence in the previous appropriation act. Further, he pressed, there would be no money for the next fiscal year unless Congress completed its work on Indian appropriations in the present session. Parker acknowledged that the Indians' pattern of scattering to the Plains was a result of insufficient food and the possibility of procuring food outside the reservation.

Throughout the spring of 1871, an exasperated Tatum reported to Gen. William Tecumseh Sherman that the Indians traveled as they pleased and that "he was not at all surprised to hear that they were a hundred miles off, killing citizens, engaged in the usual business and stealing horses and mules."[55] Sherman defended the United States Army against blame for the consequences of the Indian Office's policies when he wrote to the adjutant general that

> issues of provisions and supplies are made regularly to the families of Indians who have for years been engaged in open war with the people of Texas, having absolutely desolated several miles of its frontier, killed hundreds of people, stolen horses, mules and cattle by the thousands and are at this moment out. . . . [Citizens' complaints] are against the troops who are powerless, but should be against the [Indian] Department that feeds and harbors their Indians when their hands are yet red with blood.[56]

Though it is difficult to believe that Sherman was unaware of the Kiowas' living conditions, his misrepresentation that the Indians had and continued to be well provisioned helped to make his case that Indians were warring and that a military assault on the outside bands was justified.

Five days later Tatum reported to Sherman that a party of one hundred young Kiowa men under "big chiefs" had left for Texas where they killed several white men and stole forty-one mules. Meanwhile, Agent Tatum had begun withholding rations from the reservation Kiowas pending the return of other stolen horses and mules. Throughout the summer Kicking Bird endeavored to gather the stolen mules from the May raid. On August 12, General J. M. Schofield reported that Kicking Bird and Pacer, accompanied by a party of warriors, had delivered thirty-eight mules and one horse to the agent. Tatum accepted the animals as full return of the stolen stock and released the rations he had been withholding from the reservation Kiowas.[57] Until that point, $135,218

had remained unexpended in the agency's coffers. Agent Tatum's practice of withholding rations for the return of stock had resulted in the
recapturing of stolen goods, but it had not stopped the raiding. To the
contrary, the scarcity of rations and Tatum's practice of withholding
them ensured that the raiding would continue.

In May 1871, General Sherman proposed that the United States formally adopt Tatum's local practice of withholding rations and ratchet
up the pressure to coerce the outside bands into compliance. By intensifying the misery of the reservation Kiowas, Sherman hoped to break
the outside bands' refusal to come on the reservation. In a vigorous letter to Gen. Edwin Franklin Townsend, Sherman stated that the agency
should take a more active role in punishing the reservation families of
the raiding parties. Sherman successfully persuaded the Department of
Interior to formalize the practice Tatum had been using for the previous year.[58] However, the language of the June 12, 1871, circular from the
Department of Interior went even further, stating "that for such crimes
[murder, theft, or robbery] the tribe will be held responsible and the
annuities will be withheld until offenders are delivered up by them to
be properly punished." To this point the return of captured goods secured the release of rations. From this point on, however, returning
to the United States' good graces and receiving rations would require
reservation Kiowas to surrender perpetrators of named "crimes," their
kinsmen and only link to external sources.

The representation of Indian depredations as acts of war rationalized the Americans' refusal to distinguish between the guilty and the
innocent and their indiscriminate punishment of all tribal members
through starvation. The authorities located the cause of war in Kiowa
culture, calling the inexperienced to look to the Indians' "education
and traditions." According to Colonel Nye's *Carbine and Lance*, in the
ways of the southern Plains people "The Indian boy is taught from in-
fancy to believe that the only true road to honor or distinction is the
warpath. An Indian who cannot look out from his lodge and behold a
herd of horses or ponies and few scalps dangling from his shield, as
the result of his exploits is branded among the tribe as an old woman

or coward and fit subject for ridicule."[59] Until such notions were banished, the United States "may expect a repetition of these outrages."

Throughout 1872 the Kiowas continued to feel the deprivation of insufficient food supplies, but evidently were unwilling to collaborate with the government. The inspector general attested that the Indians had virtually abandoned the agency by mid-summer, with the main Kiowa camps moving to the branches of the north fork of the Red River. From that location, they sent out raiding parties. Some Kiowas raided the quartermaster's stock. Tatum had been withholding rations from the Kiowas pending the return of three captive settler children. He lamented that overall "the disposition of the Kiowas toward thieving and plundering is certainly more manifest this year than last." He remarked that even the reservation leader, Kicking Bird, "hitherto relied on as friendly or rather indisposed to the evil practices of the others, has not been in for more than three months." Tatum was in an unmistakably punishing frame of mind when he added,

> I have cause to believe that the Kiowas are implicated in stampeding and stealing 120 mules from Capt. Moore a short time ago somewhere north of Camp Supply. Has the Department any instructions to give in regard to withholding rations and annuity goods from the Kiowa Indians should it be shown that these atrocities as well as the principal part of raiding in Texas this Spring has been committed by the Kiowa Indians. My own view is that they should receive nothing more from the Government at present, unless they return the stolen animals, and then the leaders of the parties who commit murders. The Kiowas are uncontrollable by me and this is the only punishment that it is likely I can inflict.[60]

Asa Habit, a Comanche, summarized the Indians' view of Agent Lawrie Tatum and the impasse between them when he said the agent's "way is so straight, the Indians couldn't walk it."[61] He perfectly captured the Indians' circumstances: remain on the reservation and collaborate with the government and starve, or employ the skills that have sustained the tribes for decades and invite punishment of relatives on the reservation. The way would become even straighter when the Americans ultimately succeeded in imposing an identity system on the Kiowas for the purpose of containing and managing them.

The tide began to turn against the tribes in 1873. Where military harassment had failed, bureaucracy would have more success in cornering the Kiowas. In 1873 Capt. Henry Alvord, who had served in a supervisory capacity in the Leased District, called for a new strategy that would eventually undermine the outside bands' autonomy. Alvord employed a vocabulary that deemphasized destruction and yet was destructive. He argued, as others did before him, that assimilation of the Kiowas was desirable and should be attained through "localization" and "individualization" of the Indians. He argued that the tribes would never be coerced to surrender their arms and horses or to any form of abridgment of their personal liberties. But by confining their mobility the government could keep them under the surveillance of a "daily muster" and hold them to personal responsibility for their actions. Alvord's plan was Leavenworth's and Tatum's policies of destroying the Kiowas' economy and tribal autonomy wrapped in the seemingly progressive solution of individualism for backward tribalism. Alvord, like Tatum and others, hoped to address the persistent problem of Indian raids by making distributions to numbered individuals or heads of households. For the Kiowas the greater danger was that rations based on such enrollment would make it more difficult for off-reservation young men to have access to rations. Tatum had complained earlier about families sharing their rations with the off-reservation bands. The ongoing decimation of the buffalo herds and the U.S. military presence on the Plains had forced the outside bands to turn to rations as a secondary subsistence source. Alvord's policy would drive the final wedge between the off-reservation bands and reservation leaders in addition to stripping the rebellious bands of their anonymity.[62]

The daily muster Alvord envisioned put tribal enrollment into the service of American surveillance of the Indians through distribution of food. Without enrollment many of the Indians easily maintained their anonymity and traversed the reservation borders with impunity. The

Kiowa headmen's resistance to enrollment signaled their understanding of its significance and threat to the tribe's political autonomy. They protested that the numbering violated the Indians' dignity, and even went so far as to invoke a cultural taboo against numbering.

While "war" threatened to commence outside the reservation, inside the leaders persisted in resisting the more threatening and ominous enrollment that would close the loopholes in federal Indian policy that the Indians had successfully exploited since 1866. The combined threat of enrollment and practice of punishing the collective tribe for the depredations committed by outside Kiowas placed enormous pressure on leaders. But it was as if politics and the weather conspired against the Kiowas. Summer heat, fall rains, and freezing winter conditions plagued them. Rations became all the more dear. They had much to lose and little to gain by their continued friendliness to the off-reservation bands. The leadership began to speak out directly against their young men. In December 1873 Lone Wolf and his wife told the agent that if they knew that the young men were going out on a raid they would follow them, kill their ponies, and make them walk home. Kicking Bird proclaimed that if the military killed every young Kiowan man who went over the Texas border "we would cry for them but it would be right." Lone Wolf also abandoned the young men when he asserted that those who kill Texans are "dead."[63]

In August the Kiowa leaders capitulated to the United States' demand that they enroll individual Indians.[64] Some reservation Kiowas fought back with noncompliance. The Kiowas who enrolled lengthened the process by refusing to give their names directly to the enrolling officer, insisting instead that they give their names through the leaders. Beyond that, some refused the "certificate" of enrollment. Stumbling Bear later stated, "Of the eleven hundred Kiowas [at the time of enrollment], the enrolment of our names showed only about two hundred and seventy men, women and children as classed among the disloyal."[65] Though enrollment and the release of rations brought some relief to the reservation Kiowas, it destroyed the collaboration between off-and on-reservation Kiowas. Enrollment stripped the off-reservation Kiowas of the anonymity that protected their incursions into the reservation, and cut them off from the government rations that had become a valuable secondary source of food. Although some leaders mouthed condemnations of the young men, others threatened to "go on the warpath of their own accord the moment a movement begins against the outlaw Indians." Kiowas could not control the weather. The army undertook a policy of keeping the Indians "on the run," throughout an unusually cold fall that brought freezing rain. As the Indians made their escape, they left all their camp goods behind. When the outside bands turned themselves into the authorities at Fort Sill, which one observer said had become a "city of refuge," they had lost every material thing except the clothes on their backs.

Young men are an important segment of tribal societies that has been overlooked by history. They have served the conventional narrative of Plains Indian history as symbols of chaos and primitivism at its most savage, characterizations that justified the United States' ongoing policy of imposing control over Plains tribes. Ironically, young men in the late reservation period began to be regarded as the United States' best hope for transforming Indian tribes culturally and economically. From the perspective of American reformers and government authorities, their youth made them malleable in an environment of proper instruction and example. The Americans presumed that by cutting them off from the perceived traditional routes to manhood, such as the quest for war honors, and substituting liberal values and agrarian practices, the characteristics of tribal culture would disappear as older generations died off.

The stereotypes of *d'ogudle* have also reduced their presence in Kiowa history and the history of Native–U.S. contact to background din. As stereotyped pathological savages, young men were presumed to carry out violence instinctually, following natural impulses born of their uncivilized state to strike out in the most destructive ways. Neither "resisters" to the United States nor "traditionalists," young men are thus robbed even of limited historical agency in the academic paradigm of opposites. They are credited only with a kind of raw, brute power that terrorized settlers.

Kiowa expectations of their young men, framed in social values consistent with other acknowledged tribal practices, evidence their importance as a labor force. Their economic and social roles were joined in such practices as raiding and hunting parties, where they advanced toward respected status as a result of both providing meat and exploiting opportunities to accrue honors to their names. A young man's credibility as a provider and protector depended on both. For Kiowas, the source of male honor lay in such acts as counting coup, rescuing comrades, and charging the enemy. Under such a system relatively limited benefit derived from acts of violence.

The talk of violence in histories of the Kiowa people mirrors the talk of Kiowa war intentions that Sherman's officers and Agent Tatum fell back on to justify military solutions: discipline and punishment. Themes of violence and war have obscured evidence of sustained relations between off-and on-reservation bands as well as between generations of Kiowan men in the early reservation years. Themes of violence and war have also obscured the state's reliance on bureaucracy and civilizing discourse as weapons to be used against tribal people, a key element in colonialism historically and in the present. In analyzing identity formation, substituting the image of *d'ogudle* as perpetrators of violence with one of young men carefully and methodically groomed for the arduous pathway to respected manhood is more than a matter of shifting emphasis. Rather, the education of young men accounts for violence in the context of Kiowa social values. Violence, while not completely contained, was relatively restricted to revenge and grief, and to limited wars with other tribes and later the United States Army. Without an acknowledgment of young men as products of Kiowa training and socialization, their violence can only be interpreted as savagery, which though convenient for nineteenth-century Indian policy should not be perpetuated as an uncorrected misrepresentation.

The talk of violence also obscures the destructiveness of rations as a colonial weapon. Official American discourses represented rations as a necessary pragmatic measure to prevent starvation while the Indians underwent a transition from subsistence on buffalo and small game to a diet of domesticated beef and farm produce. Policies like the provision of rations were cloaked in the language of benevolence, holding out the promise of social and economic progress. However, rations were a Trojan horse containing the means to take control of tribal life. Rations were one face of a broad strategy to subjugate the Kiowas through a process of domesticating and disciplining Indian bodies. Theoretically, the colonial-inspired ingestion of rations mediated the internalization of Western liberal values, such as individualism and Western-style work, thereby undermining Native practices, economy, and political autonomy literally from within the bodies of Native people. In practice, however, the United States and its local representatives denied the Indians sufficient food, called Indian efforts to procure food war, and successfully pushed them to the economic margins of the United States. Withholding rations from Indians whose economies had been destroyed, the consequences of which were catastrophic for Indian peoples, belied the benevolent discourse of improvement and required the Kiowas to fashion a response or starve.

For the Kiowas, the reservation in southwestern Indian Territory, while situated in their traditional territory, represented a small fraction of the country they had previously used for hunting, procuring, and trading. Reservation policies, practices, and boundaries disrupted Kiowa modes of production in most areas of their subsistence. Exploiting an environment like the arid southern Plains required large territories in which to follow the migratory buffalo; pursue other game; procure sufficient supplies of food, medicines, and manufacturing materials from botanical sources; obtain water; and graze large horse herds. Yet hunting off the reservation was now possible only with the Indian agent's permission.

The rupturing of the conquest narrative uncovers the work of *d'ogudle* and other Kiowas whose evolving solutions to pressures of American colonialism produced economic, social, and political consequences for both the Kiowas and the United States. Cooperative relations among bands despite a reservation boundary challenges the categorizing of Indians as "progressive" versus "traditional" as a method of historical analysis of nineteenth-century Kiowa history. Both the diversion of horses and cooperation between off-and on-reservation bands demonstrated that the expansion of American domination tested the United States' practical goals for imposing control over the Indians. Stumbling Bear's remarks, which could be easily subsumed into the interpretation of Indian resentment and victimization, revealed the generative side of colonialism that arose out of the contest between colonizers and colonized where Indian agency, colonial fallibility, victimization, and violence are all evident.

Chapter 5. Fictions of the Nineteenth-Century American Assimilation Policy

By 1875 enormous change had rocked the worlds of American Indians and Americans though in different ways. Great Plains tribes had experienced the destructive forces of American hegemony like many tribes before them. Americans simultaneously grieved from the costs of the Civil War and celebrated the conquest of the American West. A project, funded by federal and private sources, was underway at Philadelphia to commemorate the one hundredth anniversary of the Declaration of Independence and to exhibit American technological progress and growth for an international audience. The Philadelphia Centennial Exhibition illustrates a nationalistic collaboration involving the state, the commercial sector, and the academy. The state and commercial sector provided funding and shared an investment in forms of national boosterism and narrative making. The interests of academics in the fledgling American field of anthropology were tied into the project through federal funds provided for fieldwork. The discipline of anthropology made significant contributions to the narrative. Ethnographic exhibitions of "traditional" Native material culture, undisturbed by the American invasion, maintained the visitors' ignorance of the reality of reservation conditions. The dioramas of "Indian life" kept Indians frozen in time and allowed Americans to deny the destructive consequences of expansion and imagine the successes of assimilation.

The "American Indian" served multiple purposes in this obvious, but unrecognized collaboration. His presence in the Philadelphia exhibition opens a window onto the varied ways in which colonialism works and is reinforced by the shared interests of various sectors of the

United States. Seeing through this window is best achieved by stepping back from Philadelphia into the world of real American Indians. They are present in the analysis of this book as an affirmative statement of tribal identity and as a Native consciousness behind colonialism. In this chapter, the Philadelphia exhibition, a model of assimilationist thinking, and a group of southern Plains men imprisoned at Fort Marion, in St. Augustine, Florida, during its unfolding offer two ways of looking at the connections between colonialism at the top and the bottom, between colonizers and colonized.

As the planners of the Philadelphia Centennial began building resources, organizing the exhibits, and making lists of dignitaries who would participate in a ceremonial role on the opening day, they likely had little if any awareness of the conditions at the Kiowa agency in Indian Territory. The off-reservation bands had come in during the fall of 1874 following the enrollment of reservation Kiowas. Kiowas not enrolled were received at Fort Sill as prisoners of war, put into an open stockade, and exposed to the elements. Soldiers threw raw meat to them over the stockade fence. In time, the privilege of being moved from the stockáde to an indoor cell for good behavior became available. Women and children were released. Kiowa leaders and the military authorities devised an arrangement by which a well-behaved prisoner would be released to a more senior man who would assume liability for him. Winter passed, and in the spring Kicking Bird picked some of the men to be incarcerated. In May, Kiowa, Comanche, Cheyenne, and Arapahoe men, seventy-two in all, plus one unidentified woman, were shackled, loaded on to wagons, and set out for Fort Marion, in St. Augustine, Florida. Relatives gathered, crying and pleading fearfully for the prisoners, destined for an unknown fate.

The trip involved traveling by wagon, train, and, finally, boat. It was an arduous and anxiety-ridden trip, leading one man to commit suicide and another to attempt escape. Placed under the supervision of Lt. Richard Pratt, they began, unknown to them at the time, a three-year term of imprisonment. These off-reservation outlaws were to be an example for the rest of the Kiowas, who had no knowledge of the punishment that awaited them and in some instances speculated that they would be put to death (see photos 1 and 2).

1. Prisoners at Fort Marion. RC 2006.011.2, National Cowboy & Western Heritage Museum, Oklahoma City OK.

2. Indian Council. 2005.043.3, National Cowboy & Western Heritage Museum, Oklahoma City OK.

Pratt had his own ideas about how the men would spend their time. He was an ardent assimilationist and saw Fort Marion as an opportunity to test his ideas. In the isolation of Fort Marion, in remote St. Augustine, Pratt had complete control of their days and nights. It was a perfect laboratory in which to test the idea of Indian civilization.

Born in 1840 at Rushford, New York, Pratt and parents moved west to Logansport, Indiana, when he was six. At a young age he took various jobs to help support his mother and two brothers. He enlisted and fought in the Civil War, returning home to Logansport to go into business for himself. In 1867 he applied for a commission in the regular army and was appointed second lieutenant in the Tenth United States Cavalry, a Negro regiment commanded by white officers. Pratt spent the next eight years in the southern Plains as part of the U.S. effort to subdue the Indian tribes of the area, including the Kiowas, Comanches, Cheyenne, and Arapahoe. In 1875 Pratt undertook the job of supervisor of the Fort Marion prisoners, seventeen of whom he took with him to Hampton Institute in Virginia following their release three years later.[1] To the casual student of Native history, Pratt is best known as an Indian educator and founder of Carlisle Indian School in Pennsylvania, which opened its doors in 1879. Pratt's famous maxim, "kill the Indian to save the man," encapsulated his belief that ethnocide and assimilation into American society were the only remaining options for the Indians. Captain Pratt, the nominal rank by which he was known, spent twenty-four years as head of Carlisle. Following his retirement in 1904 until his death in 1924, Pratt remained an intense critic of the Bureau of Indian Affairs, much as he was of the Indian reservation system.

Pratt's memoir, completed in 1923, chronicles his careers as military officer and as Indian education activist.[2] Pratt's dual military and educational perspective, shaped by his experience with American Indian affairs in the defining late nineteenth century, gives value to the memoir as an assimilationist text. As a member of the military establishment, Pratt participated in bringing the southern Plains tribes under control and confining them to reservations. His military affiliation made him a natural enemy of the Bureau of Indian Affairs, since most of the bureau's critics objected to the reservation as an obstacle to

Indian advancement. Pratt, environmental determinist, believed that Native tribes possessed weaknesses as primitive societies, which they might overcome if situated in the right conditions for learning. Formal education would get them through the gates of American society.

Pratt even went so far as to offer a parallel example of the determining power of environment by comparing Indian assimilation to the habits of wild turkeys. While out scouting with the post quartermaster, Pratt observed a wild turkey laying her eggs in a clump of bushes. Gathering the eggs, he took them home to his wife who placed them with one of her laying hens. The hatched baby birds grew large enough to leave the hencoop. Instead of leaving for the nearby woods, the wild turkey's traditional undomesticated habitat, they assumed a roosting place in the trees in the yard of the Pratt property. Mrs. Pratt continued to feed the turkeys daily. In this experience, Pratt found a lesson "to the man who was pondering much over the race question. He saw that even wild turkeys only need the environment and kind treatment of domestic civilized life to become a very part of it."[3] The wild turkey's preference for regular feeding over competition for food in the woods was evidence to Pratt of the determining power of a civilizing environment in the domestication of wild animals, an analysis he extended to Indians.

That Pratt's cultural program for the southern Plains warriors should be carried out at St. Augustine, the oldest settlement of an invading European power in North America, is an irony of history. The city was founded by Menéndez in 1565, and was associated with various colonial military operations, Franciscan missions, and the European contest for control over the continent. It was sacked by Francis Drake in 1580 and was attacked by other colonial powers before coming under British possession in 1763. After yet another brief period of Spanish control, the United States took possession of the city in 1781.

Castillo de San Marcos, later renamed Fort Marion, came into existence in 1756 during the Spanish period. It sat at the north end of the city where it occupied a commanding position over the harbor. The fort was unique in its medieval architecture and, according to one tourist publication, "a magnificent specimen of the art of military engineering as developed at the time of its construction." This "massive structure of coquina stone, with curtains, bastions, moat and outworks," occupied an acre of land. The dungeons of Fort Marion had held the famous Seminole Indian leaders Osceola and Coacoochee.

St. Augustine himself, for whom the city was named, had made an important contribution to the legal discourse of empire and conquest while serving as Bishop of Hippo in fifth-century North Africa.[4] Donatist schismatics had challenged the Catholic Church to acknowledge clerical morality as a determining qualification for worldly office. Augustine's defense of papal authority led the radicals to assume aggressive militant strategies. In the context of the conflict over clerical qualifications, Augustine extended his theory of a *jus bellum* in civil affairs to the religious realm, where resistance to papal authority signaled irrationality, and justified the church in undertaking militant corrective measures. Augustine's argument was embedded in later papal justifications of the Crusaders' attacks on infidels in the Iberian peninsula and the Spanish invasion of the Americas. In 1875, St. Augustine the city was silent witness to a microcosm of the war of ethnocide the United States government waged on American Indian peoples. In keeping with Augustinian notions of a just war, ethnocide was represented as a moral Indian policy; Native resistance to it and to assimilation measures were signs of irrationality. Thus, the legal bases of ethnocide as an Indian policy justified aggression in many forms against Native people who resisted the civilization program.

Pratt recognized that he had been given a unique opportunity to put theory into practice when the army placed him in the position of supervisor over the Fort Marion Indian prisoners. An early letter exuded optimism: "I intend they shall advance every day, and if forty or fifty of them can speak our language, ... and all have a fair knowledge and practice of labor and its benefits, I think you will be pleased with the experiment."[5] His assumptions about the prisoners were typical of the time. Having spent most of his military career in the southern Plains, Pratt would have been remarkably unusual to think of the Indians in other terms. He, like other contemporaries, had begun to think of young Plains men as the best hope for civilizing Indians; they would plant the will to civilization among their people. Pratt pointedly targeted young men as a vanguard of assimilation that would overtake the dwindling conservative generation. He envisioned interceding in a Kiowa socialization process that he believed centered exclusively on warfare. As young men who had received Western instruction aged into senior men, they would become a "great civilizing element among their people."[6] Thus, Pratt's beliefs led him to focus on cultivating only young men to accept work and studies, leaving senior men to participate voluntarily.

Fort Marion married Pratt's regard for military discipline with his belief in uplift through education. Pratt first targeted the men's bodies and physical appearance (see photo 3).

Having been beaten into submission on the Plains, deprived of liberties and life-sustaining necessities at Fort Sill, and tortured by separation from their families, the men's now pliant bodies and educable minds were ready for Pratt's regimen. Haircuts and uniforms inscribed prominent signs of reform on the men's bodies. Uniforms created the illusion of equality with American soldiers that Pratt reinforced when he permitted the Indians to drill with the regular soldiers and to organize a unit to guard fellow Indian prisoners. Drills in the common yard established symmetry between prisoners and U.S. troops. There, soldiers modeled an assimilated male body, synonymous with military discipline, for warriors whose own ideas of military discipline were undermined by the discourse of savagery. For Pratt, the blurring of lines between serving prison time and enforcing their own punishment rewarded the men for earning his trust. The integration of roles also broke down the segregating forces that withheld "equal privilege for development."

The imprinting of Western thought and practice was carried out through language study, church attendance, and especially work. Pratt made efforts to secure the men work in the nearby town of St. Augustine. They cleared palmetto stands, moved a Sunday school building, carried baggage at the train station, hauled lumber at the sawmill, and performed other kinds of day labor for wages. Work was irregular so Pratt encouraged the production of tourist goods. The

3. Indian Guard. 2003.161, National Cowboy &
Western Heritage Museum, Oklahoma City OK.

men polished sea beans for a curio merchant in town. Zotom, one of
the Kiowa prisoners, painted fans on his own initiative, which were
so popular he had at times a standing order. Pratt's belief in racial
hierarchies and in moral uplift through work was on display when a
group of African-American workers hired to clear palmettos failed to
report for a second day of labor. Pratt stepped in to assure the property
owner that the Indians could and would complete the job. He proudly
recounted their stories of the heat, blistered hands, and aching backs,
as well as their superior resolve to endure the rigors of work until
they had succeeded where the African-American laborers had failed.
It was important to Pratt to establish and convince white society that

American Indians were capable of emulating American values of work and competition even if making that case required reinforcing stereotypes about African Americans.

Pratt had noticed the prisoners' boredom and restlessness. His experience on the Plains had given him the opportunity to observe Indian men drawing pictures on paper obtained from the troops or the agency. So he drew together some paper, pencils, and crayons and presented them to the prisoners to help them pass the time. The young men became absorbed in drawing. Of the young prisoners at Fort Marion, these former outlaws straight off the Plains by way of the horrific stockade, twenty-six produced in three years over eight hundred unconventional drawings, rich in content, color, and the voices of anonymous young men.

The drawings descend from the traditional arts of Plains hide pictography. Processed buffalo hides owned by individual male warriors attested to an individual's military record and materialized his reputation. Frequently, young men were given the work of painting specific deeds reflecting the warrior's exceptional courage or risk taking on to the hide. Over time, the accumulation of discrete images filled the surface of the hide, marking it the possession of a specific individual. One might think of it as a publicly displayed résumé that kept a warrior honest in his accounts and reinforced his good name and reputation through display. The conventions of hide paintings were narrow, including a distinct pictographic style and restriction to images of horses, riders, and, perhaps, buffalo.

The young men had opportunities to be exposed to sources of stylistic inspiration during their free days. Art historian Janet Catherine Berlo argues that the drawings "conform quite closely to the traditional Plains ideals of pictorial painting," pointing to the Northern Cheyenne artist White Bird's recording of his memories of the Battle of Little Bighorn in 1876.[7] The existence of White Bird's deer hide painting does confirm that many Native male artists were responding to the life-altering period of the late nineteenth century through their art. Traditional pictographic painting with its attendant conventions was

too restrictive to accommodate the dramatic events that were unfolding in the lives of Indian men.

The Fort Marion drawings exhibited a flat, two-dimensional style
as well as dramatic departures from the traditional forms. The young
men experimented with subject matter, technique, perspective, and
color. Suddenly, their art contained landscape, romance, and ethnographic detail. They drew their journey to Fort Marion, capturing con-
temporary transportation technology, landscape, and changing environments. They also drew from events after their arrival at the Fort,
limning images of encounters with strange wildlife, St. Augustine
society, and military life at Fort Marion. Their drawings also documented Kiowa social life, camp life, and men and women engaged in
hunting, courting, and domestic work. Though some artists used their
drawings to express fantasy, even more radical is the perspective of
their experiences and observations. Perhaps the most profound drawings are those that evidence the young men's engagement with the idea
of Pratt's social experiment, expressing experiences and observations
that radically challenged the discursive patterns of the colonizers.

Wo-haw, one of the Kiowa artists, was twenty years old when his
group, led by Satanta, surrendered at Fort Sill on October 3, 1874. As
a member of one of the last groups that held out from the reservation, he was identified with the notorious perpetrators of great crimes.
Consequently, he spent his entire time at Fort Sill in the stockade. At
Fort Marion, he continued to resist, participating in a failed escape
attempt. During his incarceration at Fort Marion, Wo-haw produced
two twelve-page sketchbooks filled with drawings, which together
with three drawings are stored at the Smithsonian Anthropological
Archives.

One group of drawings captures the classroom where the young
Kiowa men took English-language lessons from imported teachers
and local St. Augustine volunteers. Identically drawn students with
haircuts and uniforms sit at desks facing the authoritative teacher. One
image, however, stands out among the classroom drawings (see photo
4). Wo-haw's representation of the classroom includes a spectral warrior, in robe-like clothing, his hair in the traditional style the young

4. Untitled (Schoolroom at Fort Marion). Museum Acc# 1882.18.15.
By Wo-Haw. Missouri Historical Society, St. Louis.

men wore before their haircuts. The spectral Indian in traditional pre-
sentation contradicts the image of the young men with short haircuts
and army uniforms, standing apart from them at their desks like a sen-
tinel watching over them as they work. The spectral warrior creates a
dramatic intervention in the representation of the assimilation environment that can be read many ways. Is the figure a reference to time
or memory? Does he represent Wo-haw's resistance to the program, an
interpretation of loss, awareness of change, or is it simply a comfort-
ingly familiar image? In most interpretations this rather complicated
image has mainly been construed as evidence of nostalgia for a disap-
pearing era, reinforcing the colonizing nation's narrative.

This drawing and one other by Wo-Haw are two of the most in-
triguing examples of the men's struggle to conceptualize the connections between past and their future. His famous image, known by a
title given it some time later, "Wo-Haw in Two Worlds" (see photo 5),
shows a Plains warrior over whom Wo-Haw has written his name strad-
dling a boundary that divides the drawing into two fields: an idealized
image of the Indians' conventional tipi on the open plains and one of

WoHAW

5. Untitled (Indian between Two Cultures). Museum Acc# 1882.18.32.
By Wo-Haw. Missouri Historical Society, St. Louis.

the Anglo-American farm. The Plains scenario includes a buffalo and celestial signs, a moon, a star, the sun. The idealized farm includes a bovine. Wo-Haw offers a pipe to each animal. As Janet Catherine Berlo has noted, "Wo-Haw holds a peace pipe out to each, although he is facing the domesticated animal. One foot stands near the buffalo herd and Kiowa tepee, but Wo-Haw's other foot is firmly planted in the tilled fields in front of a wooden house. Wo-Haw knew that he, his people, and their art had embarked irrevocably on the white man's way."[8]

Wo-Haw's classroom drawing and split-field drawing share the same binary organization, one strikingly consistent with the binary discourse of the colonizers: progressives versus traditionals, friendlies versus troublemakers, and so on. But it is equally if not more likely that the drawings reveal the double consciousness the men carried and contemplated in their own lives, futures, and identities.

In the romanticized, assimilationist interpretation of the Indians' choices in the late nineteenth century, Wo-Haw has accepted the future as a white world. This interpretation is certainly consistent with Pratt's ambitions for the young men and with the narrative he constructed in his interpretation of letters the young men later wrote each other. This was the dominant narrative, but not necessarily the Indians' narrative. Wo-Haw was hardly assimilation material. He had remained with the outside bands until the end, and he participated in a plot to escape Fort Marion. Again, it is difficult to know what was in the painter's mind as he created the split-field drawing. Acceptance of the inevitable loss of identity, as Berlo suggests, is the tragic but benign interpretation of the piece, which seemingly marks the end of a sad chapter. But it is just as likely that the drawing reflects the teachings of older Indians during this period. Many Native people, with good reason, saw their options as limited to creating a new strategy or dying. They saw themselves in a world that held no place for Indians. In this more compelling sense, Wo-Haw's drawing is a representation of his awareness that many older Indians were encouraging their children to take the best of both worlds, because they would need both to survive as a minority people in the postcontact world.

The same artist also produced a drawing of the Kiowa Sun Dance lodge (see photo 6). It is a rendering of vision-seeking to gain protection over the Sun Dance. A lodge constructed of cottonwood sits in the center of a field, an older Indian sitting off to one side. Again, the sun, moon and star float above the lodge. A young male initiate stands with open arms looking into the sky, reaching for a vision, which comes in the form of a thunderbird. The drawing is vibrant, accurate in detail, and powerful. It references a world the white man, with his assimilation programs and coercion, cannot touch. As the Cree-Chipewyan artist Jane Ash Poitras describes it, "After his ordeal, the Sun Dancer is reborn to the sacred. The more rebirth a visionary survives, the more power he has in the sacred world—power used to help, to heal, and to communicate good to the community."[9] The Sun Dance is a ceremony of pain and endurance, cleansing, and clarity. This drawing, which breaks away "from profane time through a visionary moment," is not unique in this respect; such seeking was a traditional practice of the Kiowas and other tribes. Again, romanticized interpretations of a dying culture, nostalgia, and tragedy are tempting, but Wo-Haw's

6. Untitled (Sun Dance). Museum Acc# 1882.18.46. By Wo-Haw.
Missouri Historical Society, St. Louis.

ceremony on paper is far more plausible as a representation of spirit
power seeking, which he had practiced or had seen practiced.

Pratt makes not a single mention of the drawings in his 1923 memoir *Battlefield and Classroom*, perhaps because he viewed the activity as in-
significant or benign, providing merely comfort and familiarity for the
men. Inclusion of the drawings in the memoir would also have drawn
attention to the clash between the content of the drawings and Pratt's
philosophies about assimilation. In the immediate context of Fort
Marion and Pratt's ongoing work to promote assimilation, however,
the drawings served him in important ways. The artists' references to
home and family humanized them to American visitors, tourists, and
St. Augustinians, and evoked the tragic "vanishing Indian" sentiment,
thereby diminishing non-Indian hostility. The drawings, which included scenes of the fort and St. Augustine, nevertheless contrasted
the men's unreconstructed tribal identities with Pratt's transforming
environment. The drawings underscored the urgency and struggle of
Pratt's program and narrative—that the American Indian reservation

had failed and that Indians must be removed from their communities to reach their successful assimilation into American society.

In 1878, seventeen of the prisoners, accompanied by Pratt, traveled to Hampton Institute in Virginia to continue their education; the remainder of the men returned to their respective reservations. In Pratt's view, the Indian experience under American colonialism offered two alternative narratives, the Indian who successfully assimilated and the Indian who failed. Those who went to school had a better chance at assimilating than the men who returned to their respective reservations. But the latter was where the real test took place, amidst poverty and lack of resources.

Letters written by the men who returned to the reservation to their Hampton friends provided material for Pratt's construction of a narrative in which he faithfully believed. Pratt published these letters, together with other letters by reservation-bound Indians, Indian residents, and Indian graduates to Pratt, former teachers, and friends made at St. Augustine, in the Hampton Institute's newsletter, *The Southern Workman*. Since Pratt published the letters as part of a fundraising campaign to support boarding and educating reservation children, a process of selection is implied. Despite his professed reluctance to present the Indians as begging, he titled these "Pathetic Letters from Indians" who had "little or no chance of earning money, no tools to farm with, no work to get."[10] By painting a picture of reservation failure, the letters served Pratt's critique of the reservation as an obstacle to Indian assimilation.

Some of the letters Pratt used were from a Kiowa named Awlih, who had returned from Fort Marion to the reservation, to his friend Etahleah, who had accompanied Pratt to Hampton. Of the reservation Awlih wrote, "I am tired of this place here, and wish I were back with you at school." In the meantime, Awlih would "stick to my clothes and what I know about the white man's way, but when my pantaloons and coat wear out I don't know where I shall get any more." His only means of supporting himself was working a small cornfield, but otherwise he had nothing to do. He ended, "Give my love to all the Kiowas."[11]

The students who accompanied Pratt wrote about the rewards of hard work, the desire to learn more, and their belief in an outcome that would improve their lives. In one letter, Paul Tsaitkopeta, a Kiowa prisoner, reflected on his intellectual journey in a lengthy letter to Pratt. Tsaitkopeta reminisced about his early days with Pratt at Fort Marion, where he struggled to learn to "speak good." He wrote: "White man's talk is very hard. . . . Long time ago when you first began to teach us you showed us a card and asked us what that was. It was A. B. C. but I did not know anything about it. I only laughed in my heart. . . . By and by I think yes! he wants to show us the road (poore mouth)." But looking back Tsaitkopeta saw that, "In one year I heard a little, and something I began to know of what you said. Again in one more year I understood a heap. Again in one more year I knew almost all your talk." In Pratt's hands, Tsaitkopeta's letter proved that young men would accept assimilation, that a civilized state was possible through progression, and that Indians were capable of work. At the same time, the letter also clearly exhibited the limits of Tsaitkopeta's knowledge, showing that the work of civilizing Indians was never ending. [12]

Tsaitkopeta also had more to say about Pratt and assimilation. "I took it [Pratt's 'talk'] and put it away in my head to remember. . . . It is very hard to remember what we learn. Every day I study and learn something and think I know it. At night I go to sleep and when I wake in the morning it is all gone." But he did not give up. "By and by I study again and pack it away in my head. I learn . . . I try, try, and then in a little while I know. I think a great deal—I think all the time I work. Whatever I do I think think [sic] so I may know and keep what I learn." Here Tsaitkopeta's letter underscores the idea of work, productivity, and rationality, lessons Pratt persistently incorporated into the Fort Marion program. On a practical level, Tsaitkopeta's letter served Pratt's fundraising work, but more significantly it, and other letters, complemented the assimilation narrative he was driven to realize.

In contrast, themes of failure dominated the stories of men who returned to the reservation following their release from Fort Marion. The accounts printed in the Southern Workman provided descriptions of the reservation as impoverished, lacking adequate resources, and offering few opportunities for work. Even the well-born Cheyenne Howling Wolf could not escape hard times. Writing from Darlington agency to a couple to whom he had grown close during his incarceration at St. Augustine, he assured them that "not one word [of all the instruction he had received at Fort Marion had] been lost" and that he had continued to travel the "good road" upon his return to the reservation. However, he said, "My lodge is poor, and I do not feel good to be still living in one of the old kind of houses. When the agent gives me help to build a wooden house I shall feel glad. I am very poor. All my friends Arapahoes and Cheyennes are friendly and want to learn to be like white men, but often say my white friends East have forgotten all about me."[13] Howling Wolf was no backslider, but the reservation failed him as it had failed Awlih, reinforcing the idea of his dependency on the help of his white friends in the east who would save him.

Howling Wolf's letter is representative of the returned prisoners' testimony to the reservation's poor conditions and their difficulties in establishing themselves in more independent ventures such as farming and stock raising. But other letters, such as the Cheyenne leader Minimic's to Pratt, spelled out the necessity of rejecting the old Indian ways and reconciling themselves to a new way of life. The old chief wrote: "All that you have told me I am holding close to my heart. I give none of it away. Since I returned some of my people have gone after buffalo, but I did not go. Those who went are now returning poor; found nothing but small game."[14] In the absence of buffalo Minimic channeled the energies of young men into chopping wood for sale at $1.25 per cord.[15] But their difficulties persisted, as a May 1879 letter from Chief Killer, who lived at the Cheyenne and Arapahoe agency, reflects. Though he intended to remember all that Pratt had taught him and the others at Fort Marion, he as yet had "nothing, no horses and no money." Indeed, he went on, "I think the people do not know how poor we are." Nevertheless, "the buffalo are gone. I am going to work soon to plow for corn, and push hard to make a crop." By the time of a visit Pratt had promised to make, Chief Killer hoped to have four horses and to "show you how I can make a crop."[16] Chief Killer's letter offered Pratt both personal reassurance of his commitment to the lessons of Fort Marion and affirmation of Pratt's assimilation program.

But the deprivation reservation Indians suffered from lack of resources was not the worst of their problems. Some felt threatened by their very identities. Quoyuouah's letter to Captain Pratt was filled with anxiety that other returned men shared. He wrote of himself, "I am again a Comanche," and despite his desire to adhere to the "white man's road," he had no horse of his own and was "very poor. When you [Pratt] come to see us I shall have nothing to show you—no corn—no house—nothing at all. This is a poor country and a poor ground. I don't sleep well, I am afraid."[17] The underlying point of this explicit message is unmistakable: Pratt's work at Fort Marion had erased the men's tribal identities and instilled the fear of reverting, or backsliding. Quoyuouah's letter also did the work of assigning blame to himself for the failures of the assimilation program.

The worried Comanche man and others confronted a reservation that the state conceptualized and built on destroyed tribal economies. It was a corrupt system that worked against the state's own plan of assimilation and promises of progress to tribal people in exchange for land cessions and peace. The Indians were not the failure, but that fact would not have served American history. Warriors who had once been held up as contemptible renegades, then as promising symbols of assimilation, met failure and returned full circle to irrationality, pathos, and primitiveness. The reported experiences of favored son Howling Wolf provided the language of reverted, backsliding Indians. He was accused of raping an American girl and hid out for several years to escape punishment, ultimately leaving Oklahoma for Texas. There Howling Wolf, esteemed son of a respected Cheyenne leader, performed in Old West performance theater, before eventually returning to Oklahoma to live out his life.[18]

These letters were useful to Pratt in maintaining an image of himself as the assimilationist with the answers to the Indian Problem. They reinforced ideas on the theoretical trajectory of progress, the ceaseless work to be done in civilizing the Indians, the dependency of Indians on their white friends and on Pratt, and the failure of the reservation. Indians who followed the white man's road enjoyed a different fate. Being students at Hampton opened up new channels and opportunities, such as the transfer of some students to Carlisle Indian School in Pennsylvania. Others went out into the world as converted Christians and ministers or artists; still others returned home. The *Southern Workman* provided Pratt with a forum from which to issue a comparison between the rewards of assimilation and, by implication, the costs of backsliding. For example, one story contained an account of several Indian students being asked why they liked to learn. Reportedly, the students' unambiguous response was "Because it makes me a man."[19]

Pratt's man-making pedagogy was infused with social evolutionary ideas intended to unmake young Native people and re-create them in the image of Western civilization. Before-and-after photographs of the young men at Fort Marion, like the photographs of boarding-school children, document the binary, man-making transformation that demanded the destruction of the men's Native identity and their acceptance of domestication. Such photographs were a rejection of Indian agency, noncompliance, and negotiated spaces between the colonizers and colonized. Pratt's narrative fills in the gap created by those who failed to assimilate in the form of a tale of backsliding and failure. Narratively, these were the Indians' only options.

Simultaneously, the emerging field of American anthropology had begun to develop a language of social scientific description and categorization that produced a complementary flip side of tribalism discourse. The famed nineteenth-century anthropologist James Mooney carried out fieldwork among the Kiowas for a decade beginning in 1893, the late reservation–early allotment period. His monograph *Calendar History of the Kiowa Indians*, published in 1898 was the product of his work in the southern Plains. It covers Kiowa history from its genesis according to their origin account, through their migrations to the southern Plains, to the final allotment of their lands in the late nineteenth century. Mooney's ethnography contains descriptions and analyses of Kiowa language, social organization, government, religion, and military societies. He provided an accounting of the numerous disease epidemics the tribe suffered and the effect on their population. Drawing from several individually produced calendars (individually maintained calendars organized as Kiowas measured time), including one owned by Dohausen, and government sources, Mooney dedicated the second half of the book to a year-by-year interpretation of annual calendars composed of summer and winter accounts. The calendar keeper interpreted a single event for each summer and winter count in the form of a pictograph which served as mnemonic devices, prompting memory and unlocking tribal oral history. The pictographs served as a mnemonic device, prompting memory and unlocking tribal oral history. Mooney also enjoyed close relationships with Kiowa artists, especially Silverhorn, who is perhaps best known for producing miniatures of tipis and other material culture for Mooney's contributions to the Indian exhibits at the 1893 Columbian World's Fair Exposition in Chicago.

It was common for anthropologists and government officials to draw comparisons among the tribes, ranking their character traits, measuring their cultural losses, and so on. Such contrasts varied because they were constructed on the basis of narrow experience and subjectivity, for reasons of expediency. For example, Mooney's *Calendar History of the Kiowa* asserts in a section titled "Sociology of the Kiowa" that "In character the Kiowa are below the standard." Mooney used essentialist characterizations of the Sioux as "direct and accommodating, the Cheyenne high-spirited and keenly sensitive, the Arapahoe generous and accommodating, the Comanche practical and businesslike" to emphasize the inferiority of the Kiowas. For Mooney, the Kiowas could only claim "the savage virtue of bravery," with "less of honor, gratitude, and general reliability than perhaps any other tribe of the plains." The admixture of Mexican blood was his explanation for the deficiency of Kiowa character.[20]

Mooney is a perfect example of the duality that exists in the American mind about American Indians, both in the nineteenth century and today. He was known as an Indian sympathizer, particularly after the 1890 massacre of Sioux men, women, and children at Wounded Knee. His anguished description of the bodies left on the field for three days, killing of women and children, noted absence of the missionaries to help the wounded, and the long trench in which army personnel buried the Indians "like so much cordwood" politicized his work in the eyes of John Wesley Powell and the Bureau of American Ethnology. He broke ranks with conventional wisdom, daring to draw predictably controversial comparisons between Native and Christian revitalization movements in his work on dreams and visions. Still, his work leaves a record of a judgment about Indians that was consistent with the common nineteenth-century view.

Mooney was highly respected for the careful scholarship evident in his Kiowa work, professionally isolated for his Indian sympathizing, and admonished for his criticisms of the Indian Service. But he could not carry over the affection he had for Native people practicing their traditions and using their cultural knowledge to the same people who after years under U.S. colonialism had, in his view, degenerated. Testifying before a Smithsonian committee investigating Powell's practices at the Bureau of American Ethnology, Mooney urged anthropologists to salvage what remained of Native American cultures. In doing so, he simultaneously revealed that he valued Indians of the past, but reviled real Indians living in their present conditions:

> The [Kiowa] man with whom I made my home . . . had eight rings
> in one ear and five in the other. He lived in a tipi and under an ar-
> bor in summer, always had his full buckskin on when it was time
> for buckskin; and he never went to a military post, or to a dance,
> or to anything else, without spending a couple of hours at least to
> dress and paint up. Now he is in a house, and has chickens and a
> corn field, and stoves and clocks and beds; and he has taken out
> his rings and cut his hair, and he looks like a dilapidated tramp.

Anthropologists like Mooney lost interest in Indians as they changed with the times. Ironically, for anthropologists the value of Indians lay in their tribalness, as the Philadelphia and Chicago expositions illustrated.

Anthropology abetted the United States' colonial project with its social scientific description and categorizations, Indian-focused profession making, and participation in the construction of a national narrative. About mid-century, anthropology's foremost figure was Lewis Henry Morgan, author of *Ancient Society*. In Morgan's time an-

thropology was preoccupied with origins in the context of a social development model. Societies moved through stages, he believed, from
savagery to barbarism and finally into civilization. While others were
preoccupied with philology, Morgan focused on analysis and classifi-
cation of kinship systems, resulting in his 1871 publication, *Systems of
Consanguinity and Affinity of the Human Family*. John Wesley Powell followed Morgan's ahistorical path of identifying single stages of development. Powell's advocacy of the creation of the Bureau of American
Ethnology before a review committee of the Smithsonian Institution
led to an act of Congress in 1879 that founded the bureau. The Bureau
of American Ethnology carried out its mission to complete *Contributions
to North American Ethnology* under the Smithsonian Institution.[21] Social
development models, kinship studies, and categorizations presented
in social scientific language reinforced the idea that Native tribalism
was comparatively inferior to Western societies.

   Given this context, it is at first glance grossly ironic that in 1876 and
1893 the first two American expositions, both celebrations of technological and commercial progress, included public programs intended
to elevate the study of Native America and justify salvaging Native culture for future research.[22] To further complicate the irony, the expositions manifested the nation at work in constructing a celebratory historical narrative that omitted its ongoing and current efforts to destroy
American Indian communities while they exploited their cultures com-
mercially for public entertainment. The myriad contradictory ways in
which American Indians were located in the American mind and society were evident in both the 1876 Philadelphia Centennial Exhibition
and the 1893 World's Columbian Exposition in Chicago. Both included
major ethnographic exhibitions, villages inhabited by representatives
from Native communities, and public performances. American Indians
were displayed as a professional field of research and study, amusement
for commercial exploitation, and trope for history writing. Combining
science and carnival, the expositions legitimized the emerging field of
anthropology and its subfields, the commodification of Native culture,
the federal assimilation policy, and the construction of a national narrative that naturalized the Vanishing American Indians.

National narrative writing, "salvage" anthropology, cultural com-modification, and federal assimilation policy, all mutually reinforcing projects, brought together the state, the commercial sector, and the academy. The federal government and the private sector, using their re-spective sources, shared in the cost of organizing and building the ex-positions. Men from the highest levels of the business sector, like John Wanamaker, for example, committed themselves to creating a success-ful program. Congressional appropriations funded the work of nu-merous federal agencies participating in the exposition, including the Department of Interior, Bureau of Indian Affairs, and the Smithsonian Institution's National Museum. Federal funding supported the work of government anthropologists on the National Museum's professional staff to carry out fieldwork, collect specimens of material culture, and curate exhibitions based on their expert knowledge. The collaborative work of the government and private and academic sectors was evident in the exposition exhibits, midways, and performances.

The expositions were an important steppingstone for the field of American anthropology. Scholars of American Indian anthropology enjoyed access to an international public audience, and exploited that opportunity to represent the field as a legitimate emerging scientific area of study. Anthropology had defined its work as salvaging Native material culture and documenting knowledge, languages, and ceremo-nial life before American Indians vanished altogether. The profession also carved out a place in the work of constructing a national narrative, contributing its own legitimization and rationalization of the process by which the American Indian "vanished." From budget justifications to the final exhibition installation and in virtually every decision in be-tween, a narrative of Indian identity and its disappearance along with the salvaging of both knowledge and the nation's unique history of progress was assembled.

In 1871, founding Smithsonian secretary Joseph Henry named Spencer F. Baird, assistant secretary of the United States National Museum, to represent the institution on the president's appointed Centennial Planning Board.[23] Baird's budget justification to Congress centered on the idea of the vanishing Indian. He petitioned Congress to fund an "exhibition of living representatives of the principal Indian tribes." He elaborated, "it is quite reasonable to infer that, by the expiration of a second hundred-year period of the life of the American Republic, the Indians will have entirely ceased to present any distinctive characters, and will be merged into the general population."[24] Eroded identity, racial distinction, and the eventual vanishing Indian thus merged in this U.S. public program of unprecedented scope and size. This predicted disappearance invested the public's interest in both an exhibition of living Indians and the ethnological collection, which "will be the only exposition of the past; and, with each passing year, these specimens will become more valuable and more highly appreciated." In other words, assimilation had accomplished the goal of separating Native knowledge and material culture from tribal people and creating value in their rarity, exotic status, and objectification.

Anthropology raced against the Indian's vanishing to document, describe, and categorize tribal material culture, language, and society. A propensity for description and categorization guided exhibition methodology. Anthropologist Otis Mason was appointed by the Smithsonian to "draw up a systemic schedule of the various articles of clothing, ornaments, household utensils, implements of agriculture, weapons of war and the chase, tools of trade, the apparatus used for the pursuit and capture of game, &tc."[25] The exhaustive list of items became a three-part exhibition that reflected the state of anthropological theory and methodologies. A broad category of "man" was devoted to the physical attributes of Indian people, their "peculiar pathologies," and the phenomenon of tribal organization. Mortuary evidence, cranial and bone measurements, and other human remains subjected to various measurements and evaluations all affirmed anthropology as a science given to precision in its study of humankind. The category "surroundings" explored the physical environment in which Native people lived and correlated various tribes and their habits with those environments. Everything else fell into the encompassing category of "culture." Everything from food and utilitarian goods to systems of knowledge and material culture associated with war, religion, domestic spheres, and social organization enabled taxonomies of tribal cultures. Mason's plan embodied the methodology of salvage anthropology, which not only presumed the disappearance of Native peoples, but facilitated the transfer of Native material culture from one regime of value, based on Native production and consumption, to a regime of increasing value based both on scarcity and controlled access.

The project of salvaging culture and knowledge distinguished anthropology, advanced its profession-making mission, and gave it agency in the construction of a national narrative. Anthropology constructed the connections between objects, representation, and narrative with authority derived from research, science, and status making in the academy. The government and the public accepted anthropology's assertions of academic authority, as written accounts of the ethnology exhibitions evidence. As Nicholas Thomas argues, even "if ethnology was in fact often of little practical value for administration, it can be understood at least to reinforce an imperial sense of epistemic superiority."[26] In other words, the groundwork was being laid for anthropology's belief that it possessed more authority to speak of Native history and culture than the Indians themselves, given their state of decline. The field defended this position with increasing militancy throughout the twentieth century, reaching an intense extremism during the struggle between Native people and the museum and academic communities over repatriation of Native human remains and material objects.

The Philadelphia and Chicago expositions allowed anthropology to deploy its narrative-making authority using various exhibiting methods. Frederick Putnam, director of Harvard's Peabody Museum, organized an outdoors exhibit consisting of over three hundred Indians from fifty-two tribes living on the Centennial grounds near the Japanese Building. Fear that a living exhibit of Indian culture would become a "side-show" had prompted the Department of Interior to reject the idea of building an actual Indian encampment. The following description from the Centennial guide illustrates both the tension that arose from the anthropologists' own concerns about authenticity and decorum and their simultaneous inability to completely segregate science and amusement:

Every tribe is represented by from four to eight persons of different ages and both sexes, and in order that the original inhabitants of America may appear at their best, only the very best families have been selected for the Exhibition. Many of the visitors from the frontier are the chiefs of tribes and their families, while almost all the others are persons distinguished for deeds of daring, perfection of form and feature, or the possession of other rare gifts or attainments. The red-skinned guests are in other words, the crème de la crème of Indian society. A number of lodges, utensils, weapons of warfare, implements of agriculture and manufacture were brought by the Indians, as were also a large number of ponies and dogs. They will carry on their various occupations, including the weaving of blankets and belts; the method of dressing buffalo, and other skins; the manufacture of pottery; construction of stone implements, and the making of moccasins, baskets, ornaments, etc. Among those represented are the Warm Spring braves—Charlie, a half brother of Scar-faced Charlie; Clamtaskina, chief of the tribe, and his daughter, Jennie, aged 17; Aska, a Comanche brave; Tella (Spring), chief of the Kiowas, and his daughter, Kotella (Budding Spring); Running Water, a Pawnee brave; Tontonqua, a Pawnee brave; Walking-water Bill, a Pawnee, one of the very few full-blooded Indians who can wear a moustache and beard; Buffalo Hump, chief of the Comanches; Fire-water Jim, the Comanche brave, who prevented a general massacre between Brownsville and Eagle Place, by carrying the news to Fort Sill, and several others from the Arrapahoe, Piute and Apache tribes. The two princesses accompanying the party, are pretty, modest, intelligent, and in these respects evidence the vast difference which exists between women of the higher and lower grades of Indians of the present. One great peculiarity which marks them distinct from all other races is—that they never express, either by word or sign—amazement, admiration, or disappointment; they note every detail at a glance, but never show by outward sign the effect which strange scenes produce upon their minds. Anything which pleases them they survey critically and pronounce it "good."[27]

The organization of "The Encampment," and this written description, complied with one version of the Americans' Indian, the one that was falling away in the face of expansion and civilization. The encampment Indians would represent the vanishing real Indians, undiluted, culturally authentic, and recognizable. Chiefs, braves, and princesses, collectively the nobility of Native America, were identifiable by their Indian names, Indian deeds, Indian comportment, and Indian goods. An Indian was not an Indian without his lodges and weapons of war. The encampment women's prettiness, modesty, and intelligence and the men's emotionless stoicism marked them as a higher grade of Indian in contrast to the Indians who failed to comply with expected behaviors, or stereotypes. Yet the encampment Indians had not thrown off their savagery, as evidenced by their red skins, skin lodges, skin clothing, and cohabitation with dogs and horses.

Several further outcomes of the planned encampment are evident in the quoted description. First, it bore the expected signs of descriptive anthropological method. The representation of Indians in the ethnographic past conformed to popular ideas of tribal authenticity and American stereotypes of Indians. However, ethnography's Indians failed to represent the reality of Native Americans' lives and the state of Indian–white relations. For example, the Comanche Buffalo Hump, who was featured in the encampment, was a member of a tribe that spent ten years in transition to a reservation in southern Indian Territory. During that period Buffalo Hump and his tribe experienced land loss, the destruction of the southern Plains economy, and U.S. military assaults. Only in 1875 had all Comanche bands acceded to living on the reservation. There they found themselves poor, under the pressure of assimilation, and helpless to extract from the United States government the promised compensation for tribal lands and cooperation laid out in the 1867 Treaty of Medicine Lodge Creek. Back at "The Encampment" at Philadelphia, however, this narrative of westward expansion, Native destruction, and failed assimilation policy was simply absent.

The encampment represented nineteenth-century grading and sorting of American Indians (full-blooded, higher and lower grades), phenotypes that a public audience could receive because they reinforced prevailing concepts of Native identity and authenticity and social hierarchies. Simultaneously, the quoted description suggests a hint of carnival, a parade of Indian notables on display. Meanwhile, neither authentic Indians nor the Indian spectacle at the exhibition conformed to the federal Indian policy of assimilation or to the reality of late-nineteenth-century Native life, marked by poverty and government policies to destroy tribalism.

The Indian encampment's contribution to the larger meaning of history, empire, and progress was to help erase Indians from the U.S. historical narrative of expansion and advance a sanitized version of historical progress. However, the encampment was more successful as a promotion for anthropology, although, in the context of an exposition about such muscular matters as American technological and commercial progress, it flirted with the line separating it from performance and entertainment.

The Chicago World's Fair Exposition in 1893 continued to promote anthropology and colonial ideologies through representation by displaying Native people and their material culture. Again, Frederick Putnam, the eminent anthropologist from Harvard University, seeking to showcase ethnography and Native cultures on a "dignified and decorous basis," offered a more elaborate series of exhibitions concerned with Native American culture. The Anthropology Building, situated along the banks of South Pond, housed the ethnology exhibition. It included a major exhibition on five groups of Hopewell mounds based on archaeological fieldwork and research. Another major program exhibited multiple tribes from the United States, including Alaska. According to one impressed writer, "With historic accuracy in strict chronological sequence and with the most interesting results, has Professor Putnam, the erudite chief of this important department grouped his wards." Putnam's and Franz Boaz's ethnology exhibition within the Anthropology Building was, like Philadelphia's, a taxonomy of Native society, material culture, and language.

Putnam's team also created two outdoor exhibitions, including an

"Esquimaux" (Eskimo) village built just inside the Fifty-seventh Street entrance to Jackson Park. The village was intended as anthropology's representation of Eskimo life, but the anthropologists could not control the popular perception that blurred the line between science and entertainment. One visitor wrote: "For a fee of 25 cents one can see the natives, their wolfish-looking dogs, their sledges, spears, stoves, canoes, lamps, etc. There are men, women and children in the village, and their modes of life and the sanitary conditions (or rather the want of them) peculiar to them and their crowded quarters do not 'lade the pulsing air with sweetest perfumes.'"[28]

Just outside the Anthropology Building and near the Esquimaux Village, a model of the Yucatán ruins and an exhibit on "Cliff Dwellers" from Battle Rock in Colorado were constructed.[29] A written account of a Quackahl performance at the site of the ruins put on for the benefit of Princess Eulalia, the eldest daughter of the king and queen of Spain, shows Indians both as objects of study and sources of entertainment and amusement:[30]

> Being informed that the Quackahls were preparing an entertainment for her, the princess seated herself in a rolling chair that had been covered with a gaudy red Navajo blanket and waited with an expectant face for the performance to begin. The dull thumping of a drum on the outside told the approach of Chief Wannock and his tribe. The drummer came in backward, and while he battered away at his queer shaped instrument, he set up a song. He was accompanied by the other Indians as they came in. For about five minutes the Quackahls marched in a circle, beating time with their bare feet in the sand to the wild song. The song ceased and three or four men crowded around a small square board and began beating a lively tattoo on it with bones. A woman wrapped in a gaily embroidered blanket, and with her long black hair floating in the air, began circling around in front of the princess. The drum beat louder and the rattle of bones on the board quickened until the woman danced up to the crowd and shook a lot of fine feathers from her head on the board. Then the

princess began laughing, for half a dozen of the Quackahls were rolling on the sand in front of her and scratching themselves as though infested with 10,000 fleas. She had never seen such an entertainment before.

This account evidences the vulnerability of anthropological exhibitions to public interpretations that science and amusement are interchangeable programs. Both the close proximity of Chicago's Midway Plaisance to the exposition and private businesses' appropriation of ethnographic display techniques contributed to the blurring of science and entertainment. On the Midway, "American Indians, artistically painted in chrome yellow, vermillion and green, with feathers, knives, tomahawks and all the horrid accoutrements of savage warfare, perform their war dance for the delectation of visitors, keeping time to their orchestra, which thumps out a maddening and interminable tune consisting of one note."[31]

Conversely, anthropology was using techniques to make Exposition exhibits accessible to a popular, nonscholarly audience. For example, the Smithsonian included in its exhibition a set of life-size figures taken from plaster casts. This, an impressed writer noted, was "a work of the utmost value, the last true records of a dying race of men." The Chicago World's Fair had the additional challenge of competing with Buffalo Bill's Wild West Show, which had positioned itself outside the exposition grounds between Sixty-first and Sixty-third streets. There, rent was cheaper than on the Midway, and the distance from the Midway permitted noncompetitive ticket prices. The popular cowboy and Indian spectacle drew huge audiences. As a consequence, the Wild West Show "made even more money than the most lucrative Exposition amusements." Buffalo Bill's Wild West Show gave 318 performances to audiences averaging twelve thousand over a six-month period, leaving Cody with a nearly million-dollar profit.[32] The public's reconciliation of popular entertainment and anthropological research on display as versions of one truth frustrated anthropologists but did a greater disservice to American Indians by exaggerating the distortions of Native culture and history already present at the expositions.

The anthropological exhibitions at the Philadelphia Centennial Exhibition and the World's Exposition at Chicago were predicated on anthropological theories of social evolution and were built on the expectation of popular interest in a vanishing race. However, anthropology contributed to the discourse of empire and colonialism in other fora as well. In 1893, the International Congress of Anthropology met at Chicago, where President Daniel G. Brinton connected the theoretical work of anthropology and the colonizing work of the state.[33] In his address, "The 'Nation' as an Element in Anthropology," Brinton put forth an argument that was consistent with the federal Indian policy of assimilation, colonial ideologies, and social hierarchy theories.[34] Inspired by the work of Lewis Henry Morgan and his awakening to "the potent agency of the state on the psychical nature of man," Brinton extended the idea that nationality was more determining than race, environment, religion, or culture in man's development. His argument flowed from a hierarchy of three types of social compacts—of blood, of territorial area, or of purpose—that plotted man's "upward march to conscious culture." The least-developed social compact type was that of the tribe because it organized itself around blood and kin relations, Morgan's earlier contribution. These societies, according to Brinton, were matriarchal and endogamous, which encouraged purity of descent and had over time produced distinct races. The federation, such as the Iroquois Confederacy, marked an intermediate step between tribal organization and the nation.

Brinton's speech is an anthropological expression of anti-tribalism that can also be found in congressional debates of the same period. In both, the nation represented the highest form of social compact the human race had achieved thus far. Though Brinton believed that a world community that relied on international organizations would eventually overtake the nation as dominant social compact, the characteristics of the nation affirmed it as the form of social compact above the tribe and federation. Specifically, national unity, including physical unity, national costume, and comportment, were signs of the abandonment of individual tribal traits and distinctions. Other markers of the nation included the presence of a modern army drawn from citizens through-

out the polity, linguistic unity that had successfully suppressed trib-
ally distinct languages, a unified belief in a supreme intelligence,
and a court system that followed a body of law that held individuals, rather than their kin, accountable for their actions. For Brinton,
personal liberty was the source of personal happiness. The nation,
therefore, represented humankind overcoming the limitations of
a multiplicity of parochial tribes, each possessing distinctive religi
ous beliefs, languages, governing structures, and tribal legal customs that centered on the family's responsibility for the transgres-
sions of individuals.

Brinton's address on the nation and anthropology united the field
with the state's policies of anti-tribalism and assimilation and contributed the language of scientific reasoning to turn the United States'
genocidal attack on Native institutions, cultures and economies into a
project of social advancement. Insofar as it determined man's identity,
in the case of American Indians an undesirable identity, tribalism was
appropriately targeted for destruction. It is not surprising, therefore,
that anthropologists of the late nineteenth century were single-mind-
edly devoted to salvaging Native culture before it disappeared rather
than trying to imagine how to preserve Native culture in the face of
state assaults on tribal institutions and peoples. Brinton's identification with science and his evolutionism coexisted with popular amusements such as P. T. Barnum's mocking "Congress of Nations" and
"Ethnological Congress." These scientific and popular discourses
legitimized the contemporaneous federal assaults on tribal peoples
and reified the idea of the vanishing Indian, while minimalizing the
destructive consequences of an anti-tribalism in which both the academy and the commercial sector had participated.

Three separate narratives, those produced by the state in collaboration with the academic and commercial sectors, by Pratt, and by the
Kiowa prisoners, all constructed nearly simultaneously, illuminate
competing accounts of the colonized and the colonizers. The anthropological and assimilationist narratives have enjoyed a long shelf life,
but as a result the personal statements by the Kiowa-outlaws-turned-
inspired-artists have been buried. Power constructs reality, a fact born

out by the absence of Native history in the American narrative, even today. The state dehumanized the Indians, the anthropologists encased them, and the commercial sector profited from images, goods, remains, and, most valuable of all, their resources. The Kiowa drawings, tourist goods now recategorized as art, are also, I argue, evidence of a competing narrative.

Chapter 6. **Households of Humanity**

The forces of capitalism that accompanied the American invasion were inextricably linked to federal Indian policies, which were complementary formulations that cleared Indians from the path to make way for capitalist infrastructure, privatized projects, and exploitation of resources. Simultaneously, the nineteenth-century anti-tribal "cant of conquest," an imperative to civilize the Indians, promised Indians peace and progress through adopted self-sufficiency (which Indians had been stripped of to coerce their acceptance of reservations). The promise of self-sufficiency was contingent on the Indians' acceptance of capitalism and the values on which it rested: individualism, competition, acquisitiveness, and rejection of the oppositional values of tribalism, collectivity, and communal economic strategies. The federal Indian policy of civilizing Indians, which was generated by legislation, court decisions, ad hoc innovations at the agency level, and the bureaucracy's center of oversight for Indian affairs, appeared to link the future of Native America to the rising star of American capitalism. The real connection between Indians and capitalism, however, lay in the federal trust responsibility to protect the interests of tribes, which the United States government consistently ignored or neglected.

The politics of Indian–white relations, federal Indian policies, capitalist expansion, and a colonizing ideology that justified the genocide carried out by the United States reinforced each other. The experiences of tribal people and the rhetorical ambiguities of nineteenth-century American policy makers, lawmakers, and reformers are consistent with Maureen Konkle's analysis of American colonialism. Indian–Euro-American relations sit in a framework determined by the American idea that each exists in a separate state of nature. Euro-Americans exist within their abstract concept of progress as an endless trajectory toward perfection. Native people, by contrast, exist in a both abstract and real state of nature where progress is defined by their acceptance of the Western construction of Euro-American superiority, abandonment of tribalism, and imperfect mimicry of Euro-American practices. Thus, the unattainable indigenous trajectory toward perfection is merely hypothetical.

The nineteenth-century Indian reservation system exemplifies Konkle's theory of the hypothetical trajectory. Reservations, built on the ruins of indigenous economies, were created to control American Indians. Their lives were regulated through the surveillance of reservation agents, passes issued for off-reservation hunting, government commodities, isolation, and a local military presence. Regardless of environment, the United States' policy required that Indians make the transformation through forms of work, specifically farming, that justified the practices of the government's civilization program. That Plains Indians were not, for the most part, farming people did not disturb the United States and its citizens' vision of tribal Indians transformed into independent farmers. The delusional vision was preferable to the proposal to exterminate the Indians. Together, the flawed idea and the realities of reservation life strapped Indians to the Americans' hypothetical trajectory of progress.

Local reservation experience complicates explanations that may generalize historical conditions in ways that are useful to our understanding but are still instrumental in obscuring the history of the silent colonized. The Kiowas could not have survived the reservation on government commodities and a buffalo-free environment. That they survived as a tribe, albeit with significant population loss throughout the period, begs the question of the source of their income and subsistence. When the buffalo were exterminated men had been deprived of the principle means of providing for their relations. Annual reports by the Commissioner of Indian Affairs fill in the picture of men's labor, a patchwork of irregular jobs that provided income. The reports do not reveal much about Kiowa women, however, who had also been negatively affected by the loss of the buffalo. Their responses to this catastrophe, however, were partially determined by Western ideas of gendered work, which steered them away from farming and toward the domestic sphere. As this chapter shows, Kiowa women fashioned their own responses to destitution that allowed them to interact with capitalist markets at a distance, maintain cultural practices, and sustain the social values that defined their status in the community.

Kiowa men's roles were greatly altered as a result of the reservation system. Hunting and procuring through raiding were coming to an end. Men continued to hunt and exchange hides with local traders for manufactured goods and to reduce debts, but the robe and fur trade had collapsed, falling from $70,400 in 1876 to $5,068 in 1879. In the waning years of the buffalo business, Indians benefited less and less while American hunters and merchants wrung the last of the profits out of the robe trade. One robe trader in Texas dealt "largely with the hunters on this frontier and [purchased] hides direct from them."[1] In the preceding season alone he had received seventy thousand hides, out of which he sold "some six thousand robe hides that were really *select*, as *leather* hides, not being able to place the robe hides."[2] He expected many more hides in the coming season and hoped to hire Indians from the Kiowa and Comanche reservation to process them either for a piece rate or in exchange for some of the hides.[3] Meanwhile, Agent James H. Haworth reported in January 1878 that "my Indians have not had very good success as far as I have heard, not half as many as last year. My impression is that this year will almost end the Buffalo business."[4]

Reservation-era farming was unsuccessful. After a decade of encouraging Indians to cultivate corn, Haworth summarized his observation of the Indian policy to the Superintendent of Indian Affairs at Lawrence, Kansas. "Five year's experience and observation," Haworth wrote, "satisfy me that this is not a good agricultural district, and cannot be relied upon for farming purposes."[5] He went on to suggest that "If the government would issue to them yearly $12,000 worth of cattle—heifers two years old preferable—for four years, the increase by the fifth year would be almost sufficient to supply the necessary beef ration."[6]

Haworth's advice had not been heeded by the time the Fort Marion prisoners returned to the reservation in 1878. Indians were still planting corn under difficult conditions. Malnourished ponies were harnessed to plow unbreakable ground. The fields had been left unfenced throughout the winter, permitting the animals to graze amidst stalks from the previous crop. The new agent, P. B. Hunt, could only report success at one field where three Indians managed to plow and plant.[7] Meanwhile, agents consistently reported insufficient rations and farming equipment as well as low numbers of cattle.

In 1881, Hunt pronounced the region uncultivable. He reported: "I come now to write the darkest page of the record of our year's work," he reported. "The stand had been perfect, and rains had fallen at the proper intervals. . . . But their hopes were blasted, for no more rains fell on their crops, and stalks and blades were soon dried up with not an ear upon them."[8] Within three years of his arrival at the agency, Hunt too had become convinced of the futility of forcing the Indians to grow corn. "Nothing," he wrote, "is more certain than that this country is badly adapted to agriculture, the scarcity of rainfall cutting short the crops one and sometimes two out of three years. Indeed, I am informed there has been known to be a drought three years in succession."[9] As for the Indians, Hunt said, "There is at times absolute suffering . . ."[10]

Early attempts to put Indians into stock raising were mainly unsuccessful as they either ate or sold the cattle that were issued them. Indeed, in 1875 there were merely two head of cattle for every Indian.[11] Cattle hides replaced bison and game hides as trade items. The cattle-hide trade appears to have been an important source of income, but was fraught with conflict among the licensed traders and the Indians, producing its own type of exploitation. The Indian Bureau and the local agent attempted to impose order on the contentious situation by fixing the price of hides according to grade. Haworth's goal was to set a fair price for both Indians and traders based on the assumption that cash paid out to the Indian would return to the merchant when the Indian returned to trade. Haworth questioned whether the trader should profit twice, once from the purchase and sale of robes, then from the sale of Indian goods.[12]

In the meantime, Indians and ambitious traders collaborated in circumventing the agent's attempts at regulation. A. J. Reynolds, a licensed Indian trader at Anadarko, complained bitterly about his competitors' practices. By giving Indians a higher price on hides than that fixed by the agent, some traders built up their hide business at the expense of merchants who complied with the regulations.[13] Reynolds was losing the highly valued Indian trade, but was careful to say that he did not favor a raise in the agent's fixed price. Some Indians set themselves up as middlemen in the hide business. Otter Belt, a Comanche, for example, purchased hides directly from other Indians, usually, according to Reynolds, "at the places of gambling on the evenings before issue day, and then, on issue day collecting the same taking them to Mr. Fred's Store."[14]

Fred also secured a generous percentage of the hide trade by extending loans to the Indians against future exchanges. Again, Reynolds wrote to Agent Hunt to complain, this time about SunBoy, who threatened a young man attempting to trade a hide to Reynolds when, according to the Indian's story, Reynolds reported, "this young man had received $3.25 in advance from Mr. Fred and . . . had promised to give Mr. Fred a beef hide for the loan." Unfortunately, Reynolds had also advanced a cash payment to the same young man for the hide. Reynolds defended his violation of the prohibition against advance payments to Indians for hides because Mr. Fred had broken the rule first.[15]

Indians much preferred exchanging robes, furs, and cattle hides for goods and credit to receiving cash. Traders were happy to exchange robes and hides with the Indians because the Indians would take fewer goods for hides than they would purchase with cash. Agent Haworth reported discrepancies between the amount of goods Indians received from exchange and those they obtained through cash purchases. Remedying the situation was difficult because what the Indian customer "has to pay is secondary consideration with him, the important one being the price allowed him for his robe or whatever he has to sell."[16] According to the agent, the problem rested somewhere between trader noncompliance with the regulations concerning fixed hide prices and the need for Indians to be "educated to a proper valuation."[17] In the meantime, only "some of the Indians are learning the fact that ten or twelve dollars in money buys more goods than a Robe valued at either of those sums."[18]

Indian men turned to other sources of income, such as carrying freight for seventy-five cents a pound, in between crops and the trade of hides on issue day. Freighting was the primary source of income outside hide exchanges, but traveling by wagon between the railroad and the reservation presented many challenges. Frequently, Indian ponies failed to recover during the periodic drought conditions, and during sudden rains small streams and creeks became impassable. Despite such obstacles the Indians hauled over one million pounds in 1880, for which they received $14,278.[19] Things improved in 1882, however, when the Fort Worth and Denver Railway was completed to Henrietta, Texas, reducing the trip between the agency and the railroad depot to one hundred miles.[20] In addition to working small cornfields, trading cattle hides, and freighting, men hired themselves out to the agency and worked various odd jobs such as cutting timber.

With few if any constant sources of cash, the reservation economy turned on individual credit with local traders. Traders willingly extended credit because they had some assurance of recovering the debt when annuity payments were distributed by the agency. Although traders often found it difficult to collect on Indian accounts, they were protected by agents; regulations created to safeguard against abuses to traders and Indians; and later the red card system, grass lease payments, and the allotment of Indian lands, which served as collateral.

In 1885 Comanches began leasing reservation pastures to Texas cattlemen, an arrangement that would continue until 1906.[21] The lease payments put cash into the reservation economy and contributed significantly to Comanche subsistence for the remainder of the century.[22] Cattle herds also increased. In 1885, individual herds ranged from one to two hundred head. That figure would continue to rise to five head for each Indian, or twenty-five thousand head, by 1892.[23]

The catastrophe that followed the American invasion of Kiowa territory forced major changes to women's lives and situated their experience within colonial ideology and capitalist markets. Kiowa women's work roles before the catastrophic effects of American expansion set in involved procuring resources, managing their camps, producing food, and manufacturing clothing, housing, and household items. The knowledge required to meet these responsibilities was impressive. Tipi making as a social event and economic practice reinforced the status of women. Kiowa women were also property owners and managers. Their camps and all the goods associated with it were the result of their work and under their domain. Kiowa women possessed knowledge about deriving food, medicines, and manufactures from plants, including where the plants grew, how to identify them, when to harvest them, and how to prepare and preserve them. The art of buffalo hide processing was complex and arduous, but unavoidable, and an inventory of items made from buffalo parts reveals the centrality of the buffalo to Kiowa material life. Income losses that accompanied the extermination of the buffalo were never fully replaced in the reservation period.

The Americans had introduced ideas that degraded Indian women generally. In the colonial imagination (and this would not be limited to the "frontier") Indian bodies were seen as dirty and polluted with sexual sin. Native women's bodies, being dirty and polluted, were, according to Andrea Smith's seminal work, therefore sexually violable and rape-able. Gender violence, far from being an outcome of frontier disorder, accompanied the racism contained within the colonial toolkit. Though gender violence, including murder, was the most extreme expression of colonial racism, the introduction of the construction of Kiowa womanhood as squaw drudge and prostitute wrought its own share of damage to women's dignity and humanity.

Traditional Kiowa laws prescribed punishment for such crimes against women as rape and murder. The Federal Major Crimes Act (1885) and the introduction of Western legal ideas and institutions thus deprived Native women of protections under both tribal law and federal criminal law. Although the rape of Indian women was a criminal act and prosecutable under the 1885 law, Western views of Native women's bodies as dirty and rape-able undermined the delivery of justice to violated women. There is no doubt that Native communities continued to preserve traditional practices of social control, even in the late nineteenth century. Protection for women and justice for victims eroded as a result of federal Indian policy and Native internalization of colonial racism and identity ideologies.

Analyses of Native women's experiences under capitalism have produced three interpretations: the declension model of the loss of equality that women enjoyed in undisturbed tribal societies; the increase in Native women's status as a result of Indian–white contact; and a holistic approach that emphasizes the diversity of women's experiences and approaches the dynamics of domestic and capitalist sectors of production (synonymously center and periphery) as mutually determined. The experience of Kiowa women is consistent with the implications of the third approach: in the periphery, domestic work is more attenuated because the wages earned by workers are depressed. The reservation provided limited opportunities for work and limited types of work.

Women, like men, generated alternative sources of income to carry families through crop failures, unemployment, absent rations, and insufficient stock. Sources are scant on the subject of reservation women's improvisations in struggling against a ration and annuity system that trapped them in poverty. Undernourishment, which clearly existed and presumably contributed to children's health problems, advances the likelihood that women felt compelled to supplement family incomes in a variety of ways. Prostitution, which, in the midst of economic destruction, represented income, is documented in agent reports. In 1880, Agent Hunt reported his impression of "a frightful mortality . . . of infants and children under four years old."[24] He blamed high infant mortality not on the untenable poverty in which Indians lived, but on the presence of venereal disease and the "habits of the young women," which doomed "the prospect of a better future for these people."[25] The presence of capitalist sex trade was an outcome of racism, economic destitution, and limited means to obtain food.

Native women no longer processed buffalo hides hunted by their men, but through the 1870s they continued to work hides brought by white hunters to the agent. Following the near extinction of the buffalo, women focused on cattle hides, an inferior substitute. Kiowa women's work as mothers, owners of the camp, gatherers of plants, and processors of hides continued. The onset of women's production of commercial beadwork is clearly documented in the historical record. Beginning in the reservation, allotment, and post-allotment periods Kiowa women thus held the dual roles of earning household income and preserving material culture production. Traders' records, though full of gaps, document enormous quantities of beads and other materials, beginning in the early 1880s at least, coming into the Kiowa reservation; the role of beadwork in settling accounts with traders; and the distribution of commercial beadwork through external venues such as fairs, exhibitions, and expositions. Hide processing continued, as did tribes' manufactures made from hides. Women also continued to bead for community purposes. Numerous elk-tooth dresses, beaded dresses and cradleboards, moccasins and leggings held in museum collections attest to the ongoing beadwork carried out by Kiowa women.

During this period women also diverted their labor to the production of tourist goods. The goods they made for tourist or curio trade were produced cheaply, with inferior materials and simple designs on small, quickly made items such as watch fobs, pouches or purses, bands, and moccasins. These items were not fully beaded. Later Kiowa women took up beading medallions, which evolved into a popular item for Indians and whites. Segregated from the majority society, women channeled their goods through the local Indian traders. Most frequently, women sold the goods and used the proceeds to pay down their accounts.

The volume of women's work is suggested in trader purchase invoices and receipts. Licensed trader A. J. Reynolds of Anadarko purchased impressive quantities of Indian merchandise from his supplier, S. A. Frost, in New York City. While the record is full of gaps, it suggests a significant volume of manufactured supplies for trinket production coming into the reservation. In 1879, for example, Reynolds ordered 1,073 bunches of beads in seven different colors.[26] Between May and July of 1881, Reynolds purchased 2,200 pairs of silver ear bobs, and one order called for 300 bunches of turquoise seed beads.[27] In 1881, his incomplete records documented the purchase of 1,775 bunches of beads between February and September.[28] During that same year Reynolds ordered 3,000 pairs of silver ear bobs in July, 1,000 pairs in September, and 3,800 pairs in October, for a total of 7,800 pairs of ear bobs in three months.[29] Reynolds continued to order large amounts of beads. In August 1882, for example, he ordered 1,800 pairs of beads from Frost.[30] In addition to beads and ear bobs, traders stocked cloth; ribbon; "Indian sashes"; German-silver buttons; silver- and gold-plated rings; bells; and brass, silver, and nickel studs.

There are no corresponding records of commercial beadwork inventories or of beadwork sales. Recent scholarship on Kiowa and Comanche cradleboards provides a likely reason for the influx of large quantities of beads. Grass lease payments had begun, and although they were modest by any standard, they coincide with a temporary period of more extravagant designs in Kiowa cradleboards.[31] After the brief renaissance Kiowa families in need of resources parted with the sought-after objects, which made their way into museum and private collections.

Later records from the A. D. Lawrence Red Store in Lawton (a town associated with Fort Sill) provide textual evidence of the commercial trade. A. D. Lawrence bought the Red Store at the Fort Sill subagency in 1905. Lawrence's son preserved his father's business records and donated them to the Museum of the Great Plains at Lawton, Oklahoma, where as the Lawrence Collection they document the turn-of-the-century trinket trade. He, like Reynolds, carried an inventory of beads, German silver, and notions from S. A. Frost and Marshall Field and Company.[32] He gave credit and made cash loans to his Indian customers. Lawrence had ambitions to distribute locally produced Indian goods to businesses outside of Oklahoma. Moccasins, beaded bags, leggings, baskets, beaded watch fobs, and other goods were featured prominently in a trinket business that stretched from Los Angeles to New York and from San Angelo, Texas, to Minneapolis. Letters exchanged between Lawrence and buyers of Indian trinkets suggest a steady demand for goods ranging in quality and quantity. Lawrence's network included other traders who also supplied general merchandise stores, theme parks, and curio shops. Their eclectic inventories included beaded items, leatherwork, pottery, and other locally produced goods, extending to far more exotic objects such as idols, mastodon bones, and "ancient goods."

Lawrence's letters reflect his ability to obtain a wide assortment of
Indian handmade goods, ranging from "Indian Curios" to "more expensive goods."[33] The latter category included "papoose cradles, war
bonnets, canes, belts" as well as "cradles, sashes, Indian suits, Eagle
Head Dresses, Peacock Feathers, Bow and Quiver outfits, Bows and
Arrows, Chains, Baskets, Moccasins, Quirts, etc."[34] How Lawrence
came by his "more expensive goods" is not documented. One letter,
however, indicates that he was also in the pawn business. In May 1909
Lawrence wrote to C. L. Ellis, special Indian agent at Anadarko, responding to charges of misconduct in the matter of the war bonnet
of a local Indian, Ar-rus-che.[35] Ar-rus-che had left his bonnet with
Lawrence in exchange for five dollars with the understanding that he
would retrieve it within "a few days." When Ar-rus-che failed to return
for the bonnet Lawrence exchanged it for a "bunch of peacock feathers"
with "an Indian from the North part of the state."[36] Ar-rus-che claimed
that Lawrence had failed to honor the terms and contested Lawrence's
story that he had held the bonnet for a month before trading it.[37] Such
practices have a long tradition in Anadarko, which even today is the
home to numerous pawn shops. Pawn enabled Lawrence to boast of an
inventory that included "relics" and "rare items in Kiowa, Apache and
Comanche work."[38]

As a licensed Indian trader, Lawrence was aware of the annuity payment schedule and the amount of the payment. Even when payments
were short, traders found business remained good. It left the Indians
"hard up," and "for that reason we have been able to pick up these
goods at reasonable prices." As a result, Lawrence obtained a "fur
robe, bow and arrow outfit and head dress."[39] Lawrence's revelations
about his business practices suggest that individuals parted with masculine objects through pawn or outright sales for cash.

Lawrence boasted that his Indian goods were "GENUINE" and
bought "direct from the Indians."[40] He was able to "guarantee every
piece to be GENUINE, for the write [sic] has bought them person-

ally, and knows all the Indians of whom I have bought."[41] Lawrence gave attribution to the tribe if not the producers of his Indian goods, which reinforced his claims. Invoices listed items such as "Tobacco Pouch 'Kiowa', Apache Bag, Comanche Moccasins," and "Kiowa Fob Pouch."[42]

Lawrence also had a vigorous trade in the "curio" line. He promoted his curios alongside the finer goods. Although the distinction was sometimes blurred, curios tended to include beaded bags, moccasins, beaded watch fobs, dolls, purses, and other small items. Curios had their own cachet as a line that was "changing all the time."[43] Lawrence's correspondence suggests that handmade items came into his possession somewhat regularly, and the quantities he sold in certain items, particularly beaded watch fobs, indicate a steady production pace. Other items such as beaded and partially beaded bags appear in fewer numbers.

The Lawrence Collection includes a number of store ledgers, which though somewhat cryptic, further document his trade in Indian goods. Numerous entries contain language suggesting that people brought in items to trade or sell. Some entries appear to document such transactions by including the word *from*. Typical entries read, "mdse ac Ear Bobs *from* Pecinah," "Mdse 1 pr Mox *from* Permah," and "Mdse a/c 1 Belt *from* Maggie 1.50" (italics mine).[44] Other entries do not include the preposition: "Mdse a/c 1 watch (Nah dah yaker)," "Mdse a/c Beaded chain Tochocozoo," and "Mdse a/c Ear Rings (Pemah)."[45] It appears that Lawrence was documenting part of his trade in Indian goods, but not entirely. Watch fobs, for example, never appear in cash book "c," nor does his pawn activity.[46]

Lawrence's letters never name the sources of his Indian curio line, but they were without doubt predominantly women from the reservation. Men might have produced leather goods such as moccasins and silverwork, but historically women produced clothing and regalia worn for family events and continued to do so through the reservation period. Beadwork was a prominent element of buckskin clothing, moccasins, and regalia prior to and during the reservation period. Beadwork for personal consumption might have increased in importance during the reservation period. David Penney has argued that reservation confinement and changes in economic life increased the symbolic value of ceremonial dress.[47] As a result, dress became more elaborate as a way of making a statement about ethnic identification. Dress, Penney concluded, symbolized ethnic solidarity and contrasted Indians with the dominant culture. It followed that beadwork, silk appliqué, and other applied ornament became exaggerated during this period. Those particular techniques represented traditional women's industry, which reinforced the association with symbols of cultural identity and resilience, especially when worn for celebratory events. Women who excelled at arts such as beadwork enhanced their family's standing within the community and, as a result, reinforced their own reputations. They were sought after when special circumstances required a skilled bead worker and their name as producer of a ceremonial garb added to the significance of the piece.[48]

Bernard Mishkin's *Rank and Warfare among the Plains Indians* was based on Kiowa data collected in 1935 in Oklahoma. Mishkin attached an appendix to the last chapter on rank in which he listed twenty-five of the most famous men in the tribe and twenty-one of the most famous women and the basis of their prominence. The first nine women were known for tipi making, tanning, and saddles; women ranked ten through twelve for beadwork; and thirteen through twenty-one for good looks, dancing, and cooking. Of the first twelve, all famous for proficiency in women's crafts, seven were wives of *ondei*, or the highest rank.[49] The traditional values of women's industry persisted throughout the reservation period and well into the twentieth century. Their abilities were valued within the community, enhanced their marriage opportunities, and secured their reputations within the community. It is unquestionable that a Kiowa woman's skills were and continue to be a significant social marker.

Nevertheless, women are nearly invisible in the records of licensed Indian traders and in correspondence related to outside opportunities such as expositions and fairs. For example, on only one occasion did Lawrence allude to a specific individual in his Indian goods correspondence. Writing to Frank Rush in Cache, Oklahoma, who wished to

have some unspecified item made from a buffalo hide, Lawrence con-
veyed an invitation from "the best Indian in the country for that kind of
work" to "bring the hide to Mt. Scott sometime when you are coming
that way." Rush should expect to speak to her through her daughter
who would interpret for the unnamed woman.[50]

The letter contains hints as to possible explanations for the invis-
ibility of Indian women. This unnamed woman was clearly a speaker
whose English was too poor to converse with a white man. She needed
her daughter to be able to understand what he wanted done with it,
to obtain proper measurements, and to communicate her price.[51] She
lived in Mt. Scott and was willing to do the work only if the gentleman
traveled to her home to negotiate the project. Apparently, Lawrence
traveled to Mt. Scott to do business with her, as hinted in his affirmative line, "I bought some beautiful things of her yesterday."[52] At least in
this instance, a respectable woman with proficiency in hide work and
the production of "beautiful things" did not approach Lawrence for
work. Her reputation preceded her and drew him to her, away from his
store and ledgers.

The scenario suggests an informal agreement based on mutual
awareness of the other's reputation, prices negotiated and arrived at
mutually, an exchange based on goods she had on hand, vague agreements about future exchanges when Lawrence made his next trip to
Mt. Scott, promises of payment or credit to the woman's account when
her "beautiful things" were sold, and her acceptance of those terms.
On the one hand, the scenario suggests a passive attitude on the part
of the unnamed woman. But Lawrence's letters suggest another possibility. Kiowa women's beadwork trade defied capitalist principles in
significant ways while still engaging with the capitalist market. While
women refused to have their work conform to the dictates of white customers, they were willing to produce and sell objects that fell far short
of the standards of traditional beadwork. They did not work under
externally imposed standards for their manufactures. Kiowa women
were not exploited through capitalist modes of production typical of
the time. There were no factories, and thus no direct exploitation of
women's labor. While women worked, the trader acted as intermedi-

ary, both insulating Kiowa women from and connecting them to the capitalist economy. Kiowa women set the pace of work for the tourist-curio market.

Trade documents reveal that despite their subaltern status, women maintained control over the pace and volume of trinket production. Lawrence's letters contain references to being short of curios and of his inability to fill orders to specification. In one letter he wrote: "It is quite hard to always send just what our customers want as the Indians do not make a regular line of goods." He wrote in another letter: "Our line of curios is changing all the time, that is to say, we do not have exactly the same things at all times." Indian goods were seldom produced, as Lawrence suggested, according to the dictates of a distant market. Rather, Indian producers manufactured them on a somewhat irregular basis, perhaps as the need for cash and credit arose.

Women's commercial production followed a completely different standard than beadwork made for family purposes. Beaded watch fobs, a popular turn-of-the-century item, were small, required relatively little time to make, and could be made out of inferior pieces of a cowhide. Beaded bags usually signified hide bags with minimal beadwork around the edges of the bag, or small designs within the edges. Today, Anadarko and the surrounding communities in southwest Oklahoma are an economically depressed area. A small tourist trade forces many beadworkers to specialize in making only beaded rosettes, keychains, and earrings. One very elderly bead worker with whom the author used to visit, who has since died, underscored that point. She said she herself "specialized" in beaded rosettes because they took little time and few materials.

In contrast, labors of love and cultural maintenance followed a different schedule, as Jacob Ahtone attests in the case of his mother's work habits. The rhythm of women's work was steady, even if the output of commercial goods was not. A friend's mother was a bead worker and reportedly produced eight full-sized cradleboards. She had a full-time beadwork schedule, working regularly five to seven hours per day nearly every day. She preferred to work alone, involving only her husband, who made the frames.

Between 1870 and 1910 Kiowa women had access to other outlets for their commercial work, namely, regional fairs and the American exposition. Kiowa women thus garnered opportunities to sell their beadwork off the reservation. Plains tribes had a strong identification among the public as "wild Indians," which made them especially popular with organizers of commercial fairs and federally funded expositions. Organizers of the Indian International Fair at Muskogee (1884), chaired by the Cherokee Nation, enticed Agent Hunt with the assurance that "There will be a Wild Indian Dept. so that Wild Indians will compete only with Wild Indians."[53] The "premium list," for which two hundred dollars had been set aside, included a number of beaded-object categories. A fully beaded buckskin gown was included in the top prize category of ten dollars.[54]

Out-of-state fair organizers such as the Dallas State Fair and Exposition Association also inquired about obtaining "bands of Indians."[55] In 1889, the Kiowas and Comanches were invited to participate in the Texas State Fair at Dallas. Fair organizer and local businessman Ben Cabell included in his request an appeal for about fifty Indians and "two or three older Chiefs some that have some history."[56] The Office of Indian Affairs granted the Texas fair organizers' proposal with instructions to Agent Myers to "permit representatives of Texas Fair to take an equal number of progressive and non-progressive Indians."[57]

Beadwork offered one of the more obscure categories of Indian manufacture. Columbia College anthropologist Otis Mason's systematic outline of Indian culture located beadwork by name in two categories: "other personal ornaments" and "beadwork for art purposes."[58] Beadwork would have appeared in other categories of Mason's exhibition outline, including: clothing; adornment; games and pastimes; art; religion; furniture and utensils; head ornaments; breast and body ornaments; ornaments of the limbs; badges of distinction; and instruments for beating.[59]

Beadwork found in ethnological exhibitions became subsumed within one or more anthropological categories of other objects. Although it was included in the art category, art tended to be identified with representational paintings, carvings, and drawings. Beadwork often lacked a separate category, but was instead considered a feature of some larger cultural object. These distinctions provide insights into the value attached to different kinds of objects. In the case of beadwork, organizers, mostly male, failed to give it the prominence that they accorded to other kinds of objects, such as religious items, weapons, and other "craft" forms such as basketry.

On occasion, the Indian Office exhibited discomfort with the common identification of the southern Plains tribes as "wild Indian." Instructions from the Indian Office to Agent White in 1888 concerning the Indians' participation in the Indian International Fair at Muskogee were pointed. The commissioner wrote: "You will see that such parties are composed as nearly as may be, of the most progressive and industrious of your Indians, whose attendance at the Fair would be likely to result in benefit to the tribes."[60]

The presence of southern Plains Indians in federally funded expositions increased with the arrival of government anthropologist James Mooney. Despite the Indian Office's documented objections to the "wild Indian" image, the expositions consistently emphasized the inclusion of "native dress," relics, and ceremonial objects. The distinction between large expositions and commercial affairs was science, or ethnology, versus entertainment. But that it was not always a convincing distinction can be detected in the language of some of the correspondence. One member of the National Museum wrote, concerning Indian participation in the Louisiana Purchase Exposition, "How would it do to have a family of Kiowas go to the Fair to live for sixty days or so, putting up a native shack and dressing up in their native costumes, one of which at least, would be the elk-tooth gown?"[61] It is no wonder that commissioners of Indian Affairs despaired over the prospects of civilizing the Indians when they were constantly being undermined by other agencies of their own government.

Fairs and curio trade were important opportunities for Kiowas to earn money and lower indebtedness to traders. Though other benefits from such activities might have accrued to Kiowa women, the income paid the bills. While conducting research in Lawton, Oklahoma, for this project, the author's conversations with local citizens also revealed that women's beadwork and men's handwork frequently served as payment to doctors, dentists, and other professionals well into the twentieth century. These material objects, although perhaps on a limited basis, had become an acceptable form of currency between Indian and white neighbors.

The thoroughly maintained trader records of the Lawrence Store, which continued into the second half of the twentieth century, provide a glimpse into the social world of local Indians and whites. A. D. Lawrence had transformed his desire to preserve his father's business records into an obsessive recordkeeping habit of his own. His voluminous diaries document the trader's relations with the local Indians, mainly Comanches by his time, with whom he did business. The letters suggest more than the ledgers ever could have told about his father's ties to his Indian customers. If it is fair to assume some continuity in the tenor and quality of relations between the trader's son and his Native clients during and after his father's era, then the diaries offer many insights into their world.

For an unprofitable business, Lawrence seemingly expended significant personal energy in staying on top of the local news.[62] So-and-so died at the hospital today.[63] He heard rumors of Indian payments and those of the Indian children.[64] Small-town networks allowed him to check on other debts Indians held: "Wrote to the Highway Commission" to check on payoff of car notes, he wrote, for example.[65] Bankers shared information about Indian accounts, especially when a customer made a deposit.[66]

Lawrence routinely traveled to Anadarko from Lawton to attend hearings and "file claims against dead Indian Estates." He noted upcoming hearings, his trips to Anadarko, and some of the politics involved in his efforts to recover money against the Indians' debts.[67] Sometimes relatives "objected strenuously" to the payment of relatives' debts. In any case, the local Indian office had the final word in such matters. In order to exploit such opportunities to recover his money, Lawrence had to keep his ear to the ground for local news, which was sometimes disappointing. On August 23, 1930, he noted that he "Heard that B—— (K——)

had died," only to learn "Later: not true."[68] The financial stability of his business depended in part on his recovery of debts from Indian estates. Just two months prior to the false news of B——'s death, he had noted on June 9: "R—— H—— hearing today. Attended hearing today in Anadarko. Must have money for taxes." The urgency hinted at in this entry is confirmed by the extreme relief that communicated in the next two day's entries: "August 10, 1930 Mrs. R—— B—— hearing today!", then, "August 11, 1930 P—— B—— hearing today!" And apparently, his elation was justified. Saturday, June 14, was, he wrote, the "Last day to pay last $^1/_2$ taxes without penalty. Paid taxes." By the end of 1930, Lawrence reported a total of $10,340 in Indian accounts and $9,176 in inventory, making it "an uneventful and unprofitable year."[69] The next year showed a disturbing trend for businesses like Lawrence's: "April 2, 1931 Very little trade. Our credit sales for March were the lowest they have ever been. In fact we sold more than credit. That is a good sign in one way and a bad one in another. It shows the Indian credit business is drawing to a close." Lawrence's gloomy prediction did not completely materialize, according to subsequent diaries.

The diaries never suggest that Lawrence wielded a big stick over the Indians. He needed them as much as they needed him. He was willing to trade with Indians who did not pay their accounts if they were shopping with cash, although with some reservation. In the case of one customer in similar such circumstances, Lawrence sold her a shawl and noted with resignation, "I guess we will have to get along with her as best we can even though she doesn't pay her account."[70] The local Indians had their own strategies for dealing with their indebtedness, one of which in particular dated at least to early reservation times. "March 23, 1931," Lawrence wrote. "We notice that the Kiowas are trading with us now and of course for cash." Then: "March 31 We had fair trade today. We notice more Kiowas trade with than formerly. Perhaps because they do not owe us anything. If this be true, then our Comanches are trading elsewhere because they are in debt to us."

Lawrence's diaries sometimes read like a who's who of twentieth-century Indian Country:

September 6, 1936
Allan Houser, Route #5, Apache, Oklahoma. Was in. He was a friend of Aaron Kawaykla, and is a painter, too. He may bring some of his work in for me to sell. May have found another talented artist. He says he does "flat" work—whatever that means.[71]

February 4, 1937
One of the four brilliant and talented Kiowa Indian artists Monroe Tsatoke [one of the famed Kiowa Five] has painted his last picture before death from tuberculosis took him yesterday at the Kiowa Hospital. One of his pictures hangs now in our curio section.

November 10, 1937
Spencer Asah [another of the Kiowa Five] was in with some of his paintings. They consist of a folded sheet of heavy paper upon the front of which he has painted Indian designs. Mother purchased several at .50 each.[72]

March 17, 1938
Letter from Franz Boas in the department of anthropology at Columbia University saying that he knew "Silver Moon" when the latter was in New York. Answered the Boas letter asking him about the system he used.

One of Quanah Parker's wives, Topay, appears in Lawrence's diary several times. Lawrence was one of the organizers of a ceremony at the Kiwanis Club meeting at which she was to sign a buckskin, drawn by Steven Mopope, conveying Quanah's headdress to the United States government. She agreed, but refused to give a "talk." She told Lawrence: "people are always coming to her home asking her to relate things about Quanah Parker, and she refuses them."[73] Likewise, the Cheyenne painter Archie Black Owl dropped in to sell a painting of a flute player.[74] Lawrence used his good relations with the Indians to improve his inventory, learn Comanche (his ardent pastime), and instruct white people about Indian culture. It seemed the only thing he could not do was make money: "January 14, 1936 Had a talk with Bob Gilbert. He said he made $5000 this last year. Evidence that *some* can do it—why not I?"

Local Indians seemed to trust and respect Lawrence, calling upon him at times to assist them with personal business affairs. He apparently enjoyed a long, trust-filled friendship with L—— and W—— T——, a married couple from the Comanche community, for example. He helped L—— invest in "the largest business in the United States." She held five shares of stock, which "she purchased . . . by saving it out of her income."[75] By 1937, Mr. and Mrs. T—— had saved enough money to buy a new Ford automobile. On May 13, Lawrence reported:

> They came in—one at a time—about 12:00 o'clock looking rather tired. It seems that [the dealer] had been after them again trying to get them to hurry and they had been to Apache to try to find [a friend] who was to teach W—— to drive without success. Later, (about 2:30 p.m.) we went down to the Ford Agency and after much explaining they counted out $800 in currency and the deal was complete. She insisted that she be allowed to drive her old Model T. Ford until W—— had mastered the shift on the new car, and [the dealer] brought her a written statement permitting this. She later return [sic] to the store [Lawrence's] to tell me she wanted the Ford People to tell any Indians who asked that she didn't pay cash for her car so that she wouldn't be bothered with requests for money.[76]

The car presented some problems for the T——'s. By June, W—— "hadn't learned to drive the car yet. It seemed to distress [L——] considerably for it means she has to buy groceries and supplies for her relatives who are driving the car for her. She wants me to meet them at the Mission tomorrow, and show W—— how to change gears. Started to learn Comanche words for 'push down,' 'let up or release slowly,' etc."[77] Lawrence kept his promise: "Ran across W—— on the street with a sack of groceries. 'Where is your car, father?' I asked him. 'Mission,' he answered. So I took him out and there stood the car beside their little house. It was all covered over with a duck sheeting and anchored at each end. Prevailed upon him to take a car lesson then and there. He protested he was 'coo Ya' which means 'afraid.' But he tried it. We drove down to the gate and returned."[78]

The couple relied on Lawrence to cash their dividend checks, and repaid his service with new Comanche vocabulary, which he seemed to treasure, though complaining occasionally that he could not learn it quickly enough to suit him. At L——'s request, he accompanied them to the doctor when W—— was not well. L——'s trust in Lawrence extended to the most personal matters.

> Our little couple were in today—L—— and W——. L—— wanted me to write a note to the druggist [Not-so tilpe voh] so she could purchase some kind of laxative which she called moo-se-tah. Said that she had taken some moo-se-tah without effect, and wondered if it were any good. Accompanied them down to the Lawton Drug instead of writing the note to see what I might accomplish in the way of interpreting. Found the moo-se-tah to be a patent medicine marketed by some local people. The bottle had a picture of an Indian in a war bonnet on the label.

Lawrence suggested an alternative—castor oil. "L—— asked if it wasn't oil (oh you) and if it didn't make you want to vomit (oh it). That identified castor oil all right." Their exchange continued regarding other treatments of a highly personal nature that indexed the trust existing between the trader and the couple. Lawrence continued: "Our purchases ended, the little couple left for the Yellow Mission apparently satisfied."[79]

Lawrence's help with these, other medical problems, and finances show an extraordinarily trusting and respectful relationship between him and the couple. He was also called to the bedsides of the dying. Such was the case on February 11, 1939, when E—— C—— summoned him to the bedside of M—— who lay dying. She confused Lawrence with her son O——.

> "No, I am your white son," I explained, and at once she understood. I waited. Her daughter R—— stood closely and listened to

her low spoken words. "The money, and the land I want O—— to have," she finally told me. The money was her deposit funds in the store, and the land I presumed was her allotment. I noticed her thumb was still black from ink as though she had just signed (Indian fashion) an instrument of some kind. At times her talk became disconnected, and she must have said queer things for the others in the room laughed softly. I marveled that the relatives showed no particular grief, or anxiety considering that death was probably so close. I gather this much. Old age and death is as much to be expected as the rising of the sun in the morning, so stoically they accept it, because it is natural. Rather a comforting thought to hold I felt. When I left she laid her old hand upon mine and thanked me for all I had done for her. Strange though it may sound I felt better for my changed viewpoint [about death?] than I had before I had gone out there. Another lesson the Indians had taught."[80]

L—— and W—— brought the news of M——'s death to Lawrence two days later.[81]

Lawrence was a valuable witness to trade relations that continued between Indians and whites following the reservation period. As a common trader with close Indian ties and an ear for the grapevine, he provides a window into the daily life where relations were knitted, practices resided, and social values were exhibited. His witnessing is extraordinary because it was so regularly attended to, and because his daily observations paint a picture of the local Indians and merchant engaged in something far beyond commercial transactions. The Lawrence diaries reveal the cultural, social, and political dimensions of a mixed Indian-white community. The diaries suggest Lawrence's appreciation for his ties to the Native community, a desire to have even closer relations that was prevented only by his limitations with the language, a shrewd eye for his Indian customers' practices, and, still, the occasional lapse into romanticism. His Indian customers kept him in check, never allowing him to have complete access to them, or to enjoy total familiarity with their habits. For example, when Lawrence carried his camera to the home of Indian friends and attempted to take photographs of them, they rebuffed him repeatedly. They allowed him in, but then unexpectedly reminded him that he was an outsider.

Lawrence's diaries illuminate the persistence into the twentieth century of colonial patterns of social and economic interaction between traders and Kiowa women established in the reservation period. Colonialism is not a historical artifact of nation building, with its attendant political and economic exploitation of the colonized by the colonizers. Rather, it is a persistent economic, political, and social reality in relations between Native people and "the visitors," as the author heard one Native elder refer to the Americans somewhere during in her travels. Colonialism is present on multiple fronts. One hundred years have passed since Kiowa women were beading tourist goods to ward off starvation, but tribes are only now digging out from under the weight of that history. Because colonizers are frequently inconsistent as a result of conflicting goals, overconfidence in their power to control, and simple incompetence, they have not, in this case, ever established monolithic control. Americans have victimized both Indian individuals and tribes; they have failed to realize the vanished Indian. Native people—noncompliant, driven to survive, and rarely predictable—thwart their progress and complicate their experiences. The most significant thing emerging from these complicated conditions for history is the recovery of a Native agency that is complex, imperfect, unromantic, frequently invisible, but successful in ensuring the continued existence of Native people. The historical experiences of Native people, as shown here, are legitimate and significant on their own terms.

Kiowa women's work in a capitalist colonial setting illuminates Konkle's theory of two natures and hypothetical trajectory. Americans promised Indians assimilation, but in reality, as evidenced in the reservation system, federal appropriations, and land alienation, they saw Indians as admirers and mimics of American progress. Kiowa women interacted with the capitalist system indirectly, that is, through the trader gatekeeper and mediator. Their interaction with the capitalist system, limited to hides, then tourist goods, kept them on the economic and social periphery where their domestic labor was attenuated as a result of conditions on the periphery. Women's work, however, continued to play a role in marking the status of individuals, thus sustaining a valued element of Kiowa women's identity in the late nineteenth century.

In some areas of work, like beadwork, Kiowa women retained an unexpected level of autonomy in a colonial system. Property ownership continued to exist. Women received their own allotments, one form of property ownership, but also retained ownership of their work domains, including beadwork. Women's beadwork for community purposes throughout the last quarter of the nineteenth century was, in the context of federal Indian policy, a political act. Colonial codes and Western-style institutions served to undermine tribalism, even going so far as to outlaw some aspects of Indian culture. The persistence of women's beadwork and other labor patterns defied the U.S. attack on tribalism and ensured that the Kiowas would retain specific traditional forms and patterns of work. Today, Kiowa cradles are high-prized works of art for which buyers pay thousands of dollars. Medallions continued to be produced as part of the community's traditional clothing and as a tourist good. Today, women continue to produce beaded dresses, which they also continue to count. And a trip to Anadarko or Lawton will turn up a plethora of tourist goods side by side with objects in which Kiowa women, and men, invested time, the best materials, and a wealth of cultural knowledge.

Chapter 7. **Conclusion**

No less a figure than Walt Whitman created the most seductively eloquent language of inevitability and regret with which to surround the price of American progress:

> There is something about these aboriginal Americans, in their highest characteristic representations, essential traits, and the ensemble of their physique and physiognomy—something very remote, very lofty, arousing comparisons with our own civilized ideals—something that our literature, portrait painting, etc., have never caught, and that will almost certainly never be transmitted to the future, even as a reminiscence. No biographer, no historian, no artist, has grasp'd it—perhaps could not grasp it. It is so different, so far outside our standards of eminent humanity.[1]

With that, Indians could be hustled out of history books and national memory with a clear conscience. Once the slavery issue had been dealt with, the United States enjoyed an uncluttered narrative of its nation building.

On December 2, 1952, Ella Deloria, a member of the prominent Deloria family from the Yankton Sioux Reservation in southeastern South Dakota, wrote to H. E. Beebe, who funded the typing for Deloria's *Waterlily* manuscript:[2] "This may sound a little naïve, Mr. Beebe, but I actually feel that I have a mission: To make the Dakota people understandable, as human beings, to the white people who have to deal with them. I feel that one of the reasons for the lagging advancement of the Dakotas has been that those who came out among them to teach and preach, went on the assumption that the Dakotas had nothing, no rules of life, no social organization, no ideals. And so they tried to pour white culture into, as it were, a vacuum."

Deloria, who enjoyed great respect for her abilities as an expert translator of Lakota and Dakota dialects of Sioux from an array of texts, did not intend to leave representations of Indians to the likes of Whitman and others who shared his views. She was a close associate of Franz Boaz and Ruth Benedict. At their urging, Deloria wrote *Waterlily*, a fictionalized account of a nineteenth-century Siouan women's life. Deloria's primary objective was to use a more personal approach than did the anthropological approaches of the time, which flattened Indian people into one-dimensional representations of ethnographic data. Written in the 1940s, *Waterlily* symbolized a Native woman's effort to humanize the Sioux to non-Native people.

For Native people, tribalism is the expression of their humanity. The social values that intertwine work habits, ceremonial life, gender relations, and kin relations are rooted in ideals. Deloria's heroine Waterlily, responding to the behavior of ill-kempt pioneer children, wrote:

> Here were unbelievably wild, untutored children. No one had ever said to them, "No, don't do that . . . see, nobody does so" and thereby shamed them into good behavior toward those about them. There were no others about them from whom they might learn by imitation. And so they were growing up without civility—and the results were terrifying to see. Camp-circle people were civilized; they knew how to treat one another. They had rules. These children were wild because they lacked any standards of social behavior.
>
> It came over Waterlily as she observed the unfortunate children, so unkempt and so hostile [in response to her friendly gesture], how very much people needed human companions. It was the only way to learn how to be human. People were at once a check and a spur to one another. Everyone needed others for comparison, for a standard for himself. This measuring and evaluating of self was only possible in camp-circle life, where everyone was obliged to be constantly aware of those about him[.]

At mid-century Deloria wrote to the American unwillingness to recognize Native humanity, present in all aspects of tribal life. Americans, like other colonizers before them, have resisted the simple truth that Indians were not empty vessels waiting to be filled with Christianity, Western ideas about work and productivity, an admiration for capitalism, and desire for acquisition—that is, unwilling to abandon tribalism—they pronounced them inhuman. The Western ideology that linked progress and perfection lacked an authentic acceptance of Indian civilization. Individualism was critical to the kind of progress reformers prescribed for Indians. Ella Deloria observed the vision became a program: "Those who sought to 'individualize' Indians . . . developed strategies of subjectivity and emotion production that aimed to prescribe how an 'individual' should properly pursue happiness, meaningfulness, and work—for example, by desiring an affectively intensified romantic bond, having a sentimentally privatized family, and being willing to work at just about any job to possess goods and own property."[3]

This ideology of Americanism sanctifies a sanitized national narrative that will not claim anything less than perfection in the steady march toward progress. "Regrettable," "inevitable," "necessary" are the ways Americans explain the Native genocide that made their country what it is. As the current U.S. administration never forgets to remind us, freedom takes hard work. The repetitious erasure of Indians from academic, political, and social discourses implicates everyone in the creation of not just an incomplete, but a false history. Colonialism exists in United States history, not just in the celebratory chapter on breaking from England, but in the simultaneous attack on Indian life and theft of their resources. The ongoing theft of Native resources, poverty, health crises, youth suicide, insufficient services, and diaspora, all reinforced by isolation and the unfulfilled federal trust responsibility, confirm the continued existence of U.S. internal colonialism.

Late-nineteenth-century Native North America is likely familiar to most as a study in cultural and economic declension and as the regrettable, but inevitable outcome of American progress. The near-simultaneous productions of two separate narratives in the late nineteenth century allow us to explore the machinery and politics that generated distinct accounts of internal American colonialism and complicate interpretations of the Indian reservation era and the national narrative. First, Richard Pratt the reformer accounted for the successes and failures of assimilation, a dominant aspect of federal Indian policy. Second, young Kiowa prisoners in St. Augustine, Florida, captives of Pratt's social laboratory, explored the meaning of Kiowa identity and destiny under American domination. Simultaneously, the state, commercial sector, and American intelligentsia collaborated in creating a national narrative of American progress for an international public audience at Philadelphia. Utilizing ethnographic exhibits of timeless Indian culture, the nation sanitized its history of the destruction to Indian tribes while exploiting them to reinforce the celebration of progress. The simultaneous production of these three narratives illustrates the role of power, specifically state power, in history writing, and in manufacturing the disappearance and silencing of the colonized.

The idea that individualism and competition were nonexistent in tribal societies was incorrect. Both were evident among the Kiowa men and women in the tribal processes of reputation making, although in different areas of practice. Men valued strong reputations based on extraordinary deeds in war, for example. Women valued reputations of skill based on individually produced beadwork designs, for example, which they guarded jealously. Other social conventions counterbalanced expressions of individualism and competition with practices that reinforced social cohesion. Respect correlated to men's self-sacrifice for the security of the entire party during war. Self-sacrifice was a required calculation for future reputation and potential leadership roles. Senior women ensured family distinction by passing down beadwork designs to favored daughters or other female relatives, thereby giving advantage to relatives in a specialized arena of reputation building. Americans overlooked this and other evidence of that which would have challenged their presumptions about Kiowa social and cultural primitiveness, leaving Kiowa and other Indian societies permanently associated with chaos and irrationality.

At its most modest, assimilation promised to lift some Indians out of chaos and irrationality, if not effect a complete transformation in Indian societies. Americans grasped at various explanations for the failure of assimilation—flawed policy, reformers' unrealistic expectations of Indians, or deliberate Indian noncompliance. Americans could accept that, at best, only some Indians would successfully complete a civilizing transformation. The key was the application of discipline to promote civilization. Starvation to force compliance was one form of discipline that emerged when rations were introduced into the Indians' subsistence system. Within a disciplined and disciplining environment, Christianizing, educating, and teaching Indians to farm could do the work of inscribing specific American values onto the minds and bodies of Native people. Through worship, the classroom, and labor, Indians were expected to learn to value individualism, competition, and the desire to impose order over their environment. Indians would be educated to internalize the liberal idea that the right to a life of dignity and security rested in the labor they invested in making land productive.

Thus, the role of Indians in the Philadelphia Exhibition functioned to serve the nation's history. First, exhibits of precontact or prereservation peoples allowed the nation to reinforce its claim to uniqueness while cordoning off its uncivilized beginnings to a distant prehistoric time. Second, unassimilated Indians better served the message of American political and economic progress. Third, the absence of references to assimilation and the progress it promised Indians, save for the Indian School House, prevented public criticism of the nation's failed Indian policies. Fourth, Philadelphia left American Indians hermetically sealed in the past, omitted from the present, deprived of place in the future. American Indians provided a form of entertainment now found objectionable and a useful service to the narrative by not being there as they really were. The writing was on the wall for Indians and their place, or lack of place, in the national narrative.

These three narratives share a common origin in late-nineteenth-century internal American colonialism, but they tell radically different histories. Not all the histories survived. Assimilation is now seen as a relic of a misguided era (although the idea still has currency in many contexts of domestic and international politics). The Kiowas remain identified with Plains savagery or nobility, and one can still find numerous references to Indian young men as outlaws and renegades of one kind or another in historical literature and Hollywood films. The drawings have been recategorized as art by both art critics and art historians, who have provided us with descriptive language about technique, medium, and comparisons to earlier Plains art forms. Yet the narrative that has survived fairly intact is the one produced at Philadelphia through a large-scale collaboration between the state, commercial sector, and American intelligentsia.

Appendix A. U.S. Indian Appropriations and Disbursements, 1860–1910

Year								
1860	EA	S.misdoc.79, 37-2	DAID	N/A	ARST	H.exdoc.2, 36-2	REUS	H.exdoc.12, 36-2
1861	EA	S.misdoc.79, 37-2	DAID	N/A	ARST	S.exdoc.2, 37-2	REUS	H.exdoc.36, 37-2
1862	EA / AdA	H.exdoc.1, 37-2	DAID	N/A	ARST	S.exdoc.1, 37-3	REUS	H.exdoc.8, 38-1
1863	EA / AdA	H.exdoc.3, 37-3 / H.exdoc.1, 37-2	DAID	N/A	ARST	H.exdoc.3, 38-1	REUS	H.exdoc.84, 38-1
1864	EA / AdA	H.exdoc.3, 37-3 / H.exdoc.2, 38-1	DAID	N/A	ARST	H.exdoc.3, 38-2	REUS	H.exdoc.73, 38-2
1865	EA / AdA	H.exdoc.2, 38-1	DAID	N/A	ARST	H.exdoc.3, 39-1	REUS	H.exdoc.12, 39-2
1866	EA / AdA	H.exdoc.2, 39-1 / H.exdoc.2, 38-2	DAID	N/A	ARST	H.exdoc.4, 39-2	REUS	H.exdoc.315, 40-2
1867	EA / AdA	H.exdoc.2, 39-2 / H.exdoc.2, 39-1	DAID	N/A	ARST	H.exdoc.2, 40-2	REUS	H.exdoc.29, 42-2
1868	EA	H.exdoc.2, 39-2	DAID	N/A	ARST	H.exdoc.2, 40-3	REUS	H.exdoc.36, 42-2
1869	EA	H.exdoc.3, 40-2	DAID	N/A	ARST	H.exdoc.2, 41-1	REUS	H.exdoc.37, 42-2
1870	EA	H.exdoc.3, 40-3	DAID	N/A	ARST	H.exdoc.2, 41-3	REUS	H.exdoc.57, 43-1
1871	EA	H.exdoc.5, 41-3	DAID	N/A	ARST	H.exdoc.2, 42-2	REUS	H.exdoc.57, 43-1
1872	EA	N/A	DAID	N/A	ARST	H.exdoc2, 42-3	REUS	H.exdoc.179, 43-2
1873	EA	H.exdoc.88, 42-3	DAID	H.exdoc.6, 43-2	ARST	H.exdoc.2, 43-1	REUS	H.exdoc.35, 45-2
1874	EA	H.exdoc.5, 42-3	DAID	N/A	ARST	H.exdoc.2, 43-2	REUS	H.exdoc.9, 45-2
1875	EA	H.exdoc.5, 43-1	DAID	N/A	ARST	H.exdoc.2, 44-1	REUS	H.exdoc.97, 47-1
1876	EA	H.exdoc.5, 43-2	DAID	H.exdoc.6, 44-2	ARST	H.exdoc.2, 44-2	REUS	H.exdoc. 117, 47-1
1877	EA	H.exdoc.5, 44-1	DAID	H.exdoc.6, 45-2	ARST	H.exdoc.2, 45-2	REUS	H.exdoc.121, 47-1

(cont.)

Appendix A. U.S. Indian Appropriations and Disbursements, 1860–1910 (cont.)

Year								
1878	EA	H.exdoc.5, 44-2 H.exdoc.5, 45-1	DAID	H.exdoc.6, 45-3	ARST	H.exdoc.2, 45-3	REUS	H.exdoc.93, 48-1
1879	EA		DAID	N/A	ARST	H.exdoc.2, 46-2	REUS	H.exdoc.98, 48-1
1880	EA	H.exdoc.5, 45-3	DAID	N/A	ARST	H.exdoc.2, 46-3	REUS	H.exdoc.203, 48-2
1881	EA	H.exdoc.4, 46-2	DAID	H.exdoc.6, 47-1	ARST	H.exdoc.2, 47-1	REUS	H.exdoc.29, 49-1
1882	EA	H.exdoc.5, 46-2	DAID	H.exdoc.6, 47-2	ARST	H.exdoc.2, 47-2	REUS	H.exdoc.31, 49-1
1883	EA	H.exdoc.5, 47-1	DAID	H.exdoc.6, 48-1	ARST	H.exdoc.2, 48-1	REUS	H.exdoc.365, 49-1
1884	EA	H.exdoc.5, 47-2	DAID	H.exdoc.6, 48-2	ARST	H.exdoc.2, 48-2	REUS	H.exdoc.100, 49-2
1885	EA	H.exdoc.5, 48-1	DAID	H.exdoc.6, 49-1	ARST	H.exdoc.2, 49-1	REUS	H.exdoc.124, 50-1
1886	EA AdA	H.exdoc.176, 49-1 H.exdoc.5, 48-2	DAID	H.exdoc.6, 49-2	ARST	H.exdoc.2, 49-2	REUS	H.exdoc.382, 50-1
1887	EA	H.exdoc.5, 49-1	DAID	H.exdoc.8, 50-1	ARST	H.exdoc.2, 50-1	REUS	H.exdoc.294, 51-1
1888	EA	H.exdoc.5, 49-2	DAID	H.exdoc.8, 50-2	ARST	H.exdoc.2, 50-1	REUS	H.exdoc.47, 51-2
1889	EA DEF DEF	H.exdoc.5, 50-1 S.exdoc.135, 50-2 H.exdoc.71, 50-2	DAID	H.exdoc.8, 51-1	ARST	H.exdoc.2, 51-1	REUS	H.exdoc.228, 52-2
1890	EA	H.exdoc.5, 50-2	DAID	H.exdoc.8, 51-2	ARST	H.exdoc.2, 51-2	REUS	H.exdoc.256, 52-2
1891	EA	H.exdoc.5, 51-1	DAID	H.exdoc.8, 52-1	ARST	H.exdoc.2, 52-2	REUS	H.exdoc.42, 53-2
1892	EA	H.exdoc.5, 51-2	DAID	H.exdoc.239, 52-2	ARST	H.exdoc.2, 52-2	REUS	S.rp.708/2, 53-2
1893	EA	H.exdoc.5, 52-1	DAID	H.exdoc.36, 53-2	ARST	H.exdoc.2, 53-2	REUS	S.misdoc.55, 53-1
1894	EA	H.exdoc.5, 52-2	DAID	N/A	ARST	H.exdoc.2, 53-3	REUS	H.exdoc.100, 53-3
1895	EA	H.exdoc.5, 53-2	DAID	N/A	ARST	H.doc.8, 54-1	REUS	H.doc.41, 54-1
1896	EA	H.exdoc.5, 53-3	DAID	N/A	ARST	H.doc.8, 54-2	REUS	H.doc.75, 54-2
1897	EA	H.doc.12, 54-1	DAID	N/A	ARST	H.doc.8, 55-2	REUS	H.doc.94, 55-2

1898	EA	H.doc.12, 54-1	DAID	N/A	ARST	H.doc.8, 55-3	REUS	H.doc.44, 55-3
1899	EA	H.doc.12, 55-2	DAID	N/A	ARST	H.doc.8, 56-1	REUS	H.doc.36, 56-1
1900	EA	H.doc.12, 55-2	DAID	N/A	ARST	H.doc.8, 56-2	REUS	H.doc.80, 56-2
1901	EA	H.doc.12, 55-2	DAID	N/A	ARST	H.doc.8, 57-1	REUS	H.doc.35, 57-1
1902	EA	H.doc.12, 56-1	DAID	N/A	ARST	H.doc.8, 57-2	REUS	H.doc.78, 57-2
1903	EA	H.doc.12, 57-1	DAID	N/A	ARST	H.doc.8, 58-2	REUS	H.doc.42, 58-2
1904	EA	H.doc.12, 57-2	DAID	N/A	ARST	H.doc. 8, 58-3	REUS	H.doc.64, 58-3
1905	EA	H.doc.12, 58-2	DAID	N/A	ARST	H.doc.9, 59-1	REUS	H.doc.55, 59-1
1906	EA	H.doc.12, 58-3	DAID	N/A	ARST	H.doc.9, 59-2	REUS	H.doc.152, 59-2
1907	EA	H.doc.12, 59-1	DAID	N/A	ARST	H.doc.9, 60-1	REUS	H.doc.23, 60-1
1908	EA	H.doc.12, 59-2	DAID	N/A	ARST	H.doc.1041, 60-2	REUS	H.doc.1079, 60-2
1909	EA	H.doc.12, 60-1	DAID	N/A	ARST	H.doc.102, 61-2	REUS	H.doc.236, 61-2
1910	EA	H.doc.1031, 60-2	DAID	N/A	ARST	H.doc.1001, 61-3	REUS	H.doc.1043, 61-3

EA (Estimate of Appropriations)

AdA (Estimate of Additional Appropriation)

DAID (Disbursements made from appropriations for Indian Department)

REUS (Receipts and Expenditures of United States)

ARST (Annual Report of the Secretary of Treasury on State of Finances)

Appendix B. Government Document Sources of Population Figures

Date(s)	Document Title	Reference
1867–69, 71–72	"Annual Report of the Bureau of Ethnology, 1895–96" (Includes a report on the Kiowas written by James Mooney)	H doc 316, #3836 F7
1870	"Rpt of the Commissioner of Indian Affairs, 1870"	H exdoc 1, #1449 F9
1873	"Rpt of the Commissioner of Indian Affairs, 1873"	H exdoc 1, #1601 F5
1874–95	"Indian Dept Disbursements"	See citations on "Pymts to Kiowas"
1896	"Indian Agencies of the U.S."	S exdoc 75, #3163 F1
1897	"Rpt of the Commissioner of Indian Affairs, 1897"	H doc 5, #3641 F4, p. 482
1898	"Rpt of the Commissioner of Indian Affairs, 1898"	H doc 5, #3757 F7, p. 598
1899	"Rpt of the Commissioner of Indian Affairs, 1899"	H doc 5, #3915 F6, p. 562
1900	"Rpt of the Commissioner of Indian Affairs, 1900"	H doc 5, #4101 F4, p. 331
1901	"Rpt of the Commissioner of Indian Affairs, 1901"	H doc 5, #4290 F8, p. 686
1902	"Rpt of the Commissioner of Indian Affairs, 1902"	H doc 5, #4458 F7, p. 630
1903	"Rpt of the Commissioner of Indian Affairs, 1903"	H doc 5, #4645 F6, p. 506
1904	"Rpt of the Commissioner of Indian Affairs, 1904"	H doc 5, #4798 F7, p. 594
1905	"Rpt of the Commissioner of Indian Affairs, 1905"	H doc 5, #4959 F6, p. 516
1906	"Rpt of the Commissioner of Indian Affairs, 1906"	H doc 5, #5118 F6, p. 481
1907	"Rpt of the Commissioner of Indian Affairs, 1907"	H doc 5, #5296 F2, p. 173
1908	"Rpt of the Commissioner of Indian Affairs, 1908"	H doc 1046, #5453 F3, p. 184
1909	"Rpt of the Commissioner of Indian Affairs, 1909"	H doc 107, #5747 F2
1910	"Rpt of the Commissioner of Indian Affairs, 1910"	H doc 1006, #5976 F1, p. 56

Notes

CHAPTER 1. THE AMERICAN PROBLEM

1. Primo Levi, *Survival in Auschwitz*, trans. Guilio Einaudi, with "A Conversation with Primo Levi" by Philip Roth (New York: Simon and Schuster, 1996), 56–64.

2. Robert C. Miller to A. M. Robinson, *Report of the Central Superintendency*, 1858, 98–99.

3. Jeffrey Ostler, *The Plains Sioux and U.S. Colonialism from Lewis and Clark to Wounded Knee* (Cambridge: Cambridge University Press, 2004), 40.

4. Jill Norgren, *The Cherokee Cases: Two Landmark Federal Decisions in the Fight for Sovereignty* (Norman: University of Oklahoma Press, 2004), 6–7.

5. Robert Williams, *The American Indian in Western Legal Thought: The Discourses of Conquest* (Oxford: Oxford University Press, 1990), 15–18, 22–26 (on Pope Gregory and "irrationality").

6. Maureen Konkle, *Writing Indian Nations: Native intellectuals and the Politics of Historiography, 1827–1863* (Chapel Hill: University of North Carolina Press, 2004), 15.

7. O'Brien, *Dispossession by Degrees: Indian Land and Identity in Natick, Massachusetts, 1650–1790* (Cambridge: Cambridge University Press, 1997); Saunt, *A New Order of Things: Property, Power, and the Transformation of the Creek Indians, 1733–1816* (Cambridge: Cambridge University Press, 1999); Hoxie, *Parading through History: The Making of the Crow Nation in America, 1805–1935* (Cambridge: Cambridge University Press, 1997).

8. Nicholos Arjun Thomas, *Colonialism's Culture: Anthropology, Travel and Government* (Princeton NJ: Princeton University Press, 1997); Appadurai, ed., *The Social Life of Things: Commodities in Cultural Perspective* (Cambridge: Cambridge University Press, 1986). See also Nancy Shoemaker, ed., *Clearing a Path: Theorizing the Past in Native American Studies* (New York: Routledge, 2002). Shoemaker's anthology has made an important contribution to situating Native American studies in a theoretical context.

9. *Washington Post*, December 29, 2005, A01.

CHAPTER 2. THE KIOWA SCHEME OF LIFE

1. Nineteenth-century travelers and scholars have contributed to our understanding of the southern Plains environment with descriptions, climate studies, ecological analyses, and histories. H. Bailey Carroll, writing in 1941, characterized the descriptions by Lt. James William Abert as "the record of an intimate visit with the tribe made by a close

observer at a time when Anglo-American observations of the Kiowa are indeed scarce." See Lt. James Williams Abert, *Expedition to the Southwest: An 1845 Reconnaissance of Colorado, New Mexico, Texas and Oklahoma*, introduction by John Miller Morris (Lincoln: University of Nebraska Press, 1999), 6.

2. The Kiowas lived on the Plains long before 1790, when they took up permanent residence in the southern Plains. Some writers, like Nancy Hickerson, claim that segments of the Kiowa were in the southern Plains as early as the sixteenth century. See Nancy Hickerson, "Ethnogenesis of the South Plains, Jumano to Kiowa," in *History, Power, and Identity: Ethnogenesis in the Americas, 1492–1992*, ed. Jonathan D. Hill (Iowa City: University of Iowa Press, 1996), 70–89.

3. See Patricia Albers, *The Home of the Bison: An Ethnographic and Ethnohistorical Study of Traditional Cultural Affiliations to Wind Cave National Park*, Cooperation Agreement #CA606899103 between the U.S. National Park Service and the Department of American Indian Studies, University of Minnesota, September 29, 2003, 23, 34–37.

4. James Mooney, Calendar History of the Kiowa Indians, introduction by John C. Ewers (Washington DC: Smithsonian Institution Press, 1979), 153–54.

5. Rufus B. Sage, *Rocky Mountain Life; or, Startling Scenes and Perilous Adventures in the Far West* (Dayton OH: Edward Canby, 1850), 313. Also, see Abert, *Expedition to the Southwest*, 34.

6. Abert, *Expedition to the Southwest*, 61.

7. Albers, *The Home of the Bison*, 48, 49, 55, 56.

8. Sage, *Rocky Mountain Life*, 361. Sage's description matches those of Indian potatoes by Miss Dorothy W. Smith, Home Demonstration Agent, Kiowa Agency, Anadarko, Oklahoma, in *Kiowa Recipes* (Anadarko OK: Kiowa Agency, 1934). This volume is a wonderful primary source of twentieth-century Kiowa recipes and makes references to many plants mentioned in this chapter.

9. Abert, *Expedition to the Southwest*, 29, 57, 62, 70. Abert and Lt. William Peck, leading the U.S. Corps of Topographical Engineers, explored the Canadian River, the junction of the Canadian and Arkansas Rivers, and the North Fork of the Red River in the summer of 1845.

10. Richard Irving Dodge, *The Plains of North America and Their Inhabitants*, ed. Wayne R. Kime (Newark: University of Delaware Press, 1989), 79.

11. Dodge, *The Plains of North America*, 79.

12. Andrew C. Isenberg, *The Destruction of the Bison, An Environmental History, 1750–1920* (Cambridge: Cambridge University Press, 2000), 17.

13. William Temple Hornaday, *The Extermination of the American Bison* (Washington DC: Smithsonian Institution Press, 2002), 427. This volume was initially published in 1889 as part of the 1887 *Annual Report of the Board of Regents of the Smithsonian Institution*. Hornaday (1854–1937) was the Smithsonian's chief taxidermist.

14. Isenberg, *The Destruction of the Bison*, 18–20.

15. Alice L. Marriott Papers, Box 9, Folder 18, Alice Marriott Manuscript Collection, Western History Collections, University of Oklahoma Libraries, University of Oklahoma (hereafter Alice L. Marriott Papers). This oral history by a Kiowa man contains references to "my mother's camp."

16. See, for example, "Partial List of Articles Manufactured from the Products of the Buffalo," which includes: scrapers, fleshers, drills, handles, awls, tipis, clothing, food, shields, footwear, containers, saddles, bridles, ropes, *material medica*, ornaments, beds, bedding, robes, water buckets, sausage casings, quivers, bow strings, pillows, sweat-lodge covers, swings, cradles, powder horns, tinder horns, spoons, written records, fish lines, rabbit snares, quirts, ceremonial offerings, fuel, dice, musical instruments, altars, and balls. Alice L. Marriott Papers, Box 9, Folder 1.

17. Jerrold E. Levy, "Ecology of the Southern Plains," *AES Proceedings of the Annual Spring Meetings* (Seattle, 1961). Cited in Benjamin R. Kracht, "Kiowa Religion: An Ethnohistorical Analysis of Ritual Symbolism, 1832–1987" (PhD diss., Southern Methodist University, 1989), 376.

18. Hornaday, *The Extermination of the American Bison*, 415–26.

19. Albers, *The Home of the Bison*, 53.

20. Mooney, *Calendar History of the Kiowa Indians*, 161.

21. Clark Wissler, "The Influence of the Horse in the Development of Plains Culture," *American Anthropologist* 16, no. 1 (1914): 1–25. Bernard Mishkin offers a critique of Wissler's theory.

22. Mooney, *Calendar History of the Kiowa Indians*, 161.

23. Mooney, *Calendar History of the Kiowa Indians*, 167.

24. Roe, *The Indian and the Horse*, 80. Zebulon Montgomery Pike, *The Expeditions of Zebulon Montgomery Pike* (Reprint, New York: Dover, 1987), 744.

25. George Bird Grinnell, *The Fighting Cheyenne* (Norman: University of Oklahoma Press, 1956 [1915]), 67–68.

26. Mooney, entry for Winter Count, 1872–73, *Calendar History of the Kiowa Indians*, 336.

27. Abert, *Expedition to the Southwest*, 18n27.

28. For wild onion, see Kelly Kindscher, *Medicinal Wild Plants of the Prairie: An Ethnobotanical Guide* (Ames: Iowa State University Press, 1992), 27; Kelly Kindscher, *Edible Wild Plants of the Prairie: An Ethnobotanical Guide* (Lawrence: University Press of Kansas, 1987), 12; Muriel Sweet, *Common Edible and Useful Plants of the West* (Healdsburg CA: Naturegraph Publishers, 1976), 61; Thomas S. Elias and Peter A. Dykeman, *Field Guide to North American Edible Wild Plants* (New York: Outdoor Life Books, Times Mirror Magazines, 1982), 58. For snakeroot, see William Boon and Harland D. Groe, *Nature's Heartland: Native Plant Communities of the Great Plains* (Ames: Iowa State University Press, 1990), 184; Paul Anthony Vestal and Richard Evans Schultes, *The Economic Botany of the Kiowa Indians as it Relates to the History of the Tribe* (Cambridge MA: Botanical Museum, 1939), 33; Albers, *The Home of the Bison*, 404. For prairie potato, see Waldo R. Wedel, "Notes on the Prairie Turnip among the Plains Indians," *Nebraska History* 59 (1978): 162; Kindscher, *Edible Wild Plants of the Prairie*, 183; Elias and Dykeman, *Field Guide*, 150; *Kiowa Recipes*, 5. For sumac, see Sweet, *Common Edible and Useful Plants*, 28; Vestal and Schultes, *Economic Botany of the Kiowa Indians*, 39, 72; Boon and Groe, *Nature's Heartland*, 132.

29. *Kiowa Recipes*, 4.

30. *Kiowa Recipes*, 5.

31. Vestal and Schultes, *Economic Botany of the Kiowa Indians*, 61.

32. Mooney, entry for Summer 1838, *Calendar History of the Kiowa Indians*, 273.

33. Albers, *The Home of the Bison*, 404.

34. For chokecherry, see Kindscher, *Edible Wild Plants*, 176; Kindscher, *Medicinal Wild Plants*, 170; Vestal and Schultes, *Economic Botany of the Kiowa Indians*, 30, 72; Gustav G. Carlson and Volney H. Jones, "Some Notes on Uses of Plants by the Comanche Indians," *Papers of the Michigan Academy of Science, Arts & Letters* 25 (1939): 526; Robert A. Vines, *Trees of Central Texas* (Austin: University of Texas Press, 1984), 157; Elias and Dykeman, *Field Guide*, 204. For currant, see Michael Moore, *Medicinal Plants of the Mountain West* (Albuquerque: Museum of New Mexico Press, 1979), 132; Kindscher, *Medicinal Wild Plants*, 275; Kindscher, *Edible Wild Plants*, 195; Vestal and Schultes, *Economic Botany of the Kiowa Indians*, 29, 73; Vines, *Trees of Central Texas*, 118; Elias and Dykeman, *Field Guide*, 168–70; Carlson and Jones, "Uses of Plants by the Comanche Indians," 527; Abert, *Expedition to the Southwest*, 29; Sage, *Rocky Mountain Life*, 311. For elderberry, see Sweet, *Common Edible and Useful Plants*, 18; Kindscher, *Edible Wild Plants*, 249; Vestal and Schultes, *Economic Botany of the Kiowa Indians*, 52; Vines, *Trees of Central Texas*, 359; Elias and Dykeman, *Field Guide*, 190. For grapes, see *Kiowa Recipes*, 9; Vestal and Schultes, *Economic Botany of the Kiowa Indians*, 42; Carlson and Jones, "Uses of Plants by the Comanche Indians," 526; Elias and Dykeman, *Field Guide*, 214; Abert, *Expedition to the Southwest*, 50. For hackberry, see *Kiowa Recipes*, 7; Kindscher, *Edible Wild Plants*, 241; Vestal and Schultes, *Economic Botany of the Kiowa Indians*, 22; Carlson and Jones, "Uses of Plants by the Comanche Indians," 527; Vines, *Trees of Central Texas*, 89–96; Elias and Dykeman, *Field Guide*, 220. For plum, see *Kiowa Recipes*, 9; Kindscher, *Edible Wild Plants*, 170; Kindscher, *Medicinal Wild Plants*, 273; Vestal and Schultes, *Economic Botany of the Kiowa Indians*, 29–30, 72; Carlson and Jones, "Uses of Plants by the Comanche Indians," 526; Vines, *Trees of Central Texas*, 158–63; Elias and Dykeman, *Field Guide*, 206; Abert, *Expedition to the Southwest*, 29; Sage, *Rocky Mountain Life*, 311; Wedel, "Notes on the Prairie Turnip," 2. For prickly pear, see Kindscher, *Edible Wild Plants*, 154; Vestal and Schultes, *Economic Botany of the Kiowa Indians*, 45; Carlson and Jones, "Uses of Plants by the Comanche Indians," 527; Vines, *Trees of Central Texas*, 299; Elias and Dykeman, *Field Guide*, 140; Abert, *Expedition to the Southwest*, 62. For persimmon, see Elias and Dykeman, *Field Guide*, 238; Vines, *Trees of Central Texas*, 314–18; Carlson and Jones, "Uses of Plants by the Comanche Indians," 526; James A. Duke, *Handbook of Edible Weeds* (Boca Raton FL: CRC Press, 1992), 88; *Kiowa Recipes*, 9; Abert, *Expedition to the Southwest*, 102.

35. For lamb's-quarter, see Kindscher, *Edible Wild Plants*, 80; for pokeweed, see Kindscher, *Edible Wild Plants*, 54; Vestal and Schultes, *Economic Botany of the Kiowa Indians*, 26; Elias and Dykeman, *Field Guide*, 96; for prairie clover, see Kindscher, *Edible Wild Plants*, 109, and Kindscher, *Medicinal Wild Plants*, 80.

36. Mooney, entry for Summer 1856, *Calendar History of the Kiowa Indians*, 301.

37. For button snakeroot, see Vestal and Schultes, *Economic Botany of the Kiowa Indians*, 51; Vines, *Trees of Central Texas*, 357; Carlson and Jones, "Uses of Plants by the Comanche Indians," 533; Moore, *Medicinal Plants of the Mountain West*, 135; for bush morning glory, see Kindscher, *Medicinal Wild Plants*, 126; Abert, *Expedition to the Southwest*, 44.

38. "They were taking the bark off of trees, cottonwood trees (ahi—real wood). It has a kind of nutty taste when you chew the inside bark." Alice L. Marriott Papers, Box 9, Folder 18.

39. For beardtongue root, see Kindscher, *Medicinal Wild Plants*, 267; for black raspberry root, see Kindscher, *Medicinal Wild Plants*, 276; for buffalo gourd root, see Kindscher, *Medicinal Wild Plants*, 76.

40. For purple prairie clover, see Kindscher, *Edible Wild Plants*, 109, and Kindscher, *Medicinal Wild Plants*, 80.

41. For prairie willow, see Kindscher, *Medicinal Wild Plants*, 194; for purple cone flower, see Kindscher, *Medicinal Wild Plants*, 86; for soapweed, see Kindscher, *Edible Wild Plants*, 224; Kindscher, *Medicinal Wild Plants*, 220; for white sage, see Kindscher, *Medicinal Wild Plants*, 46.

42. For crane's bill, see Kindscher, *Medicinal Wild Plants*, 82; Boon and Groe, *Nature's Heartland*, 190; Moore, *Medicinal Plants of the Mountain West*, 68; Abert, *Expedition to the Southwest*, 32.

43. For bee balm, see Kindscher, *Edible Wild Plants*, 149, and Kindscher, *Medicinal Wild Plants*, 155.

44. For gay-feather, see Kindscher, *Edible Wild Plants*, 142; Kindscher, *Medicinal Wild Plants*, 136; for ragweed, see Kindscher, *Edible Wild Plants*, 23.

45. For silvery wormwood (sage), see Carlson and Jones, "Uses of Plants by the Comanche Indians," 532; Kindscher, *Medicinal Wild Plants*, 46; Kindscher, *Edible Wild Plants*, 240; Vestal and Schultes, *Economic Botany of the Kiowa Indians*, 56, 74; Moore, *Medicinal Plants of the Mountain West*, 162. See also, Vestal and Schultes, *Economic Botany of the Kiowa Indians*, 41.

46. For chinaberry, see Vines, *Trees of Central Texas*, 235; Vestal and Schultes, *Economic Botany of the Kiowa Indians*, 41. Kiowa calendar keeping also documents the use of chinaberry as a sacred medicine. See Mooney, entry for Summer Count 1857, *Calendar History of the Kiowa Indians*, 301.

47. Albers, *The Home of the Bison*, 402.

48. Albers, *The Home of the Bison*, 420.

49. Alice L. Marriott's field notes include interviews that document the work of processing buffalo hides.

50. Alice L. Marriott Papers, Box 9, Folder 1.

51. Alice L. Marriott Papers, Box 9, Folder 1.

52. Alice L. Marriott Papers, Box 9, Folder 1.

53. Sometimes women painted transverse stripes on their leggings, indicating the scalps or coup won by warrior kinsmen. Mooney, *Calendar History of the Kiowa Indians*, 260.

54. Oral history, Alice L. Marriott Papers, Box 9, Folder 18. "I made seven tipis. Seven tipis of my very own. I trimmed my own poles. I had a stick, and each time I finished a tipi completely, I put a notch in the stick." This woman must have been the cutter. She described women coming and having sinew and hides prepared for their work.

55. Kracht, "Kiowa Religion," 247.

56. Mishkin, *Rank and Warfare among the Plains Indians*, 55–56.

57. Alice L. Marriott Papers, Box 9, Folder 10.

58. Alice L. Marriott Papers, Box 9, Folder 10.

59. Alice L. Marriott Papers, Box 9, Folder 10.

60. Mishkin, *Rank and Warfare among the Plains Indians,* 39.

61. Kracht, "Kiowa Religion," 244–46.

62. William Meadows, *Kiowa, Comanche and Apache Military Societies: Enduring Veterans, 1800 to the Present* (Austin: University of Texas Press, 1999), 40.

63. The customs of Qoichegau military society included an escape clause. A comrade might come to the aid of the warrior, release the sash, and free him of his obligation with honor.

64. Mishkin, *Rank and Warfare among the Plains Indians,* 35.

65. Mishkin, *Rank and Warfare among the Plains Indians,* 37–41.

66. Mishkin, *Rank and Warfare among the Plains Indians,* 45.

67. Meadows, *Kiowa, Comanche and Apache Military Societies,* 39.

68. Meadows, *Kiowa, Comanche and Apache Military Societies,* 40–41.

69. Meadows, *Kiowa, Comanche and Apache Military Societies,* 51.

70. Alice L. Marriott Papers, Box 9, Folder 25.

71. Oral history, Alice L. Marriott Papers, Box 9, Folder 18. "I went with my father to chase and kill and skin them. That way we learned to butcher, and the names of the parts. . . . That way I learned the thing I would need to know later."

72. Kracht, "Kiowa Religion," 363–64.

73. Kracht, "Kiowa Religion," 365. *Topadoga* is the Kiowa word for band and refers to the ten to twenty residence groups attached to a headman or camp chief.

74. Alice L. Marriott Papers, Box 9, Folder 25.

75. Mooney, *Calendar History of the Kiowa Indians,* 221.

76. Mishkin, *Rank and Warfare among the Plains Indians,* 35–39.

77. Kracht, "Kiowa Religion," 247.

CHAPTER 3. VALUES OF THE STATE AND U.S. INDIAN POLICY

1. Treaty of Medicine Lodge, Oct. 21, 1867 (15 Stat. 581), ratified, July 25, 1868, proclaimed, Aug. 25, 1868; Treaty with the Kiowa, Comanche, and Apache, 1867, 982–984, Oct. 21, 1867 (15 Stat. 589), ratified, July 25, 1868, proclaimed Aug. 25 1868; Raymond J. DeMallie and Lynn Shelby Kickingbird, *The Treaty of Medicine Lodge, 1867 Between the United States and the Kiowa, Comanche and Apache Indians* (Washington DC: Institute for the Development of Indian Law, 1976). Charles J. Kappler, ed., *Indian Affairs, Laws and Treaties,* vol. 2: *Treaties* (Washington DC: Government Printing Office, 1904) is online at http://digital.library.okstate.edu/kappler/.

2. A. A. Taylor, "Medicine Lodge Creek," *Chronicles of Oklahoma* 2, no. 2, June 1924, 98–118.

3. Scholarly sources on federal Indian policy and law include Vine Deloria Jr., *Custer Died for Your Sins* (New York: Macmillan, 1969; rpt. Norman: University of Oklahoma Press, 1988); Vine Deloria Jr. and David E. Wilkins, *Tribes, Treaties and Constitutional Tribulations* (Austin: University of Texas Press, 2000); Sidney L. Harring, *Crow Dog's Case, American Indian Sovereignty, Tribal Law, and United States Law in the Nineteenth Century* (Cambridge:

Cambridge University Press, 1984); Norgren, *The Cherokee Cases*; Andrea Smith, *Conquest: Sexual Violence and American Indian Genocide* (Cambridge: South End Press, 2005); Williams, *The American Indian in Western Legal Thought*; Robert A. Williams Jr., *Like a Loaded Weapon: The Rehnquist Court, Indian Rights and the Legal History of Racism in America* (Minneapolis: University of Minnesota Press, 2005); David E. Wilkins and Tsianina Lomawaima, *Uneven Ground: American Indian Sovereignty and Federal Law* (Norman: University of Oklahoma Press, 2002); Charles Wilkinson, *Blood Struggle: The Rise of Modern Indian Nations* (New York: W.W. Norton, 2005); Frederick E. Hoxie, *A Final Promise: The Campaign to Assimilate the Indians, 1880–1920* (Cambridge: Cambridge University Press, 1984).

4. See Konkle, *Writing Indian Nations*, particularly the introduction.

5. Elizabeth A. H. John, "An Earlier Chapter of Kiowa History," *New Mexico Historical Review* 60, no. 4 (1985): 380.

6. Daniel Tyler, "Mexican Indian Policy in New Mexico," *New Mexico Historical Review* 55, no. 2 (1980).

7. Paul Francis Prucha, *The Great Father: The United States Government and the American Indians* (Lincoln: University of Nebraska Press, 1984), 339.

8. Prucha, *The Great Father*, 340.

9. From Professor Wilkins's guest lecture to my class, "Introduction to American Indian History and Policy," University of Iowa, November 2003.

10. See Norgren, *The Cherokee Cases*, for a discussion of Marshall's decisions rendered in the cases of *Cherokee Nation v. Georgia* (1831) and *Worcester v. Georgia* (1832) as the foundation for a law of American continental real estate.

11. Harring, *Crow Dog's Case*, 34–35.

12. Contained in "Report to the President by the Indian Peace Commission, January 7, 1868" in *Annual Report of the Secretary of the Interior*, 1868, 500.

13. President U. S. Grant nominated Lawrie Tatum as agent for the Kiowa, Comanche, and Apache Indians (*Senate Executive Journal*, April 21, 1869). The Senate confirmed his appointment on April 22, 1869 (http://memory.loc.gov).

14. Treaty with the Kiowa, etc., 1837 (7 Stat. 533), proclaimed February 21, 1838.

15. Treaty with the Comanche, Kiowa, and Apache, 1853 (10 Stat., 1013), ratified April 12, 1854, proclaimed February 12, 1855; see Raymond J. DeMallie, *The Kiowa Treaty of 1853* (Washington DC: Institute for the Development of Indian Law, 1977).

16. Treaty with the Comanches and Kiowas, October 18, 1865 (14 Stat. 717), ratified May 22, 1866; proclaimed May 26, 1866; see Raymond DeMallie, *The Treaty on the Little Arkansas River, 1865* (Washington DC: Institute for the Development of Indian Law, 1977).

17. S136, 40th Cong., 1st Sess., *Journal of the House of Representatives*, July 20, 1867.

18. Senate debate, *Congressional Globe*, July 18, 1867, 706, 714; House debate, *Congressional Globe*, December 8, 1868, 20; House debate, *Congressional Globe*, February 27, 1869, 1706; Senate debate, *Congressional Globe*, March 6, 1869, 22–23; House debate, *Congressional Globe*, March 19, 1869, 166.

19. House debate, *Congressional Globe*, February 27, 1869, March 12, 1869, March 19, 1869.

20. Senate debate, *Congressional Globe*, March 27, 1867, 377–81. See especially Sen.

John Sherman of Ohio, chairman of Committee on Finance, 378; *Biographical Directory of the United States* (http://bioguide.congress.gov/). Hereafter, BDUS.

21. Senate debate, *Congressional Globe*, March 27, 2867, 380; BDUS.

22. House debate, *Congressional Globe*, February 4, 1869; House debate, *Congressional Globe*, February 27, 1869; Senate debate, *Congressional Globe*, July 18, 1867; House debate, *Congressional Globe*, February 25, 1870.

23. Senate debate, *Congressional Globe*, July 18, 1867, 714.

24. *Congressional Globe*, March 27, 1867, 380; BDUS.

25. House debate on "Indian Appropriation Bill" (FY1870), *Congressional Globe*, February 27, 1869, 1701. The House could not reach a resolution. See also BDUS.

26. Sen. Edmund Ross (Ohio), Senate debate over establishing a treaty commission, *Congressional Globe*, July 18, 1867, 706. See also BDUS.

27. Sen. Edmund Ross (Ohio), Senate debate over establishing a treaty commission, *Congressional Globe*, July 18, 1867, 706.See also BDUS.

28. Sen. Edmund Ross (Ohio), *Congressional Globe*, July 18, 1867, 706.

29. *Congressional Globe*, December 8, 1868, 17; BDUS.

30. Senate debate, *Congressional Globe*, April, 1, 1869, June 4, 1870, June 8, 1870, February 22, 1871.

31. Senate debate, *Congressional Globe*, April 1, 1869; House debate, *Congressional Globe*, March 2, 1870; Senate debate, *Congressional Globe*, June 4, 1870; House debate, *Congressional Globe*, Febuary 28, 1870.

32. Senate debate, *Congressional Globe*, July 18, 1867; House debate, *Congressional Globe*, December 8, 1868; House debate, *Congressional Globe*, January 28, 1869; House debate, *Congressional Globe*, February 4, 1869.

33. Senate debate, *Congressional Globe*, February 19, 1869.

CHAPTER 4. YOUNG KIOWA MEN, KIOWA SOCIAL VALUES, AND THE POLITICS OF RATIONS

1. Robert Utley, *The Indian Frontier of the West, 1846–1890* (Albuquerque: University of New Mexico Press, 1984), 63.

2. DeMallie, *Treaty on the Little Arkansas River*, p. 23.

3. Edwin Stanton to N. Taylor, June 8, 1867, transmitting April 26, 1867, communication of Frederick Jones, interpreter, to Lt. Gen. W. T. Sherman, commanding the Military Division of the Missouri. Letters Received, Office of Indian Affairs (hereafter LR/OIA).

4. Contemporaneous reports and histories have represented Kicking Bird as being the government-appointed leader of the peaceful element who drew much criticism from "conservatives and the war party" (Mooney, *Calendar History of the Kiowas*, 217). His "attachment" to the whites strained his relations with other members of the tribe.

5. Levy places Kicking Bird, Stumbling Bear, Heidsicke, and Goosaudle'te in the category of "Peacefuls," and Lone Wolf, Set'Tainte, Big Bow, White Horse, and Big Tree in the category of "Hostiles," 34.

6. Mooney, *Calendar History of the Kiowas*, 176; Report of the Secretary of the Interior, 1869, 504.

7. Mooney, *Calendar History of the Kiowas*, 327.

8. Kracht, "Kiowa Religion," 215–22.

9. Alfred Gell, *Art and Agency: An Anthropological Theory* (Oxford: Clarendon Press, 1998), 20–21.

10. Kracht, "Kiowa Religion," 208–29.

11. DeMallie, *The Kiowa Treaty of 1853*, 8.

12. J. P. Hatch to Assistant Adjutant General, March 31, 1877, Letters Received, Office of Adjutant General (hereafter LR/OAG).

13. Isenberg, *The Destruction of the Bison*, 93–163.

14. Isenberg, *The Destruction of the Bison*, 137.

15. Robert C. Miller, *Report of the Commissioner of Indian Affairs*, 1858, 143.

16. Robert C. Miller, *Report of the Commissioner of Indian Affairs*, 1858, 19.

17. Leavenworth to Murphy, December 4, 1866, LR/OIA M234; G. W. Todd to Office of Indian Affairs, August 28, 1866, LR/OIA, M234.

18. Isenberg, *The Destruction of the Bison*, 16.

19. Lorenzo Labadi to A. B. Norton, August 28, 1867, Report of the Secretary of the Interior, 1867.

20. J. R. Mead to Thomas Murphy, September 6, 1866, LR/OIA M234.

21. Leavenworth to D.W. Cooley, December 1, 1865, LR/OIA M234.

22. Patrick Henry Healey to Commissioner of Indian Affairs, October 15, 1866, LR/OIA M234.

23. "Investigating Affairs of Kiowa and Comanche and Wichita and Affiliated Bands Agencies," submitted by Agent Col. A. G. Boone to N. G. Taylor, January 26, 1869, LR/OIA M234 (hereafter, Boone's Report).

24. Stanton to Commissioner of Indian Affairs, June 8, 1867, LR/OIA M234.

25. Testimony of S. J. Walkley in Boone's Report; A. G. Boone to N. G. Taylor, December 29, 1868, LR/OIA M234.

26. George Ransome, employee of Leavenworth, gave this testimony, Boone's Report. John Brown, an employee of merchant Griffenstein, also testified that "Indians claimed to be starving," Boone's Report.

27. S. J. Walkley's testimony, Boone's Report.

28. S. J. Walkley's testimony, Boone's Report.

29. S. J. Walkley's testimony, Boone's Report.

30. S. J. Walkley's testimony, Boone's Report.

31. A. G. Boone to N. G. Taylor, December 13, 1868, LR/OIA M234.

32. Thomas Murphy to Charles E. Mix, Report of the Commissioner of Indian Affairs, 1868.

33. W. T. Sherman to J. M. Schofield, September 17, 1868, *Report of the Commissioner of Indian Affairs*, 1868.

34. Grierson to Assistant Adjutant General, September 25, 1869, LR/OIA M234.

35. Grierson to Assistant Adjutant General, September 25, 1869, LR/OIA M234.

36. Lawrie Tatum to E. S. Parker, July 24, 1869, LR/OIA M234.

37. Lawrie Tatum to E. S. Parker, July 24, 1869, LR/OIA M234.

38. Grierson to Assistant Adjutant General, September 25, 1869, LR/OIA M234.

39. Grierson to Assistant Adjutant General, September 25, 1869, LR/OIA M234.

40. Affadavit of Philip McCusker, submitted to E. S. Parker, July 22, 1869, LR/OIA M234.

41. Affadavit of Philip McCusker, submitted to E. S. Parker, July 22, 1869, LR/OIA M234.

42. Agent Boone's compilation of events included in Boone's Report.

43. Agency correspondence and military reports attest to the young men's activities, including persistent raiding and trading throughout the 1867–75 period. J. R. Mead (Butler Co.) to Thomas Murphy, September 7, 1866; Phillip McCusker to Leavenworth, April 6, 1868; R. H.Grierson to Assistant Adjutant General, July 14, 1870; Statement of Horse Back, Comanche Chief, July 22, 1879; Phillip McCusker to Major General Hazen, December 21, 1868; Laurie Tatum to CIA E. Parker, May 7, 1870; Laurie Tatum to E. Hoag, April 14, 1871; E. Hoag to Laurie Tatum, June 26, 1871; Cyrus Beede to Enoch Hoag, April 4, 1873; Agent Haworth to Cyrus Beede, May 8, 1873; Thomas Battey to Agent Haworth, July 31, 1873; Agent Haworth to Enoch Hoag; August 18, 1873; Agent Haworth to Hon. C. Delano, December 15, 1873; Agent Haworth to Enoch Hoag, August 21, 1873; J. W. Davidson to Assistant Adjutant General, October 8, 1873, NARG 75, LR, Kiowa Agency. Beede to Enoch Hoag, April 4, 1873, NARG 75, LR, Kiowa Agency. Edwin Stanton to the Commissioner of Indian Affairs, June 8, 1867, NARG 75, LR, Kiowa Agency.

44. Documenting raids is dependent on descriptions like Boone's, anecdotal accounts, and depredations claims. Depredations claims were collected on three separate occasions from the counties of Texas by the Governor's Office. County officials varied in the ways they presented pertinent information, but usually included names of claimants, date or year of loss, number of animals stolen, value of stolen animals, corollary murders or kidnappings, and, if possible, tribal identity of raiders. Indian depredations claims were submitted by Medina, Llano, Wise, Stephens, Palo Pinto, Kendall, and Blanco Counties, Texas, for 1870 to the Governor's Office. It is questionable whether the raids in Medina, Llano, Kendall, and Blanco counties were carried out by Kiowas and Comanches. Wise, Stephens, and Palo Pinto were common Kiowa and Comanche targets. Kiowas and Comanche raids were most common in the North Texas, West Central Texas, North Central Texas, and Texoma regions, although it was not out of the realm of possibility for them to attack settlers in other areas (*Texas Indian Papers*, vol. 5).

45. Tatum attested that the reservation Indians divided their rations with off-reservation Indians (Lawrie Tatum to E. S. Parker, May 7, 1870, LR/OIA M234).

46. Lawrie Tatum to E. S. Parker, May 7, 1870, LR/OIA M234.

47. Voucher No. 42, Abstract D. to Property Returns; Issues to Indians of Annuity Goods and Supplies by P.B. Hunt, Indian Agent at Kiowa, Comanche and Wichita Agency, Indian Territory, for the quarter ending December 31, 1879 cited in Dana O. Jenson, "Good Art from a Bad Indian: Wo-Haw: Kiowa Warrior," *Bulletin of the Missouri Historical Society*, VII (October 1950) , 82.

48. Lawrie Tatum to Enoch Hoag, February 11, 1870, LR/OIA; Grierson to Assistant Adjutant General, April 12, 1870, LR/OIA; Secretary of War J. M. Belknap to Secretary of Interior, April 16, 1870.

49. Grierson to Assistant Adjutant General, June 14, 1870; Tatum to Hoag, August 19, 1870, LR/OIA M234.

50. Lawrie Tatum to Enoch Hoag, May 14, 1870, LR/OIA M234; Grierson to Assistant Adjutant General, August 7, 1870.

51. Lawrie Tatum to Enoch Hoag, May 14, 1870, LR/OIA M234.

52. Lawrie Tatum to Enoch Hoag, September 6, 1870, LR/OIA M234.

53. Tatum to Hoag, September 6, 1870, LR/OAG 234/376.

54. Tatum to Hoag, September 6, 1870, LR/OAG 234/376.

55. Tatum to Hoag, August 19, 1870, LR/OAG 234/376.

56. Grierson to Assistant Adjutant General, May 13, 1871, LR/OIA, 234/377.

57. W. T. Sherman to E. D. Townsend, May 24, 1871, LR/OAG.

58. W. T. Sherman to E. D. Townsend, May 24, 1871, LR/OAG.

59. G. W. Schofield to Assistant Adjutant General, August 12, 1871, LR/OAG.

60. D. Delano to Ely S. Parker, June 21, 1871, LR/OAG.

61. Colonel W. S. Nye, *Carbine and Lance: The Story of Old Fort Still*, 12th ed. (Norman: University of Oklahoma Press, 1869 edition), 203–4.

62. Nye, *Carbine and Lance*, 188.

63. Haworth to C. Delano, December 15, 1873, NARG 75, Kiowa Agency.

64. Edward P. Smith to E. G. Davis, Governor of Texas, October 7, 1873; August 14, 1874; Cyrus Beede to Enoch Hoag, April 4, 1873; Agent Haworth to Cyrus Beede, May 8, 1873; Agent Haworth to the Hon. C. Delano, December 15, 1873, NARG 75, LR, Kiowa Agency; Nye, *Carbine and Lance*, 203–4.

65. Frank Nattby, interpreter, to President of the United States, November 23, 1875. LR/OAG 1874.

CHAPTER 5. FICTIONS OF NINETEENTH-CENTURY AMERICAN ASSIMILATION POLICY

1. E. D. Townsend, Adjutant General, Special Orders No. 88, War Department, May 11, 1875, LR/OAG 1874.

2. Richard Pratt, *Battlefield and Classroom, Four Decades with the American Indian, 1867–1904* (New Haven: Yale University Press, 1964).

3. Pratt, *Battlefield and Classroom*, 24.

4. Williams, *The American Indian in Western Legal Thought*, 62–63.

5. Pratt to Sheridan, March 17, 1876, LR/OAG 1874.

6. Pratt to Sheridan, March 17, 1876, LR/OAG 1874.

7. Janet Catherine Berlo, "Wo-Haw's Notebooks: 19th Century Kiowa Indian Drawings in the Collections of the Missouri Historical Society," *Gateway Heritage* (Autumn 1982): 3–13.

8. Berlo, "Wo-Haw's Notebooks," 13.

9. Janet Berlo, ed., *Plains Indian Drawings, 1865–1935, Pages from a Visual History* (New York: Harry N. Abrams, 1996), 69.

10. *Southern Workman* 8, no. 6 (June 1879): 68.

11. Aw-Lih to Etahleah, May 26, 1878, *Southern Workman* 7, no. 7 (July 1878): 50.

12. Tsaitkopeta to Richard Pratt, April 1878, R. H. Pratt box, Hampton University Archives.

13. Howling Wolf to L. E. L. Zalinski, Fort Marion, December 21, 1878, *Southern Workman* 8, no. 2 (February 1879): 19.

14. Minimic to Richard Pratt, January 24, 1879, *Southern Workman* 8, no. 3 (March 1879): 31.

15. Minimic to Pratt, January 24, 1879, *Southern Workman*, 31.

16. Chief Killer to Richard Pratt, February 4, 1879, *Southern Workman* 8, no. 5 (May 1879): 55–56.

17. Quoyuouah to Richard Pratt, June 1879, *Southern Workman* 8, no. 6 (June 1879: 68.

18. Petersen, *Howling Wolf*, 24–30.

19. *Southern Workman* 7, no. 7 (July 1978): 50.

20. Mooney, *Calendar History of the Kiowa Indians*, 233–34. Mooney's passage is also cited in Dougles C. Jones, *The Treaty of Medicine Lodge: The Story of the Great Treaty Council as Told by Eyewitnesses* (Norman: University of Oklahoma Press, 1966), 65, and Mildred P. Mayhall, *The Kiowas*, 2d ed. (Norman: University of Oklahoma Press, 1962), 144.

21. Curtis M. Hinsley Jr., *Savages and Scientists: The Smithsonian Institution and the Development of American Anthropology, 1846–1910* (Washington DC: Smithsonian Institution Press, 1981), 147. Lewis Henry Morgan, *Ancient Society* (New York: Holt, 1878); and Lewis Henry Morgan, *Systems of Consanguinity and Affinity of the Human Family*, Smithsonian Institution Contributions to Knowledge, vol. 17, Article 2 (Washington DC: Smithsonian Institution, 1868).

22. The Centennial Exhibition was, according to Robert Rydell, an escape from and response to postwar economic and political uncertainties. The "colossal edifices" of the major buildings, the exuberant celebration of technological progress, and self-conscious assertions of American artistic achievement encouraged renewed confidence in the nation recently torn apart by the bloody Civil War. See Robert W. Rydell, *All the World's a Fair: Visions of Empire at American International Expositions, 1876–1916* (Chicago: University of Chicago Press, 1984), 11–13.

23. Baird's report was attached to House Executive Document 148, 44th Cong., 2d Sess., which contained the request for an "additional appropriation for the executive departments of the United States at the Centennial Exhibition."

24. See Frederick E. Hoxie, *A Final Promise: The Campaign to Assimilate the Indians, 1880–1920* (Cambridge: Cambridge University Press, 1984), particularly chapter 4, "Frozen in Time and Space." Hoxie's work highlights the differing opinions among anthropologists of the period.

25. Otis T. Mason, *Ethnological Directions Relative to the Indian Tribes of the United States* (Washington DC: Government Printing Office), 1875. This document was "Prepared under direction of the Indian Bureau," but as Smithsonian secretary Joseph Henry noted in his introduction, "the display in question will be exhibited under the joint auspices of the Smithsonian Institution and of the Indian Bureau of the Interior Department, both departments joined in making collections for a common object." Mason, formerly a professor of anthropology at Columbia College, was contracted "to draw up a systematic schedule of the various articles of clothing, ornaments, household utensils, implements of agriculture, weapons of war and the chase, tools of trade, the apparatus used for the pursuit and capture of game, &c., and a pamphlet was accordingly prepared by this gentleman, and printed by the Indian Bureau, embracing over six hundred subjects." House Executive Document 148, 44th Cong., 1st Sess., "Additional Appropriation for the Executive Departments of the United States at the Centennial Exhibition," 5–33.

26. Thomas, *Colonialism's Culture*, 7.

27. *Magee's Illustrated Guide of Philadelphia and the Centennial Exhibition* (New York: Nathan Cohen Books 1876; reprinted 1975), 173. The *Guide* goes on to say that George Anderson of Sherman, Texas, and an Indian expert, was the encampment Indians' guide and interpreter. Fort Sill was built in 1868.

28. *Rand, McNally & Co.'s Handbook of the World's Columbian Exposition with Special Descriptive Articles* (Chicago: Rand, McNally, 1893), 182.

29. *Rand, McNally & Co.'s Handbook*, 91; Stanley Appelbaum, ed., *The Chicago World's Fair of 1893: A Photographic Record* (New York: Dover, 1980), 95.

30. Appelbaum, *Chicago World's Fair*, 106.

31. Marion Shaw, *World Fair's Notes: A Woman Journalist Views Chicago's 1893 Columbian Exposition* (St. Paul MN: Pogo Press, 1992), 59.

32. Appelbaum, *Chicago World's Fair*, 103.

33. Daniel G. Brinton, "The 'Nation' as an Element in Anthropology," in *International Congress of Anthropology* (Chicago: Schulte, 1894), 19–34.

34. The emphasis of Brinton's presidential address in Chicago in 1893 was on the "importance of the broad term anthropology as the whole study of man." He was averse to the existence of specialized fields of linguistics, archaeology, and ethnology. Regna Darnell, *Daniel Garrison Brinton: The "Fearless Critic" of Philadelphia*, Publications in Anthropology, No. 3 (Philadelphia: University of Pennsylvania Press, 1988), 37.

CHAPTER 6. HOUSEHOLDS OF HUMANITY

1. F. Conrad to Gen. R. L. Mackenzie, Commander, Fort Sill, September 8, 1877, Kiowa File, Roll 80, Oklahoma Historical Society.

2. Conrad to Mackenzie, September 8, 1877. Other requests came into the agency to hire Indians for preparing hides. Arnold to "Indian Agent," July 18, 1882, Kiowa File, Roll 80, Oklahoma Historical Society.

3. F. Conrad to General R. L. Mackenzie, Commander, Fort Sill, September 8, 1877, Kiowa File, Roll 80, Oklahoma Historical Society.

4. Haworth to Williams, January 11, 1878, Kiowa File, Roll 80, Oklahoma Historical Society.

5. Haworth to Nicholson, *Report of the Commissioner of Indian Affairs*, 1877, p. 87.

6. Haworth to Nicholson, *Report of the Commissioner of Indian Affairs*, 1877, p. 87.

7. Hunt to Commissioner of Indian Affairs, August 15, 1878, *Report of the Commissioner of Indian Affairs*, 1878, p. 59.

8. Hunt to Commissioner of Indian Affairs, September 1, 1881, *Report of the Commissioner of Indian Affairs*, 1881, p. 79.

9. Hunt to Commissioner, September 1, 1881, p. 79.

10. Hunt to Commissioner, September 1, 1881, p. 79.

11. Morris W. Foster, *Being Comanche: A Social History of an American Indian Community* (Tucson: University of Arizona Press, 1991), 80.

12. Foster, *Being Comanche*, 80.

13. A. J. Reynolds to P. B. Hunt, August 10, 1882, Kiowa File, Roll 80, Oklahoma Historical Society.

14. Reynolds to Hunt, August 10, 1882.

15. Reynolds to Hunt, August 10, 1882.

16. Haworth to Commissioner of Indian Affairs Smith, March 16, 1875, NARG 75, LR, Kiowa Agency.

17. Haworth to Commissioner, March 16, 1875.

18. Haworth to Commissioner, March 16, 1875.

19. P. B. Hunt to Commissioner of Indian Affairs, September 1, 1880, *Report of the Commissioner of Indian Affairs*, 1880, p. 75. The government supplied sixty wagons and the Indians about twenty more. All animals were supplied by the Indians (Hunt to Commissioner, September 1, 1880). In 1881, the freighting money dropped to $11,445 for 935,160 (Hunt to Commissioner, September 1, 1881, *Report of the Commissioner of Indian Affairs*, 1881, 79). It should be noted that Indians competed with American freighters.

20. P. B. Hunt to Commissioner of Indian Affairs, September 1, 1882, *Report of the Commissioner of Indian Affairs*, 1882, p. 65.

21. Foster, *Being Comanche*, 81.

22. Foster, *Being Comanche*, 81.

23. Foster, *Being Comanche*, 80.

24. P. B. Hunt to the Commissioner of Indian Affairs, September 1, 1880, *Report of the Commissioner of Indian Affairs*, 1880, p. 72.

25. Hunt to the Commissioner, September 1, 1880.

26. S. A. Frost invoice to A. J. Reynolds, October 28, 1879, Kiowa Agency Traders, Roll KA 79, Oklahoma Historical Society.

27. Frost to Reynolds, May 25, May 28, June 10, June 24, July 15, July 31, 1880, Kiowa Agency Traders, Roll KA 79.

28. Frost to Reynolds, February 15, May 9, September 29, 1881, Kiowa Agency Traders, Roll KA 79.

29. Frost to Reynolds, July 11, July 15, September 24, October 13, October 27, 1881, Kiowa Agency Traders, Roll KA 79.

30. Frost to Reynolds, August 3, 1882, Kiowa Agency Traders, Roll KA 79.

31. Hail, *Gifts of Pride and Love*, 22.

32. Frost to A. D. Lawrence and Son, February, 9, 1907, Lawrence Correspondence Files, A. D. Lawrence Collection, Museum of the Great Plains, Lawton, Oklahoma. This order from S. A. Frost included 607 bunches of beads in thirty-one colors. In July 1909 Lawrence ordered 500 bunches of beads in assorted colors from Marshall Field and Company (Marshall Field and Company to A. D. Lawrence, July 7, 1909, Lawrence Correspondence Files).

33. A. D. Lawrence to A. F. Hatfield, April 2, 1908, Lawrence Correspondence File. Lawrence's business transactions concerning the sale of Indian goods were also recorded in the store ledger, Day Book, April 29, 1905–September 22, 1913, A. D. Lawrence Collection, Museum of the Great Plains, Lawton, Oklahoma.

34. Day Book, April 29, 1905–September 22, 1913, A. D. Lawrence Collection, and A. D. Lawrence to A. F. Hatfield, July 17, 1908, Lawrence Correspondence File.

35. A. D. Lawrence to C. L. Eliis, May 19, 1909, Lawrence Correspondence File.

36. Lawrence to Eliis, May 19, 1909, Lawrence Correspondence File.

37. Lawrence to Eliis, May 19, 1909, Lawrence Correspondence File.

38. A. D. Lawrence to Ed Estes, November 18, 1907, December 3, 1907, Lawrence Correspondence File.

39. A. D. Lawrence to E. A. Estes, December 3, 1907, Lawrence Correspondence File. The beaded leather fob, a small pocket for a watch, became very popular during this period, according to the correspondence between Lawrence and his business associates.

40. A. D. Lawrence to M. Loeb, June 15, 1908, Lawrence Correspondence File.

41. A. D. Lawrence to E. A. Estes, November 18, 1907 and December 3, 1907, Lawrence Correspondence File.

42. For example, A. F. Hatfield to A. D. Lawrence, January 21, 1909, and Purdy Brothers, Galveston, Texas, to A. D. Lawrence, May 28, 1909, Lawrence Correspondence File.

43. A. D. Lawrence to M. Loeb, June 15, 1908, Lawrence Correspondence File.

44. Cash Book "C," A. D. Lawrence Collection, Museum of the Great Plains, Lawton, Oklahoma.

45. Cash Book "C."

46. Cash Book "C."

47. David Penney, *Art of the American Indian Frontier: The Chandler-Pohrt Collection* (Seattle: University of Washington Press, 1992), 49–50. The Chandler-Pohrt collection was exhibited at the National Gallery of Art, the Seattle Art Museum, the Buffalo Bill Historical Center, and the Detroit Institute of Art between May 1992 and February 1994. Penney's book is a companion to the traveling exhibition.

48. Penney, *Art of the American Indian Frontier,* 49.

49. Mishkin, *Rank and Warfare among the Plains Indians,* 54–56.

50. A. D. Lawrence to Frank Rush, October 23, 1908, Lawrence Correspondence File, A. D. Lawrence Collection, Museum of the Great Plains, Lawton, Oklahoma.

51. Lawrence to Rush, October 23, 1908.

52. Lawrence to Rush, October 23, 1908.

53. Israel G. Vork to P. B. Hunt, April 7, 1884, Kiowa File, Roll KA 49, Oklahoma Historical Society.

54. Vork to Hunt, April 7, 1884.

55. Sydney Smith to Lee Hall, July 16, 1886, Kiowa File, Roll KA 49, Oklahoma Historical Society.

56. Ben Cabell to Myers, September 29, 1889, Kiowa File, Roll KA 49.

57. T. J. Morgan to Henry Exall, October 12, 1889, Kiowa File, Roll KA 49.

58. Mason, *Ethnological Directions,* 12, 23.

59. Mason, *Ethnological Directions,* 5–31.

60. Blepshaw to E. E. White, August 17, 1888, Kiowa File, Roll KA 49, Oklahoma Historical Society.

61. S. M. McCowan to Randlett, November 27, 1903, Kiowa File, Roll KA 49.

62. Lawrence's information gathering, interactions, and relationships resulted in an impressive knowledge of the Lawton-area Native community, and beyond. Because his knowledge is of such a personal nature, at times involving family finances, health, and secret keeping, I have chosen to adopt the nineteenth-century convention of using only first letters of names out of respect for these extraordinary confidences.

63. February 20, 1931.

64. February 14, 1931.

65. May 12, 1931.

66. April 25, 1931.

67. The debt included the amount charged to account over the years in many cases, plus interest.

68. K—— died less than a year later at the Mission. Lawrence recalled that "He was one of the first Indian Police," and that "he lived just east of Cox's store" (June 8, 1931). Lawrence attended his estate hearing on August 11, 1931.

69. January 14, 1931.

70. August 15, 1930.

71. Allan Houser, Chiricahua Apache, is one of the most important twentieth-century Native artists. His graceful sculptures are included in many museum collections around the world. The National Museum of the American Indian opening in September 2004 featured an exhibit of Houser's work.

72. Asah was one of the famed Kiowa Five painters who mastered the "flat" two-dimensional style mimicked by other artists. Steven Mopope was another of the Kiowa artists.

73. May 21, 1938; May 27, 1938.

74. December 14, 1938.

75. January 19, 1937.

76. May 13, 1937.

77. June 12, 1937.

78. June 13, 1937.

79. February 15, 1939. See also, February 4 and March 1, 1939.

80. February 11, 1939.

81. February 13, 1939.

CHAPTER 7. CONCLUSION

1. Ed Folsom, *Walt Whitman's Native Representations* (New York: Cambridge University Press, 1994), p. 91.

2. Ella Cara Deloria, *Waterlily* (Lincoln: University of Nebraska Press, 1988), 237.

3. Joel Pfister, *Individuality Incorporated: Indians and the Multicultural Modern* (Durham NC: Duke University Press, 2004), 12.

Bibliography

ARCHIVES

Hampton Institute, Hampton, Virginia, Photography Collection, "Southern Workman," Student Files.

Museum of the Great Plains, Lawton, Oklahoma, A.D. Lawrence Collection, "Red Store Ledgers," "Lawrence Correspondence," "A.D. Lawrence Diaries"; Tingley Collection, "Objects Collection."

National Archives, Washington DC, microfilm Letters Received by the Office of the Adjutant General, Letters Received by the Office of Indian Affairs.

National Cowboy and Western Heritage Museum, Oklahoma City, Oklahoma, Arthur and Shifra Silberman Native American Art Collection, Kiowa Interviews and Contacts File, Archives files, Art of Fort Marion series.

Newberry Library, Chicago, Illinois, Edward E. Ayer Collection, Complete Set of Annual Reports of the Commissioners of Indian Affairs, Photograph Collection.

Oklahoma Historical Society, Oklahoma City, Oklahoma, Fairs and Exhibitions Files, Kiowa Agency Files, Trader Files.

Smithsonian Institution, Washington DC, National Anthropological Archives, Ledger Drawings file, Smithsonian Institution Archives, 1893 Columbian Exposition files, Centennial Exhibition of 1876 file.

University of Oklahoma, Norman, Oklahoma, Western History Collections, Alice Marriott Manuscript Collection, Box 9; Photograph Collection.

PUBLISHED WORKS

Abert, Lt. James William. *Expedition to the Southwest: An 1845 Reconnaissance of Colorado, New Mexico, Texas, and Oklahoma.* With an introduction and notes by H. Bailey Carroll. Lincoln: University of Nebraska Press, 1999.

Afton, Jean, David Fridtjof Halaas, and Andrew E. Masich. *Cheyenne Dog Soldiers: A Ledgerbook History of Coups and Combat.* Niwot & Denver: University Press of Colorado and Colorado Historical Society, 1997.

Ahern, Wilbert H. "'The Returned Indians': Hampton Institute and its Indian

Alumni, 1879–1893." Paper presented at the Organization of American Historians 1981 Annual Meeting, Detroit, Michigan, April 1–4, 1981.

Albers, Patricia, and Beatrice Medicine, eds. *The Hidden Half: Studies of Plains Indian Women*. Lanham MD: University Press of America, 1983.

———. *The Home of the Bison: An Ethnographic and Ethnohistorical Study of Traditional Cultural Affiliations to Wind Cave National Park*. Unpublished. Washington DC: U.S. National Park Service and University of Minnesota, 2003.

Anderson, Gary Clayton. *The Indian Southwest, 1580–1830: Ethnogenesis and Reinvention*. Norman: University of Oklahoma Press, 1999.

Appadurai, Arjun, ed. *The Social Life of Things: Commodities in Cultural Perspective*. Cambridge: Cambridge University Press, 1988.

Appelbaum, Stanley. ed. *The Chicago's World Fair of 1893: A Photographic Record*. New York: Dover Publications, 1980.

Beadle, J. H. *The Undeveloped West; or, Five Years in the Territories: Being a Complete History of That Vast Region between the Mississippi and the Pacific, Its Resources, Climate, and Inhabitants, Natural Curiosities, etc., etc*. Philadelphia: National Publishing, 1873.

Beers, Henry Putney. "Military Protection of the Santa Fe Trail to 1843." *New Mexico Historical Review*. 12, no. 2 (1937): 113–33.

Bell, Robert E., Edward B. Jelks, and W. W. Newcomb. *Wichita Indians: Wichita Indian Archaeology and Ethnology, A Pilot Study*. New York: Garland Publishing, 1974.

Bender, A. B. "Military Posts in the Southwest, 1848–1860." *New Mexico Historical Review* 16, no. 2 (1941): 125–47.

Berlo, Janet Catherine, ed. *Plains Indian Drawings 1865–1935: Pages from a Visual History*. New York: Harry N. Abrams, 1996.

———. "Wo-Haw's Notebooks: 19th Century Kiowa Indian Drawings in the Collections of the Missouri Historical Society," *Gateway Heritage* (Autumn, 1982).

Betts, John Rickards. "P. T. Barnum and the Popularization of Natural History." *Journal of the History of Ideas* 20, no. 3 (June–September 1959): 353–68.

Boon, William, and Harlen D. Groe. *Nature's Heartland: Native Plant Communities of the Great Plains*. Ames: Iowa State University Press, 1990.

Bourdieu, Pierre. *The Logic of Practice*. Translated by Richard Nice. Stanford CA: Stanford University Press, 1990.

———. *Outline of a Theory of Practice*. Translated by Richard Nice. 10th ed. Cambridge: Cambridge University Press, 1993.

Brinton, Daniel G. "The 'Nation' as an Element in Anthropology." *International Congress of Anthropology*. Chicago: Schulte Publishing, 1894.

Brooks, James F. *Captives and Cousins: Slavery, Kinship, and Community in the Southwest Borderlands*. Chapel Hill: University of North Carolina Press, 2002.

Carlson, Gustav G., and Volney H. Jones. "Some Notes on Uses of Plants by the Comanche Indians." *Papers of the Michigan Academy of Science, Arts & Letters* 25 (1939): 517–42.

Catlin, George. *Letters and Notes on the North American Indians.* North Dighton MA: JG Press, 1995.

Clark, Blue. *Lone Wolf v. Hitchcock: Treaty Rights and Indian Law at the End of the Nineteenth Century.* Lincoln: University of Nebraska Press, 1994.

Collier, Jane Fishburne. *Marriage and Inequality in Classless Societies.* Stanford CA: Stanford University Press, 1988.

Congressional Globe. Washington DC: Blair & Rives, 1834–73.

Crawford, Isabel. *Kiowa: A Woman Missionary in Indian Territory.* With an introduction by Clyde Ellis. Reprint ed. Lincoln: University of Nebraska Press, 1998.

Dale, Edward Everett. "The Cheyenne-Arapaho Country." *Chronicles of Oklahoma* 20 (1942): 360–71.

———. "Ranching on the Cheyenne-Arapaho Reservation, 1880–1885." *Chronicles of Oklahoma* 6 (1928): 35–59.

Darnell, Regna. *Daniel Garrison Brinton: The "Fearless Critic" of Philadelphia.* Publications in Anthropology. No. 3. Philadelphia: University of Pennsylvania Press, 1988.

Davis, Michael G. *Ecology, Sociopolitical Organization, and Cultural Change on the Southern Plains: A Critical Treatise in the Sociocultural Anthropology of Native North America.* Kirksville MO: Thomas Jefferson University Press, 1996.

Deloria, Ella Cara. *Waterlilly.* Lincoln: University of Nebraska Press, 1988.

Deloria Jr., Vine. *Behind the Trail of Broken Treaties: An Indian Declaration of Independence.* New York: Dell Publishing, 1974.

———. *Custer Died for Your Sins.* New York: Macmillan Publishing Company, 1969.

DeMallie, Raymond J. *Comanche Treaty of 1867 with the United States (Medicine Lodge Treaty).* Washington DC: Institute for the Development of Indian Law, 1977.

———. *The Jerome Agreement between the Kiowa, Comanche & Apache Tribes and the United States Government.* Washington DC: Institute for the Development of Indian Law, 1977.

———. *The Kiowa Treaty of 1853.* Washington DC: Institute for the Development of Indian Law, 1977.

———. *The Treaty on the Little Arkansas River, 1865.* Washington DC: Institute for the Development of Indian Law, 1977.

———. *The Unratified Treaty between the Kiowas, Comanches and Apaches and the United States of 1863.* Washington DC: Institute for the Development of Indian Law, 1977.

DeMallie, Raymond J., and Lynn Shelby Kickingbird. *The Treaty of Medicine Lodge, 1867 between the United States and the Kiowa, Comanche and Apache Indians.* Washington DC: Institute for the Development of Indian Law, 1976.

Dockstader, Frederick J. *Indian Art of the Americas.* Photographs by Carmelo Guadagno. New York: Museum of the American Indian, Heye Foundation, 1973.

Dodge, Richard Irving. *The Indian Territory Journals of Colonel Richard Irving Dodge.* Edited by Wayne R. Kime. Norman: University of Oklahoma Press, 2000.

———. *Our Wild Indians: Thirty-Three Years' Personal Experience among the Red Men of the Great West. A Popular Account of their Social Life, Religion, Habits, Traits, Customs, Exploits, etc. with Thrilling Adventures and Experiences on the Great Plains and in the Mountains of our Wide Frontier.* Hartford CT: A.D. Worthington, 1883.

———. *The Plains of North America and Their Inhabitants.* Edited by Wayne R. Kime. Newark: University of Delaware Press, 1989.

Dodge, Richard Irving, and David E. Wilkins. *Tribes, Treaties and Constitutional Tribulations.* Austin: University of Texas Press, 2000.

Doran, Michael F. "Antebellum Cattle Herding in the Indian Territory." *Geographical Review* 66 (1976): 48–58.

Dugan, Kathleen Margaret. *The Vision Quest of the Plains Indians: Its Spiritual Significance.* Lewiston NY: Edwin Mellen Press, 1985.

Duke, James A. *Handbook of Edible Weeds.* Boca Raton FL: CRC Press, 1984.

Dyer, Mrs. D. B. *"Fort Reno;" or, Picturesque "Cheyenne and Arapahoe Army Life," before the Opening of "Oklahoma."* New York: G.W. Dillingham, 1896.

Dykstra, Robert R. *The Cattle Towns.* Lincoln: University of Nebraska Press, 1968.

Eastman, Elaine Goodale. *Pratt: The Red Man's Moses.* Norman: University of Oklahoma Press, 1935.

Elias, Thomas S., and Peter A. Dykeman. *Field Guide to North American Edible Wild Plants.* New York: Van Nostrand Reinhold, 1982.

Ellis, Clyde. *To Change Them Forever: Indian Education at the Rainy Mountain Boarding School, 1893–1920.* Norman: University of Oklahoma Press, 1996.

Ellis, Richard N. *General Pope and U.S. Indian Policy.* Albuquerque: University of New Mexico Press, 1970.

Errington, Shelly. *The Death of Authentic Primitive Art and Other Tales of Progress.* Berkeley: University of California Press, 1998.

Estin, Ann Laquer. "Lone Wolf v. Hitchcock: The Long Shadow." In *The Aggressions of Civilization: Federal Indian Policy since the 1880s*, ed. Sandra L. Cadwalader and Vine Deloria Jr. Philadelphia PA: Temple University Press, 1984.

Ewers, John C. *Plains Indian History and Culture: Essays on Continuity and Change.* Norman: University of Oklahoma Press, 1997.

Feder, Norman. *Two Hundred Years of North American Indian Art.* New York: Pralger, 1971.

Flores, Dan. *The Natural West: Environmental History in the Great Plains and Rocky Mountains.* Norman: University of Oklahoma Press, 2001.

—————, ed. *Journal of an Indian Trader: Anthony Glass and the Texas Trading Frontier, 1790–1810.* College Station: Texas A&M University Press, 1985.

Folsom, Ed. *Walt Whitman's Native Representations.* New York: Cambridge University Press, 1994.

Foster, Morris W. *Being Comanche: A Social History of an American Indian Community.* Tucson: University of Arizona Press, 1991.

—————. *Being Comanche: A Social History of an American Indian Community.* Tucson: University of Arizona Press, 1991.

Foucault, Michel. *Discipline & Punish: The Birth of the Prison.* Translated by Alan Sheridan. New York: Vintage Books, 1979.

Gell, Alfred. *Art and Agency: An Anthropological Theory.* Oxford: Clarendon Press, 1998.

Gilbert, B. Miles. "Some Aspects of Diet and Butchering Techniques among Prehistoric Indians in South Dakota." *Plains Anthropologist* 14 (1969): 253–76.

Grinnell, George Bird. *The Cheyenne Indians, Their History and Ways of Life.* Vol. 2. New York: Cooper Square Publishers, 1962.

Hagan, William T. *Indian Police and Judges: Experiments in Acculturation and Control.* Reprint ed. Lincoln: University of Nebraska Press, 1980.

—————. *Quanah Parker, Comanche Chief.* Norman: University of Oklahoma Press, 1993.

Hail, Barbara A., ed. *Gifts of Pride and Love: Kiowa and Comanche Cradles.* Bristol RI: Haffenreffer Museum of Anthropology, Brown University, 2000.

Harring, Sidney L. *Crow Dog's Case, American Indian Sovereignty, Tribal Law, and United States Law in the Nineteenth Century.* Cambridge: Cambridge University Press, 1984.

Harris, Moira F. *Between Two Cultures: Kiowa Art from Fort Marion.* St. Paul MN: Pogo Press, 1989.

Harrison, Lowell. "The Two Battles of Adobe Walls." *Texas Military History* 5, no. 1 (1965): 1–11.

Hickerson, Nancy. *History, Power, and Identity: Ethnogenesis in America, 1492–1992.* Edited by Jonathan D. Hill. Iowa City: University of Iowa Press, 1996.

Hornaday, William Temple. *The Extermination of the American Bison.* Washington DC: Smithsonian Institution Press, 2002.

House Executive Executive Document 148, 44th Cong., 1st Sess., "Additional Appropriation for the Executive Departments of the United States at the Centennial Exhibition," 5–33. Washington DC: Government Printing Office.

Howard, Kathleen L. "Weaving a Legend: Elle of Ganado Promotes the Indian Southwest." *New Mexico Historical Review* 74 (April 1999): 127–53.

Hoxie, Frederick E. *A Final Promise: The Campaign to Assimilate the Indians, 1880–1920.* Cambridge: Cambridge University Press, 1989.

———. *Parading Through History: The Making of the Crow Nation in America, 1805–1935.* Cambridge: Cambridge University Press, 1997.

Hurt, R. Douglas. *Indian Agriculture in America.* Lawrence: University Press of Kansas, 1987.

Hutton, Paul Andrew. *Phil Sheridan and His Army.* Lincoln: University of Nebraska Press, 1985.

Isenberg, Andrew C. *The Destruction of the Bison: An Environmental History, 1750–1920.* Cambridge: Cambridge University Press, 2000.

Jablow, Joseph. *The Cheyenne in Plains Indian Trade Relations, 1795–1840.* With an introduction by Morris W. Foster. Lincoln: University of Nebraska Press, 1994.

James, Bernard J. "Continuity and Emergence in Indian Poverty Culture." *Current Anthropology* 11 (1970): 435–52.

Jay, Martin. "Force Fields: European Intellectual History and the Specter of Multi-culturalism." *Salmagundi* 96 (1992): 21–26.

Jemison, Verna Mae McDanial. "The Indian Traders of the Southern Plains, 1845–1875." Master's thesis, University of Oklahoma, 1932.

Jennings, Carl, and Vanessa Paukeigope Jennings. "Kiowa Beadwork." *Gilcrease Journal* 3, no. 2 (1995): 44–50.

Jenson, Dana O. "Good Art from a Bad Indian: Wo-Haw: Kiowa Warrior." *Bulletin of the Missouri Historical Society* 7 (October 1950): 2.

John, Elizabeth A. H. "An Earlier Chapter of Kiowa History." *New Mexico Historical Review* 60, no. 4 (1985): 379–97.

———. "Nurturing the Peace: Spanish and Comanche Cooperation in the Early Nineteenth Century." *New Mexico Historical Review* 59, no. 4 (1984): 345–69.

Jones, Douglas C. *The Treaty of Medicine Lodge: The Story of the Great Treaty Council as Told by Eyewitnesses.* Norman: University of Oklahoma Press, 1966.

Kappler, Charles J. *Indian Affairs. Laws and Treaties.* Vol. 1, *Treaties.* Washington DC: Government Printing Office, 1904.

Kavanagh, Thomas W. *Comanche Political History: An Ethnohistorical Perspective, 1706–1875.* Lincoln: University of Nebraska Press, 1996.

Keeling, Henry C. "My Experience with the Cheyenne Indians." *Chronicles of Oklahoma* 3 (1925): 59–68.

Kenner, Charles L. "The Great New Mexico Cattle Raid—1872." *New Mexico Historical Review* 37, no. 4 (1962): 243–59.

Kindscher, Kelly. *Edible Wild Plants of the Prairie: An Ethnobotanical Guide.* Lawrence: University Press of Kansas, 1987.

———. *Medicinal Wild Plants of the Prairie: An Ethnobotanical Guide.* Lawrence: University Press of Kansas, 1992.

Kiowa Indian Recipes. Anadarko OK: Department of the Interior, Office of Indian Affairs, Division of Extension, Kiowa Indian Agency, 1934. Reprint, Excelsior MN: Melvin McCosh, Bookseller, 1985.

Klein, Julia M. "Art That Defies Categories." *Chronicle of Higher Education*, May 24, 2002.

Konkle, Maureen. *Writing Indian Nations: Native Intellectuals and the Politics of Historiography, 1827–1863.* Chapel Hill: University of North Carolina Press, 2004.

Kracht, Benjamin R. "Kiowa Powwows: Continuity in Ritual Practice." *American Indian Quarterly* 18, no. 3 (summer 1994): 321–48.

———. "Kiowa Religion: An Ethnohistorical Analysis of Ritual Symbolism, 1832–1987." Ph.D. diss., Southern Methodist University, 1989.

Larson, Pier M. "Reconsidering Trauma, Identity, and the African Diaspora: Enslavement and Historical Memory in Nineteenth-Century Highland Madagascar." *William and Mary Quarterly*, 3d ser., 56, no. 2 (April 1999): 335–62.

Leach, John A. "Search and Destroy: Counter-Insurgency on the American Plains."

Levi, Primo. *Survival in Auschwitz: The Nazi Assault on Humanity.* New York: Simon & Schuster, 1996.

Linderman, Frank B. *Pretty-Shield, Medicine Woman of the Crows.* Lincoln: University of Nebraska Press, 1932.

Llewellyn, K. N., and E. Adamson Hoebel. *The Cheyenne Way: Conflict and Case Law in Primitive Jurisprudence.* 4th ed. Norman: University of Oklahoma Press, 1967.

Loeb, Barbara. "Crow Beadwork: The Resilience of Cultural Values." *Montana: The Magazine of Western History* 40.4 (1990): 48–59.

Lovett Jr., John R., and Donald L. DeWitt, comp. *Guide to Native American Ledger Drawings and Pictographs in United States Museums, Libraries, and Archives.* Westport CT: Greenwood Press, 1998.

Magee's Illustrated Guide of Philadelphia and the Centennial Exhibition. New York: Nathan Cohen Books, 1876.

Manning, Richard. *Grassland: The History, Biology, Politics, and Promise of the American Prairie.* New York: Penguin Books USA, 1995.

Mason, Otis T. *Ethnological Directions Relative to the Indian Tribes of the United States.* Washington DC: Government Printing Office, 1875.

Mayhall, Mildred P. *The Kiowas.* 2d ed. Norman: University of Oklahoma Press, 1971.

McPherson, Robert S. "Naalayéhé Bá Hooghan—'House of Merchandise': The Navajo Trading Post as an Institution of Cultural Change, 1900–1930." *American Indian Culture and Research Journal* 16, no. 1 (1992): 23–43.

Meadows, William C. *Kiowa, Apache & Comanche Military Societies: Enduring Veterans, 1800 to the Present.* Austin: University of Texas Press, 1999.

Meline, James F. *Two Thousand Miles on Horseback. Santa Fe and Back. A Summer Tour through Kansas, Nebraska, Colorado, and New Mexico in the Year 1866.* New York: Hurd and Houghton, 1868.

Meyer, Melissa L. "'We Can Not Get a Living as We Used To': Dispossession and the White Earth Anishinaabeg, 1889–1920." *American Historical Review* 96, no. 2 (April 1991): 368–94.

Mishkin, Bernard. *Rank and Warfare among the Plains Indians.* With an introduction by Morris W. Foster. Reprint ed. Lincoln: University of Nebraska Press, 1992.

Momaday, N. Scott. *House Made of Dawn.* New York: Harper & Row, 1977.

Monahan, Jr., Forrest D. "Trade Goods on the Prairie, the Kiowa Tribe and White Trade Goods, 1794–1875." Ph.D. diss., University of Oklahoma, 1965.

Mooney, James. *Calendar History of the Kiowa Indians.* With an introduction by John C. Ewers. Reprint ed. Washington DC: Smithsonian Institution Press, 1979.

———. "The Cheyenne Indians." *Memoirs of the American Anthropological Association* 1 (1905–7): 361–442.

Moore, John H. *The Cheyenne.* Cambridge MA: Blackwell Publishers, 1996.

———, ed. *The Political Economy of North American Indians.* Norman: University of Oklahoma Press, 1993.

Moore, Michael. *Medicinal Plants of the Mountain West.* Santa Fe: Museum of New Mexico Press, 1979.

Morgan, Lewis Henry. *Ancient Societies.* New York: Holt, 1878.

———. *Systems of Consanguinity and Affinity of the Human Family.* Smithsonian Contributions to Knowledge Vol. 17, Article 2. Washington DC: Smithsonian Institution, 1868.

Morris, John W., and Edwin C. McReynolds. *Historical Atlas of Oklahoma.* Norman: University of Oklahoma Press, 1965.

Musser, R. S. "'Counts Coup on Crow': Ledger Book Art: History, Hot and Worth a Bundle." *Indian Country Today*, October 27, 1993.

Norgren, Jill. *The Cherokee Cases: Two Landmark Federal Decisions in the Fight for Sovereignty*. Norman: University of Oklahoma Press, 2004.

Nye, Colonel W. S. *Carbine and Lance: The Story of Old Fort Sill*. 12th ed. Norman: University of Oklahoma Press, 1988.

Nye, Wilbur Sturtevant. *Plains Indian Raiders: The Final Phases of Warfare from the Arkansas to the Red River*. 4th ed. Norman: University of Oklahoma Press, 1987.

O'Brien, Jean M. *Dispossession by Degrees: Indian Land and Identity in Natick, Massachusetts, 1650–1790*. Cambridge: Cambridge University Press, 1997.

Osburn, Katherine M. B. *Southern Ute Women: Autonomy and Assimilation on the Reservation, 1887–1934*. Albuquerque: University of New Mexico Press, 1998.

Ostler, Jeffrey. "'The Last Buffalo Hunt' and Beyond: Plains Sioux Economic Strategies in the Early Reservation Period." *Great Plains Quarterly* 21 (spring 2001): 115–30.

———. *The Plains Sioux and U.S. Colonialism from Lewis and Clark to Wounded Knee*. Cambridge: Cambridge University Press, 2004.

Paul, Rodman W. *The Far West and the Great Plains in Transition, 1859–1900*. New York: Harper & Row, 1988.

Peake, Nancy. "If It Came from Wright's, You Bought It Right": Charles A. Wright, Proprietor, Wright's Trading Post." *New Mexico Historical Review* 66 (July 1991): 261–86.

Pennington, William D. "Government Policy and Indian Farming on the Cheyenne and Arapaho Reservation: 1869–1880." *Chronicles of Oklahoma* 57 (1979): 171–89.

Penney, David W. *Art of the American Indian Frontier: The Chandler-Pohrt Collection*. Seattle: University of Washington Press, 1992.

Peters, Virginia Bergman. *Women of the Earth Lodges: Tribal Life on the Plains*. North Haven CT: Archon Books, 1995.

Petersen, Karen Daniels. *Howling Wolf: A Cheyenne Warrior's Graphic Interpretation of His People* (Palo Alto CA: American West, 1968).

Pevar, Stephen L. *The Rights of Indians and Tribes*. 2d ed. Carbondale: Southern Illinois University Press, 1992.

Pfister, Joel. *Individuality Incorporated: Indians and the Multicultural Modern*. Durham NC: Duke University Press, 2004.

Philips, Ruth B. "Native American Art and the New Art History." *Northeast Indian Quarterly* 7, no. 4 (winter 1990): 37–40.

———. *Trading Identities: The Souvenir in Native North American Art from the Northeast, 1700–1900*. Seattle: University of Washington Press, 1998.

Phillips, Ruth B., and Janet C. Berlo. *Native North American Art*. Oxford History of Art Series. Oxford: Oxford University Press, 1998.

Phillips, Ruth B., and Christopher B. Steiner. *Unpacking Culture: Art and Commodity in Colonial and Postcolonial Worlds*. Berkeley: University of California Press, 1999.

Pike, Zebulon Montgomery. *The Expeditions of Zebulon Montgomery Pike*. Reprint, New York: Dover, 1987.

Poitras, Jane Ash. "Paradigms for Hope and Posterity: Wo-Haw's Sun Dance Drawing," *Plains Indian Drawings, 1865–1935, Pages from a Visual History*. Edited by Janet Berlo. New York: Harry N. Abrams, 1996.

Powell, Father Peter J. "Artists and Fighting Men: A Brief Introduction to Northern Cheyenne Ledger Book Drawing." *American Indian Art Magazine* 1 (1975): 44–48.

Pratt, Richard. *Battlefield and Classroom, Four Decades with the American Indian*. New Haven: Yale University Press, 1964.

Price, Sally. *Primitive Art in Civilized Places*. 2d ed. Chicago: University of Chicago Press, 2001.

Priest, Loring Benson. *Uncle Sam's Stepchildren: The Reformation of United States Indian Policy, 1865–1887*. New Brunswick NJ: Rutgers University Press, 1942.

Prucha, Francis Paul. *Atlas of American Indian Affairs*. Lincoln: University of Nebraska Press, 1990.

———. *The Great Father: The United States Government and the American Indians*. Lincoln: University of Nebraska Press, 1984.

Rand, McNally & Co.'s *Handbook of the World's Columbian Exposition with Special Descriptive Articles*. Chicago: Rand, McNally, 1893.

Riley, Glenda. "Some European (Mis)Perceptions of American Indian Women." *New Mexico Historical Review* 59, no. 3 (1984): 237–66.

Rister, C. C. "Harmful Practices of Indian Traders of the Southwest, 1865–1876." *New Mexico Historical Review* 6, no. 3 (1931): 231–48. .

Robertson, Lindsay G. *Conquest by Law: How the Discovery of America Dispossessed Indigenous Peoples of Their Lands*. Oxford: Oxford University Press, 2005.

Roe, Frank Gilbert. *The Indian and the Horse*. Vol. 41 of Civilization of the American Indian Series. Norman: University of Oklahoma Press, 1955.

Rogers, Jerry L. "The Flint and Steel: Background of the Red River War of 1874–1875." *Texas Military History* 7, no. 3 (1969): 153–75.

Ronda, James P. *Lewis & Clark among the Indians*. Bicentennial ed. Lincoln: University of Nebraska Press, 2002.

Ross, Luana. *Inventing the Savage: The Social Construction of Native American Criminality*. Austin: University of Texas Press, 1998.

Rydell, Robert W. *All the World's A Fair: Visions of Empire at American International Expositions, 1876–1916*. Chicago: University of Chicago Press, 1984.

Sage, Rufus B. *Rocky Mountain Life; or, Startling Scenes and Perilous Adventures in the Far West*. Dayton OH: Edward Canby, 1850.

Saunt, Claudio. *A New Order of Things: Property, Power, and the Transformation of the Creek Indians, 1733–1816*. Cambridge: Cambridge University Press, 1999.

Schorger, A. W. *The Wild Turkey: Its History and Domestication*. Norman: University of Oklahoma Press, 1966.

Sciama, Lidia D. "Gender in the Making, Trading and Uses of Beads: An Introductory Essay." In *Beads and Bead Makers: Gender, Material Culture and Meaning*, ed. Lidia D. Sciama and Joanne B. Eicher, 3–45. Oxford: Berg, 1998.

Seger, John H. *Early Days Among the Cheyenne and Arapahoe Indians*. Edited by Stanley Vestal. Norman: University of Oklahoma Press, 1956.

Seigel, Jerrold. "Going Primitive, Staying Civilized." *Salmagundi* 97 (1993): 115–24.

Shaw, Marion. *World Fair's Notes: A Woman Journalist Views Chicago's 1893 Columbian Exposition*. Lakeville MN. Pogo Press, 1992.

Sherwin, Martin J. "Hiroshima as Politics and History." *Journal of American History* 82, no. 3 (December 1995): 1085–93.

Shoemaker, Nancy, ed. *Clearing a Path: Theorizing the Past in Native American Studies*. New York: Routledge, 2002.

Skogen, Larry C. *Indian Depredation Claims, 1796–1920*. Norman: University of Oklahoma Press, 1996.

Smith, Andrea. *Conquest: Sexual Violence and American Indian Genocide*. Cambridge: South End Press, 2005.

Spielmann, Katherine A., ed. *Farmers, Hunters and Colonists: Interaction between the Southwest and the Southern Plains*. University of Arizona Press, 1991.

Spivey, Towana, C. Reid Ferring, et. al. *Archaeological Investigations along the Waurika Pipeline*. Contributions of the Museum of the Great Plains, No. 5. Lawton OK: Museum of the Great Plains, 1977.

Sweet, Muriel. *Common Edible and Useful Plants of the West*. Healdsburg CA: Naturegraph Publishers, 1976.

Szabo, Joyce M. *Howling Wolf and the History of Ledger Art*. Albuquerque: University of New Mexico Press, 1994.

Tate, Michael L. *The Indians of Texas: An Annotated Research Bibliography*. Native American Bibliography Series, No. 9. Metuchen NJ: Scarecrow Press, 1986.

Tatum, Lawrie. *Our Red Brothers and the Peace Policy of President Ulysses S. Grant*. Reprint ed. Lincoln: University of Nebraska Press, 1970.

Taylor, Morris F. "Plains Indians on the New Mexico Colorado Border: The Last Phase, 1870–1876." *New Mexico Historical Review* 46, no. 4 (1971): 315–36.

Thomas, Nicholas. *Colonialism's Culture: Anthropology, Travel and Government.* Princeton NJ: Princeton University Press, 1994.

———. *Entangled Objects: Exchange, Material Culture, and Colonialism in the Pacific.* Cambridge MA: Harvard University Press, 1991.

Trennert, Robert A. "Fairs, Expositions, and the Changing Image of Southwestern Indians, 1876–1904." *New Mexico Historical Review* 62 (April 1987): 127–50.

Turgeon, Laurier. "Beads, Bodies and Regimes of Value in France and North America (ca. 1500–ca. 1650)." Paper presented to the McNeil Center for Early American Studies Seminar Series, MCEAS, University of Pennsylvania, Philadelphia, February 2001.

Tyler, Daniel. "Mexican Indian Policy in New Mexico." *New Mexico Historical Review* 55, no. 2 (1980): 101–20.

United States. Indian Peace Commission. *Proceedings of the Great Peace Commission of 1867–1868.* Edited by Vine Deloria Jr. and Raymond DeMallie. Washington DC: Institute for the Development of Indian Law, 1975.

———. Office of the Solicitor, Department of the Interior. *Federal Indian Law.* Washington DC: Government Printing Office, 1958.

Utley, Robert M. *Frontier Regulars: The United States Army and the Indian, 1866–1891.* New York: MacMillan, 1973.

———. *The Indian Frontier of the American West, 1846–1890.* Albuquerque: University of New Mexico Press, 1984.

Verbicky-Todd, Eleanor. *Communal Buffalo Hunting among the Plains Indians: An Ethnographic and Historic Review.* Occasional Paper No. 24, Archaeological Survey of Alberta. Edmonton: Alberta Culture Historical Resources Division, 1984.

Vestal, Paul A., and Richard Evans Schultes. *The Economic Botany of the Kiowa Indians as it Relates to the History of the Tribe.* Cambridge MA: Botanical Museum, 1939.

Vines, Robert A. *Trees of Central Texas.* Austin: University of Texas Press, 1984.

Wallace, Ernest, and E. Adamson Hoebel. *The Comanches, Lords of the South Plains.* 9th ed. Norman: University of Oklahoma Press, 1986.

Wedel, Mildred Mott. "The Wichita Indians in the Arkansas River Basin." In *Smithsonian Contributions to Anthropology.* Edited by Douglas H. Ubelaker and Herman J. Viola. Washington DC: Smithsonian Institution Press, 1982.

Wedel, Waldo R. "Environment and Native Subsistence Economies in the Central Great Plains." *Smithsonian Miscellaneous Collections* 101 (1941): 1–29.

———. "Notes on the Prairie Turnip among the Plains Indians." *Nebraska History* 59 (1978): 154–79.

Wilkins, David and Tsianina Lomawaima. *Uneven Ground: American Indian Sovereignty and Federal Law.* Norman: University of Oklahoma Press, 2002.

Williams, Robert. *The American Indian in Western Legal Thought: The Discourses of Conquest.* Oxford: Oxford University Press, 1990.

———. *Like a Loaded Weapon: The Rehnquist Court, Indian Rights and the Legal History of Racism in America.* Minneapolis: University of Minnesota Press, 2005.

Williams, Walter L. "United States Indian Policy and the Debate over Philippine Annexation: Implications for the Origins of American Imperialism." *Journal of American History* 66 (1980): 810–31.

Winfrey, Dorman H., and James M. Day, eds. *Texas Indian Papers.* Vol. 5: *The Indian Papers of Texas and the Southwest, 1825–1916.* Austin: Texas State Historical Association, 1966. Reprint, Austin: Texas State Library and Archives Commission, 1995.

Wissler, Clark. "The Influence of the Horse in the Development of Plains Culture." *American Anthropologist* 16, no. 1 (1914): 1–25.

———. *North American Indians of the Plains.* Reprint ed. New York: Burt Franklin Reprints, 1974.

Worcester, D. E. "The Spread of Spanish Horses in the Southwest, 1700–1800." *New Mexico Historical Review* 20, no. 1 (1945): 1–13.

Wood, W. Raymond, and Margot Liberty, eds. *Anthropology on the Great Plains.* Lincoln: University of Nebraska Press, 1980.

Wooster, Robert. *The Military and United States Indian Policy, 1865–1903.* New Haven CT: Yale University Press, 1988.

Wright, Mary C. "Economic Development and Native American Women in the Early Nineteenth Century." *American Quarterly* 33, no. 5 (winter 1981): 525–36.

Index